Kolbe
and the
Kommandant

Two Worlds in Collision

By
Ladislaus Kluz, OCD

A dual biography of
Maximilian Maria Kolbe, O.F.M. Conv.
and
Rudolph Franz Hoess, Kommandant
Auschwitz Concentration Camp
Oswiecim, Poland

Translated by
Sr. M. Angela Santor, SSJ. TOSF., M.A

Marytown Press
1600 West Park Avenue
Libertyville, Illinois 60048-2593
847-367-7800

NIHIL OBSTAT:
Rev. Robert J. O'Donnell
Censor Deputatus
Imprimatur: Most Rev. Elden F. Curtiss
Bishop of Helena Montana, U.S.A.
November 8, 1982

First Printing May, 1983

Published by Marytown Press
1600 West Park Avenue
Libertyville, IL 60048
800-743-1177
(847) 367-7831 (fax)
KolbeShrine.org

Library of Congress Catalog Card #83-71126
ISBN: 978-0-913382-70-7
Marytown Press #101-54

Printed in the United States of America

Dedicated to the Martyrs of
Auschwitz Concentration Camp

Then Jesus said to his disciples: If any man will come after me, let him deny himself, and take up his cross, and follow me.

For he that will save his life, shall lose it; and he that shall lose his life for my sake, shall find it.

For what doth it profit a man, if he gain the whole world, and suffer the loss of his own soul? Or what exchange shall a man give for his soul? For the Son of man shall come in the glory of his Father with his angels: and then will he render to every man according to his works.

Amen I say to you, there are some of them that stand here, that shall not taste death, till they see the Son of man coming in his kingdom.

—Mt. 16, 24-27

Contents

Why This Book?

As a dual biography of a great saint and of one of the greatest criminals ever to scourge mankind, this book accomplishes what separate biographies of the two men could only suggest. It shows the inevitable deadly collision of the two worlds that each represented, a collision that also produced unexpected atonement, conversion and healing.

In the process this double biography reveals mankind's last real hope for deliverance from the crazed, satanic forces that still afflict it.

Rarely has the conflict of two opposing worlds been so dramatized and epitomized as in the stories of Maximilian Kolbe and Rudolph Hoess. Catholic priest and Nazi Kommandant, these two men sum up within themselves all the dreams and hopes, all the ideals and total commitment of self, all the courage and self-sacrifice that brought on the horrifying, purifying clash of the Church and Hitler's Third Reich.

There were, of course, many heroes and many criminals whose lives could well typify the struggle between Christianity and the Nazi empire. What elevates the story of Kolbe and Hoess to the level of an epic, is that both men were strikingly alike in their early lives and ideals. Both later became leaders who radically changed the lives of countless millions of people.

The glory and the horror is that Kolbe became one of the foremost Christian apostles and evangelists of all time, leading millions to God and eternal life; Hoess, on the other hand, became one of the world's greatest genocides, a cruel and efficient executioner who directly and personally engineered the murders of around 3,000,000 innocent men, women and children. These included Poles, English, Bulgarians, Gypsies, Czechs, Danes, French, Greeks, Spaniards, Belgians, Serbs, Croatians, Germans, Norwegians, Russians, Rumanians, Hungarians and Italians. The majority of these were Jews, though a great many were not.

Hoess was an ardent, committed militant who planned and worked for the complete extermination of the whole Jewish people and of all enemies of Hitler's dream. In the end, the lives of both men came together, and each in a terrifying, redeeming way became a victim of the other.

It is a haunting, incredible story. These two lives began only six years and a few hundred miles apart. Both children belonged to staunch Catholic families. Both were altar boys. Both wanted to be Catholic priests and missionaries. Both were highly intelligent and deeply sensitive. Both were taught to be responsible and obedient, courageous and resolute. Both developed resourcefulness and perseverance in confronting difficulties.

Later the parallel paths of the two boys' lives begin to diverge. Raymond Kolbe (Maximilian's baptismal name) and his brother Francis decide to be Catholic priests and enroll in a Franciscan high school seminary. Rudolph, embarrassed and humiliated when a priest-friend thoughtlessly informs his parents of a reprimand and punishment he had received in school, loses his enthusiasm for the priesthood and cools in the practice of his religion.

Both young men subsequently decide on military careers. When young Kolbe informs his mother he is not going to be a Franciscan but a soldier instead, she listens, and then convinces him that his true vocation is to fight God's battles under Mary's sponsorship as a Franciscan priest. Hoess, who by then has lost his father, abandons his faith entirely and sets out on a path that leads to war, many brave exploits, involvement in the Nazi party, political assassination and prison.

Kolbe is sent to Rome to study philosophy and theology, and while still a student there, founds the *Knights of the Immaculata* movement. Its purpose is the evangelization of the whole world under the sponsorship of the Immaculate Mother of Jesus. He is ordained and begins to implant the movement and its ideals in Poland. It grows rapidly, and he later establishes centers for the movement in Poland and Japan.

Hoess marries after leaving prison, and begins a new life on a farm. He is recruited for the SS, however, as Hitler comes to power. He wholeheartedly supports Hitler's plan to conquer Europe and eventually the world. As World War II begins, Hoess is given the task of developing a concentration camp at Oswiecim (Auschwitz), and then later to reorganize it as a kind of death factory for the extermination of hundreds of thousands of political enemies and other undesirables from all over Europe, and finally of indefinite millions of Jews.

It is at Auschwitz that the two men's lives converge at last. Although apparently there was never any personal confrontation between them, Kolbe surely knew who the Kommandant of Auschwitz was. Hoess was probably aware of the well-known Kolbe; at the very least, he surely came to know of him after Kolbe's heroic death.

Hoess' rule of killing ten or more prisoners for every prisoner who escaped and was not immediately recaptured, provided Kolbe with the opportunity for his final act of loving service and Christian witness.

Kolbe, after the incredible immolation of his extraordinary life, does not fade away. His name and his exploits are told and retold around the world. Unknown millions, confident that Kolbe now receives all he asks, from God, since he always remained in Christ and kept Christ's word even to the ultimate act of heroic love, begin to invoke his powerful help in prayer. Increasingly they experience amazing answers to these prayers. Hoess himself is kept from self-destruction after the crumbling of his world. Later, in prison, he finally capitulates to the gentle, ineffable mercy of God whom Kolbe served, becoming in the end a citizen of Kolbe's world.

Two chapters of this book report rather graphically the horrible cruelty and savage atrocities of the Nazis, especially in the death camp. Frankly, we felt such nausea upon reading these chapters that we seriously considered deleting most of that material. Merely to read it makes one feel dirty and degraded. We were encouraged to keep it intact, however, by the penetrating words of Pope Paul VI regarding these events.

"It is necessary to scan this dark picture again," he said at Kolbe's beatification, "in order to pick out, here and there, the gleams of surviving humanity. Alas, history cannot forget these frightful and tragic pages. And so it cannot but fix its horrified gaze on the luminous points that reveal, but at the same time overcome, their inconceivable darkness.

"One of these points, perhaps the one glowing most brightly, is the calm, drained figure of Maximilian Kolbe."

For most of us, it is hard to appreciate and believe the tremendous power of Kolbe's faith, love and life until precisely we see something of the "inconceivable darkness" that they overcame. Having seen a little of that darkness horrible as it is, and the light of God shining in Maximilian Kolbe which did indeed overcome it we will then more readily turn to God through Jesus to overcome the darkness in our own lives.

This book is basically factual and historical, although some of the dialogue is of necessity conjectural. In preparing this book for English-speaking and especially American readers, we have done some editing to adapt it to their interests and needs. We have taken most of the documentary material out of the final two chapters and included it in the appendices. We have shortened the sections on the beatification process and the account of the beatification festivities. We added the paragraphs in italics at the end of chapters, 10, 11 and 12 to further clarify the significance of these events for American readers. Finally we added the material relating to Kolbe's canonization.

We are indebted to the translator, Sister Angela Santor, for her prayers and persistence in encouraging us when apparently insurmountable difficulties threatened to prevent the publication of this book. We are grateful also to Sister M. Constantine Sobieszczyk, SSJ. TOSF, Ph.D. for her initial editing of the manuscript; and to Patrick Riley of the DeRance Foundation in Milwaukee who also helped edit it. In fact Patrick's contribution and his suggestions for the final editing were of decisive importance in preparing the book for publication.

We are especially grateful to Harry John, president of the DeRance Foundation, who showed interest in this book from the beginning, and who made Mr. Riley's services available to us. Marion Goodwin's services as copy editor and typist were also indispensable, as was the enthusiasm, encouragement, faith and hard work of Jerome Borkoski. It was he who sought and found the funds necessary for the publication of this book, and who handled all the practical details of getting bids and ordering the typesetting and printing. Bonnie Nesbitt helped with the final editing of the last chapters and the typing of the appendices.

September 27, 1982
Fr. Bernard M. Geiger, OFM CONV.

Publisher's note for the second edition: For greater accuracy of the quotes from St. Maximilian's Writings and Letters used in "Kolbe and the Kommandant" I have substituted the wording as found in the two volume work "The Writings of St. Maximilian Maria Kolbe" Vol. 1 Letters, and Vol. 2 Various Writings. The number after the Vol. 1 or 2 in each quote refers to the number of the particular writing from that volume.

Bro. Charles Madden, OFM CONV., Revision editor,
Feast of Our Lady of Lourdes, Feb. 11, 2018

1894–1913
Altar Boy to Franciscan Friar:
Kolbe

On January 8, 1894 in Zdunska Wola, Poland, a son, Raymond, was born in the home of Julius Kolbe. The attractive mother, Maria Kolbe (nee Dabrowska), held the precious treasure most tenderly in her arms. "Little son, what will become of you when you grow up?" She asked the question that penetrates each mother's heart as soon as the trauma of childbirth has passed.

In reply, little Raymond without opening his eyes, murmured something unintelligibly, while visiting neighbors hastened to add, "He will positively be a priest!" they predicted. "That's just what he will not be," interjected the father to the excited women. "Francis, my oldest son will be a priest. And this son will probably be a weaver like his parents. We can't afford to educate two sons in the priesthood."

After the neighbors departed and the children were fast asleep, Maria confided to her husband, "When I was a young girl, I frequently dreamed of entering a convent. Unfortunately, here in the Congress Kingdom, [i.e. Poland partitioned after the Congress of Vienna in 1815] the Russian authorities suppressed all convents. This repression (1863) was for cooperating with the January Insurrection. I was, therefore, forced to change the plans for my life. Then I began to pray most fervently for a husband who would neither curse, drink, or spend his time in taverns. God gave me you, Julius, and you are the type I dreamed of and desired.

"If you keep praising me like that you're going to spoil me," teased Julius.

The Kolbe parents worked very hard for a living. They were self-employed in their cottage as was customary in Lodz and the region around

1

it. They wove cloth from the yarn distributed to them by the warehouses of private factories. The completed material was then taken to the foreign owners of the factories, who paid them. Since there was no labor law regulating payment for such work, the wages were hardly enough for food and clothing.

The Kolbe family had only one large room in which to live. In one corner stood a large kitchen stove, in another were four looms for weaving, and behind a partition was the sleeping area. In a niche between the cupboards on a small table stood a little statue of the Blessed Mother amid tiny angels and candle-holders. Before this little altar, the family began and ended the day with fervent prayer. Julius with a journeyman and two apprentices labored at the looms for twelve hours a day.

Seeking a better livelihood, Julius moved with his family to Lodz, and shortly after that to Pabianice where besides his regular workshop, he opened a small business. After a time he discontinued his work as a weaver and contented himself with the management of the store. His wife became a midwife. Through the years three more sons were born, but only one, Joseph, survived; the other two died in infancy.

Although many years passed, Francis the eldest son, as well as Raymond, did not attend any school. There were no Polish schools during the Russian occupation. The parents resented the idea of having their children Russianized, and so they themselves began to teach their children reading, writing, and the basics of mathematics. The remaining studies were completed through the efforts of the Polish priests of Pabianice, who gave whatever time they had to the education of the children and youth of Poland.

In spite of these rather weak beginnings, Francis passed his examination in a trade school, the only secondary school in Pabianice. Meanwhile, little Raymond who from his earliest years gave evidence of mathematical genius, helped in his parents' business.

One day his mother sent him to the drug store to have a prescription filled. Instead of passing the prescription to the pharmacist, he read it to him.

"Please give me the medicine 'Venenum graecum'."

Mr. Kotowski, the pharmacist, was greatly astonished at the boy's resoluteness and natural intelligence.

"Do you attend any school?" he inquired.

"My older brother does, but I am being tutored privately by Father Jakowski."

"And would you like to continue studying?" "Oh yes, indeed! My parents, however, cannot afford it."

"The important thing is whether you really want to study. Starting tomorrow, come to me in the evening, and I shall prepare you for a trade school."

Mr. Kotowski belonged to those noble Poles who, after the disastrous January Insurrection, abandoned empty rhetoric for concrete action and, whenever and wherever possible, built new foundations of consciousness, knowledge and national responsibility in society. Among others, those people dedicated to the Polish cause guarded and trained the young generation, who in time would take upon themselves the fate of Poland.

Perhaps this bright boy will play some dynamic role in the history of Poland, reflected the apothecary, looking at Raymond. And in this way Kotowski, too, would share in the future of the nation.

The parents most willingly agreed to further the education of their son Raymond, especially after a thought-provoking incident. The observant mother had become aware of the fact that her son now prayed longer and longer each day before the statue of the Blessed Mother.

"Raymond, why so pensive?"

Obviously disturbed by his mother's question, the boy lowered his head. She, however, did not stop.

"A good child never keeps any secrets from his mother."

"But this secret concerns not only me, but also the Blessed Mother."

A devout woman can with difficulty allow her child a secret, but what if it concerns the Blessed Mother?

So she begged him to reveal his secret to her. The boy, touched by his mother's pleading, finally relented.

"One day when I was praying in church before the picture of Mary Immaculate, she suddenly became alive and showed me two crowns. One was white, the other red. The first was a symbol of purity, the second, of martyrdom. She asked me if I would like to have them."

"And what did you say?" asked the anxious mother.

"I chose both."

The mother's eyes filled with tears as she embraced her ten-year-old son. Overwhelmed as she was with joy and pride that Mary, the Mother of God, had chosen her son, she knew that the martyrdom of a son is always the martyrdom of the mother. To share the crown one must share in Golgotha.

During their annual pilgrimage to Czestochowa, the parents with their son, prayed long and fervently before the Black Madonna. They beseeched the Mother of God for a vocation to the priesthood for Francis and Raymond. The latter, seeing his father absorbed in prayer, asked him,

"Daddy, what are you asking the Blessed Virgin?"

"I'm imploring the Mother of God that you become a holy priest. She will never abandon you unless you yourself leave her."

". . .unless I myself leave her," repeated Raymond slowly after his father.

After returning home from the pilgrimage, young Raymond progressed in his studies with great enthusiasm under the supervision of Mr. Kotowski. As a result, he surpassed his older brother in studies and successfully passed his examination to enter the second year of the trade school.

In 1907 Kolbe's parish at Pabianice, for the first time in many decades, had mission retreats sponsored by a Franciscan, Father Peregrine Haczela, from Lwow. A new evangelical spirit was permeating the parish. Young people of the parish, contemplating the edifying example of the friar, heard the voice of Christ, "Follow me." But, where could one go to become a missionary priest? The response came during the mission. Father Peregrine announced to the congregation that the Franciscan Order was inviting boys who desired to dedicate their lives to the priesthood in a friary, to come to their secondary school in Lwow. This invitation was accepted most joyfully by the two brothers, Francis and Raymond Kolbe. Rejoicing with the news, they rushed home to tell their parents.

"Get that out of your heads," the parents cautioned the boys. "We can't afford to have you educated even here in provincial Galicia."

"But the Missionary Father announced," the boys continued to explain, "the cost of our training and studies will be covered by the Franciscan Order."

"And while in high school, if you change your minds about becoming priests and friars where will we get the money to repay the debt incurred to the Order?"

"The Missionary Father told us that even those who leave the path to priesthood have no obligatory debts. The Order will be satisfied if it trains a certain group of people into wise and noble citizens. You may speak to the Missionary Father yourselves."

The conversation with Father Peregrine brought about fruitful results, for the boys' parents whole-heartedly acceded to their sons' wishes. Consequently, the two zealous, capable boys found themselves in Lwow, the capital of Galicia.

Raymond distinguished himself from his colleagues through an aptitude for the physical sciences. Mathematics and physics were his two favorite subjects. He wasn't content with class material only but pursued his research in the sciences far more broadly and deeply.

On the other hand, he was also highly imaginative. Some of his educators remarked that the physical sciences and a vivid imagination in a young person are irreconcilable and this would later be his downfall. Others predicted that Raymond had a real genius for inventing and that fantasy in this case could enhance scientific discovery.

"Well, yes," agreed one of the former, "but fantasy in this case must also have its limits. The fact that Kolbe proves his fantasies about a manned flight to the moon with mathematics and the laws of physics makes no difference."

"Is this such a great fantasy if it has rather a real possibility?"

The first ones contemptuously shrugged their shoulders as a sign that it was useless to argue about it.

Nevertheless, Raymond continued his dreams about the conquest of space. He concentrated, likewise, on military problems. For example, how could Lwow, the Capital of Galicia, be fortified so that it would be impregnable? At another time he proved to his astonished colleagues the manner in which the Poles could, through military tactics, cast off the yoke of the

The Kolbe children as members of a boys' choir in Pabianice in 1907: 1) Francis, the eldest; 2) Raymond (Father Maximilian); 3) Joseph (Father Alphonse). The Kolbes could afford to send only the oldest son to school.

three conquerors and regain the freedom desired by many generations. His proof was based on the advantages of guerilla warfare.

In the stillness of the Franciscan church, before the picture of the Immaculate Mary, he prayed most humbly for the greatest victory over his "ego"—for the glory of his God, his Immaculate Mary and his neighbor! He dreamed of combat by which he could conquer the whole world for the Madonna of his heart, for the Immaculata, and through her, for her Son Jesus Christ!

In the spring of 1910, the boys in Raymond's class were informed that, at the end of the school year, they must decide whether they would enter the Order, or whether they would pursue further studies for a secular occupation. Raymond meditated a long time on his future. Indeed, he thought seriously of the priesthood, but he also thought of an academic career in the area of the physical sciences. He was equally fascinated by modern military problems. Since his calling to religious life was not clear to him, he decided to give a negative answer to the Provincial of the Franciscan Order. On his way to see him he was informed that his mother had come to visit him. With sheer pleasure he ran to the visitor's parlor. At once he began to tell his mother that he and Francis had decided on a military career. They wanted to fight for the freedom of Poland. They wouldn't be entering the Franciscan Order.

"Beloved son," his mother replied kindly, "I understand your desire to fight for Poland. But you will never get a martyr's crown for that. I'm sure our Lady wants you to be a soldier, but a soldier for God and the Church. Remember how St. Francis became a Knight for Christ. He fought against the devil, error and sin to win vast numbers of souls for God. Don't let the devil deceive you. You are called to follow St. Francis! And now I came to tell you that Joseph, your youngest brother wants to be a priest and a Franciscan too."

Raymond was stunned. His mother's words shot through his mind like a flash of lightning conquering darkness. All his dreams of a military career and all his doubts about his vocation dissolved suddenly. He was embarrassed he hadn't seen it before. As he discussed it with his mother peace and certainty took hold of his heart.

"Now the whole family will be in the service of God," his mother exclaimed. "Your father has already gone to join the Franciscans at Cracow. I have been living with the Benedictine Sisters here in Lwow for two years. How beautiful!"

"Yes, Mamma, very beautiful," replied Raymond softly. At the same time, he felt a strange contraction in his heart.

He soon found himself in the presence of the Provincial.

"I ask humbly for admission to the Order of St. Francis," he said in a soft but decisive tone.

On September 4, 1910, he received the habit and a new name, Maximilian, as a sign that with a new name he was beginning a new life, dedicated entirely to God.

The year spent in the novitiate was the time during which under the experienced guidance of the Master, Father Dionysius Sowiak, he tended toward closer union with God through prayer and practice of the evangelical virtues. In this period of time he suffered an attack of scrupulosity. Thanks to the kindliness and patience of his confessor as well as his superiors, the painful ordeal passed and serenity of the soul returned. Through this trying experience he acquired angelic patience in dealing with scrupulous penitents in later years. In this tranquility of spirit he pronounced his first vows on September 5, 1911. As a friar he completed his high school studies in 1912. His superiors transferred him to Cracow for further studies. Here, unexpectedly, he was called to see the Provincial.

"Friar Maximilian," he declared, "I have decided to send you with six other clerics to Rome for further studies at the Gregorian University."

This was a complete surprise. The eyes of the cleric filled with tears.

"But, Father Provincial, I won't be able to manage philosophy. In fact, I have an aptitude for the physical sciences, but not for philosophy. And, furthermore, my health is a problem. I feel a certain rasping in my lungs."

"If that's the case, you will not go to Rome," the well-experienced spiritual director and guide, Father Peregrine Haczela, calmly replied.

As soon as Friar Maximilian found himself at prayer, he began to experience qualms of conscience. "How could I, a friar, who only a year ago made a vow of obedience, now exercise my own will in preference to God's will manifested in the desires of my superiors? No, that I can not do, without betraying the ideal of the Order."

"What brings you to me, Friar?" smiled the Provincial, seeing the timid cleric standing before him again.

"I am very sorry, Father Provincial, for opposing your will."

"I knew you would do this," declared the superior smilingly. "I was counting on the action of the grace of God in your noble soul. So pack your belongings, and have a happy journey to the Eternal City!"

In his farewell letter to his mother, the young cleric expressed an ardent request.

"Finally, I ask only for one thing, a special prayer; this is the only thing I need—the rest will be taken care of by the holy religious Order, just like a good mother" (KW Vol 1, #1, para. 4).

After his arrival in Rome on November 10, he wrote to his mother. "Of our trip, which lasted two days and two nights, there is much to tell, because we saw many new landscapes. But we will talk about this, with our Lord's permission, face to face at the appropriate time" (KW Vol. 1, #2, para.1).

In Rome there was a specified time for lectures at the Gregorian University, time for preparation for examinations and time for visiting the magnificent basilicas and churches. Despite this, he didn't forget the most essential thing, developing his interior life. His spiritual guide at this time was the Servant of God, Therese of the Infant Jesus, a Discalced Carmelite. He was intensely interested in her autobiography, entitled the *Story of a Soul*, from which he learned that to become great one must become little. This brought to his mind the words of Christ to his disciples who came up to Jesus with the question, "Who is of greatest importance in the kingdom of God?" He called a little child over and stood him in their midst and said: "I assure you, unless you change and become like little children, you will not enter the kingdom of God. Whoever makes himself lowly, becoming like this child, is of greatest importance in that heavenly reign" [Mt. 18, 2-4]. A thread of sympathy grew between Friar Kolbe and the Servant of God little Therese. In prayer, therefore he turned to her as a brother turns to his sister. "If you obtain for me the grace of perseverance In the Order, and the attainment of priesthood, I will pray for your beatification and canonization. Drop upon me the shower of roses, which you promised before your death."

He was enraptured with the image of St. Joseph Cotolengo, who during his lifetime, performed great works of charity without possessing any money, but trusting whole-heartedly in the Providence of God. From the book Depth of the Soul by Gemma Galgani, he learned to endure pain with resignation to the will of God.

His devotion to the Immaculata was constantly deepening. The guides and masters of his initiation into the Marian mysteries were St. Alphonse Liguori, St. Louis Grignion de Montfort, and his class work in Mariology.

During his visits in Rome, he was overwhelmed by great emotion at the sight of the Colosseum, the site of the martyrdom of thousands of Christians in the first centuries after Christ. He recalled the red crown promised him by the Immaculata.

"And where will the Colosseum of the twentieth century be located, that Colosseum which will become my Golgotha?" The friar from distant Poland pondered at length.

1894–1913
An Altar Boy Betrayed:
Hoess

On November 25, 1900 in Baden-Baden, Germany great rejoicing prevailed in the home of Franz Xavier Hoess. His wife, Pauline Hoess (nee Speck), gave birth on this day to her first son.

With great joy and pride the father was showing his son to relatives and friends gathered there to congratulate the proud parents of the plump, blue-eyed blond with a roguish smile.

"A beautiful child," the delighted women loudly declared.

"He will be a valiant soldier!" predicted the men.

"He will definitely not be a soldier!" responded the father vehemently.

"Incredible," responded the amazed friends of Franz. "Yet, whole generations of your ancestors served in the army, bringing glory to the German army. Didn't your father, a Colonel, die a hero in the battle with the French in 1870? And didn't you as an officer of the Colonial Army, fight valiantly in German Southeast Africa? Has your wife influenced you so much in her business enterprise that you now desire to have your son a merchant? Leave the commercial business to the English. Our German nation is, above all, a nation of soldiers. We are created to fight and rule over the whole world."

"My son," replied Franz emphatically, "will neither be a soldier nor a merchant. He will be a priest."

"A priest?" questioned the guests, quite astonished at this announcement.

"Yes," the master of the house decidedly answered. "He will be a missionary priest. He will go to Africa, not with a carbine, but the Gospel, the Good Tidings which announce that God is the Father not only of the whites, but also the blacks, and that we are all brothers, members of the one human family."

Further conversation somehow was stinted. Under various pretexts the guests began to leave, musing over what passed.

"And you, Paula, do you agree that our first son should become a priest?" Franz tenderly questioned his wife.

"Oh, would to God he did become one!" whispered the pale, exhausted mother of little Rudolph, who slept peacefully in her arms.

For the health of their children, the Hoess family moved into a country house beyond Baden-Baden. In the neighboring area and even farther, they found only a few people engaged in agriculture. On the other hand, a neat stand of tall fir trees began nearby in the Black Forest.

Little Rudolph was not fond of playing with his younger sisters. Neither did he have any playmates his age, for all the neighboring children were much older than he was. As a result, he associated with older persons unsuited to his age; this resulted in a withdrawal into solitude. Whenever he could break away from his mother, he secluded himself in the forest. During one such escapade he was carried off by wandering gypsies. Fortunately, a neighbor passing near-by caught sight of the boy struggling with his hands and feet to get away from the gypsies and managed to rescue him.

Most of his time, however, was spent in grooming horses. He loved horses. For hours at a time he caressed them, talked to them most tenderly and fed them with sweets. Whenever he found a cleaning tool, he immediately brushed the horse and combed its hair. The stable masters observed with consternation how little Rudi coolly slipped between the horses' feet, and how he played with the strong and ferocious bull which was the terror of the whole vicinity. Similarly, he befriended all the dogs of the neighborhood; under his mere glance they would become docile as lambs.

The parents, particularly the mother, were disturbed by their son's behavior.

"What will become of him when he grows up?" she consulted with her husband. "He avoids people, and he won't talk with anyone or play with his sisters. He is interested only in solitary jaunts and is too fond of animals."

"We will just have to move into a neighborhood where there are no domestic animals," decided Franz.

On this account the family moved into the vicinity of Manheim. This place, too, was beyond the town. However, nearby lived a few families having quite a group of children of Rudolph's age. His parents realized soon enough they had made a mistake. Seven year old Rudi, instead of joining his playmates, hid himself in the corners of their home, cried quietly, or would sit and brood for hours.

"What are you thinking of so long?" inquired his troubled mother. Rudi was silent.

One day his mother noticed a book in his hands which he was examining most passionately. At an opportune time, the mother looked through the book and was much surprised to find it filled with animal illustrations.

Weeks passed. Rudi continued his silence; he refused to eat and play. After long deliberation the parents made a decision. For his seventh birthday, they presented him with a wonderful pony named Hans, black as coal, with a long mane and large glistening eyes. Rudolph was overwhelmed with joy. Instantly, all melancholy left him. He jumped on his pony and rode into the nearby woods. He returned after a few hours, tired but beaming with joy.

"Thank you, dearest parents, thank you!" He kissed their hands for their thoughtfulness.

Rudi never left his pony. Whenever his parents were not at home, he led his pony into his room. Hans gratefully reciprocated with an attachment to him. He walked after Rudi step by step like a pet dog.

From the year 1906 Rudolph began to attend the elementary school (Grundschule) in Manheim. He was attentive in school and behaved very well. After returning from school, he did his homework quickly in order to have leisure time with Hans. While the family lived in Baden-Baden, the father was away on business very frequently. Now, at Manheim, he had ample time to devote to his son. He questioned him and checked his homework.

Evenings were spent in chatting' with his son. He related his army experiences from service in East Africa: the combat, the injuries he received in battle; and his distinguished awards which brought him promotions and finally the rank of major. He also related the untiring activities of missionary Orders, of those courageous persons in habits who tread into every corner of Africa without arms and ammunition, but with the cross of Christ, with charity and civilization.

These talks awakened in the child a desire to become either a valiant soldier like his father, or a missionary. The latter aspiration was becoming stronger in him, particularly at the time when the family was visited by certain guests, bearded priests from Africa, old friends of the father, who presented to the boy's imagination a most attractive image of their human- itarian and religious activities. Rudi could listen for hours to their stories. These were the only moments during which he was lost to the world, even to his pet pony.

"Daddy," he exclaimed to his father after such meetings, "I shall be a missionary!"

"I am extremely happy for you. But, dear son, you must pray, pray much and fervently for perseverance in that vocation. We shall therefore make a pilgrimage to Lourdes, to plead with the Immaculate Mother for protection over you and your calling."

Finding themselves before the grotto at Lourdes,

Rudolph observed tears rolling down from his father's eyes. They were rather unbecoming to the masculine, soldierly face of a mature person. Rudolph, troubled about it, clung to his father.

"Daddy," whispered Rudi, "why are you crying?"

"Dearest son, a strange uneasiness about you filled my heart. I don't know how to explain that. I'm begging the Blessed Mother that you be- come a noble-minded man."

From his earliest years, Rudi was trained by his parents in deep responsi- bility to duty. At home he was closely observed so all orders were carried out accurately and conscientiously. Everyone had certain activities which had to be performed perfectly. Franz especially made sure that Rudolph complied with all his orders most accurately. One night he awakened the boy.

"Where did you put the horse cloth from under the saddle?" he asked his son sternly.

"I left it in the garden."

"And where did I tell you to put it?"

"You told me to hang it in the shed so it would dry."

"So, now rise immediately and follow the order. I taught you many times that a small carelessness, seemingly of no importance, very often leads to great damage."

As a zealous Catholic, Franz was decidedly opposed to the current government and its policies. Oftentimes the precocious Rudolph heard his father say to his friends:

"In spite of the fact that I disagree with the government, and, indeed, am its opponent, the laws and unjust decrees of the government must be unconditionally observed."

The perceptive boy, observant of the mutual relationship of his parents towards one another, never heard any unkind words between them, nor was he ever aware of any tenderness between them. Cold human feeling engulfed little Rudolph. While his two sisters were tenderly attached to the mother, he, on the contrary, would not show any love to his aunts and relatives from his earliest years, to the sorrow of his mother. A handshake and a few stinted words of thanks were all that could be expected of him.

Although the parents were always very kind and considerate of him, he never confided to them either his small or big heartaches. He always tried to be self-sufficient. His only confidant was Hans, his pony, to whose ear he whispered many, many things, and the pony shaking his head, seemed to understand.

Both of his sisters tried their best to gain the heart of their older brother. Unfortunately, it was all in vain. He played with them only when his mother expressly told him to do so. But then, he teased them so much that they were hurt, and ran crying to their mother.

With his school friends he played in a frenzied manner in the wildest games and fights. He wouldn't allow anyone to force anything on him; he always managed to have his say.

"I am created to be a leader and not a slave," he declared conceitedly.

When any wrong was done to him, he couldn't rest until, in his opinion, it was revenged. He was without mercy in dealing with others, and his friends feared him. They knew he was ready to do anything.

The school authorities decided that through his years of grammar school, he would sit at a single desk with a Swedish girl because none of his other classmates could get along with him. Rudi understood his girl companion quite well, and she understood him, for throughout the years of school they never quarreled.

From his early school years he was an exemplary altar boy. In church he was an entirely different person: calm, quiet and dignified. Every Saturday he received the Sacrament of Penance and on Sunday, to the joy of his parents, he received Holy Communion.

In his 13th year, an incident occurred which made a decided mark on his future. While scuffling at the entrance to the gymnasium, he accidentally pushed one of his classmates down some stairs. Unfortunately, the fall resulted in a fractured ankle. For this Rudi was punished and detained by his teacher after school for two hours. He took this very seriously especially since his school-mates did not conceal their joy and satisfaction because Rudi was punished.

The incident occurred on a Saturday before noon. As usual on Saturday afternoon, Rudi went to confession. His confessor was an old friend of the Hoess family. After confession Rudi decided to confide the morning incident to the priest. To relieve himself, he told the priest everything clearly and sincerely.

Since Rudi had no intention of spoiling Sunday either for himself or his parents, he made no mention of the incident when he returned from school. That very evening, however, the old priest-friend of the family visited them. During his conversation with the father, the priest casually related the school incident. The following morning the father called his son, requesting an explanation of the incident in school, and the reason for not telling it to him immediately upon his return from school.

Rudi was hurt and he felt it was a breach of confidence on the part of the priest. This brought about quite a change in him. He gradually began to drift away from the idea of becoming a priest, and moreover, from his religious practices. The deep, true faith of his childhood was destroyed.

1914–1918
A Student Challenges Satan:
Kolbe

On April 6, 1914 Friar Maximilian Kolbe wrote from Rome:

"Dearest Mamma ...
I do not wish for your health or success. Why? Because I wish you some-
thing more beautiful, something so good that no one, not even God him-
self, could wish you better. Therefore, I wish that in all things, you will
carry out the will of God, He who is the greatest Father of all, and that
you can carry out His will in all you do" (KW Vol. 1, #12 , para. 1 & 2).

Letters are always mirrors of the personal experience of the author. In
this case the continuation of the letter cited above confirmed Kolbe's great
understanding of sanctity. In this letter, he also mentioned a miraculous
cure.

"I very nearly lost a finger on my right hand. I developed something like
an abscess. Despite the care of the college doctor, pus kept forming. At a
certain moment the doctor saw that the bone itself was beginning to be
infected; a minor surgical curettage of the bone was necessary. After I
heard this, I told him that I possessed a better medicine. In fact, I had re-
ceived from the Fr. Rector (Luigi Bondini) a little miraculous water from
Lourdes. While he gave it to me, he told me the story of a prodigious cure.
At the age of twelve he injured his foot; a bone in the sole of his foot was
slowly turning gangrenous and the pain would not let him sleep; some-
times he screamed in pain. It was necessary to amputate the foot. One
evening the physicians had to meet for a consultation. His mother, seeing

Friar Maximilian Kolbe (back row, left) as a seminarian in Rome in 1914 at the Collegio Serafico, the Conventual Franciscans' international seminary. Picture was probably taken after Maximilian and his confreres had pronounced their solemn vows as Franciscans in the seminary chapel on November 1.

what was happening, in a desperate gesture tried a completely new treat-
ment; she threw away the bandages that covered the foot, washed it with
soap, and then rinsed it with the miraculous water of Lourdes. The Fr.
Rector, after all this time, for the first time went to sleep. After 15 minutes
he awoke, and he was healed. The miracle was evident, but the doctor, a
nonbeliever, tried to explain the fact otherwise. However, a few days later
when a piece of rotten bone extruded from the foot, the doctor realized
that he was confronted with an extraordinary fact: the bone was actually
turning gangrenous, but had broken off and had miraculously exited the
wound. Following this event the doctor converted and undertook to build
a church at his own expense. The Fr. Rector, after the application of the
miraculous water, was healed and was able to walk, but could not wear
his shoe because of the swelling that remained. However, after the bone
detached, everything returned to normal.

Our doctor, after he knew that I had the water of Lourdes, applied it
himself with joy. And what happened? The day after, I was told by the
surgeon of the hospital that surgery was no longer necessary. After a few
medications it was completely healed. Glory be to the Lord God, and also
to the Immaculata (KW Vol. 1, #12, para. 4 & 5).

On August 1, 1914 World War I broke out. Friars from the Austrian
occupation zone received orders, presumably from the civil authorities, to
leave Rome in May, 1915 and return to their native country. Friar Maximilian Kolbe left for San Marino, where he remained about a month until he
received a legal passport enabling him to return safely for further studies
in Rome.

The atmosphere in the International Franciscan College in the Eternal
City was tense. Here were friars from countries that were at war with each
other. Father Rector Ignudi, with dynamic tact and kindness, reminded the
friars that in spite of everything, they constituted one family,

God's and the community's. Friar Maximilian was at a loss. He
hoped that from this eventful conflagration, a free Poland would
emerge. But when? At this moment the Poles belonging to the annexed
regions, now warring against each other, found themselves facing their
fellow Poles at the front. How dreadful the thought; brother against
brother, and that in foreign interests. But from the beginning, attempts
were made to create Polish armies to fight for the freedom of their
country. Friar Maximilian discovered that his older brother, Francis,

had left the Franciscans and joined the Polish Legions. Their father, Julius, as a legionnaire, lost his life between Olkusz and Miechow. The young cleric contemplated whether he, too, should leave the friendly threshold of Rome, return to his country deluged in blood, and actively join the battlefront for tomorrow's Poland. Perhaps his share of action in the battle for freedom was needed. At prayer he regained his peace. Poland would need young, learned priests. And now he could help too, with prayer and interior work, imploring God, who governs the whole world, for the freedom of his nation.

On October 20, 1914 Friar Kolbe received his tonsure and minor orders. Friar Maximilian dedicated himself to God entirely and forever through his final profession on November 1st. To his religious name he added another, Maria. With that he unified his whole life.

He received more of the minor orders on November 29, 1914. Then on October 28, 1915, at the Gregorian University he completed his doctoral studies in philosophy and passed his exams with great success.

Now he was to begin his studies in the Pontifical Theological Faculty of St. Bonaventure of the Franciscan Friars Minor Conventual in Rome. On New Year's Day of 1917, together with his confreres, he attended Mass celebrated privately by the Holy Father from whose hands he received Holy Communion.

That year was to be a decisive one for him and his work. On January 20, during meditation, he was inspired to organize an association that would be dedicated to the service of the Immaculata, and through this service to get closer to God. Exactly 75 years earlier the Blessed Mother had appeared to the Jewish agnostic, Alphonse Ratisbonne, in St. Andrew delle Fratte Church in Rome. This resulted in his conversion to the Catholic faith.

Reflecting on this fact, Friar Maximilian came to the conclusion that the Blessed Mother was endowed by God's grace with the dynamic power to change the whole world, if that world would only cooperate with her. Friar Kolbe's desire was to gain full liberation from sin and total inner transformation in Christ for every human person who lives now or who will ever live, through Mary's intercession.

Images of the past moved before the prayerful eyes of the cleric. He recalled that while still a young boy he had purchased a little statue of the Immaculate Virgin for five pennies. Later, in Lwow, in the friary choir where the students were hearing Mass he promised the Immaculata while bowing his head to the floor that he would fight for her. But, how? At that time he still didn't know. During his novitiate he confided this matter to the Master of Novices, Father Dionysius Sowiak, who changed that resolution to a daily offering of the prayer, "We fly to thy patronage." Now, he became more aware of the need for a spiritual rebirth through the Immaculata. There was much evil in the world as well as in the Community. At times he talked with his confreres on the future of their Community. And then he firmly concluded that they should either place the Community on its feet, or demolish it. As a Christian, he knew only one solution, namely, that the more evil there is, the more work there will be. Instead of criticizing and brooding, it was necessary for him to work and reform. The Immaculata would help in this work. The evil prevailing at the time in Rome was not strange to him. He witnessed an unforgettable scene on the 200th anniversary of the founding of Masonry when right under the window of the Pope in Vatican Square, a gigantic banner was carried with the inscription: Satan will take over the Vatican—the Pope will be Satan's slave." Friar Maximilian was greatly upset at this audacity. He went to the Rector for permission to go to Palazzo Verde, Headquarters of the Masons, to convert their Grand Master himself. The Rector smiled. He recalled the incident of St. Francis who, permeated with similar zeal, prepared to go to the great Sultan to convert him and all his subjects to the true faith.

"Dear Friar," the Rector replied most kindly, "your prayer and study will accomplish more good for the Church than your direct apostleship. Every conversion must necessarily be preceded by the propitiatory prayers of the faithful."

During vacation Friar Maximilian experienced a lung hemorrhage for the first time. He wondered whether this illness might be the red crown offered him by the Immaculata.

On July 16, 1917, he was ordained Subdeacon. Despite his studies and illness, the idea of organizing a powerful association embracing the whole world, whose members would learn humble service to God and to mankind from the Immaculata, never left him. He was not alone in his desires. With the permission of the Rector, six men volunteered to join him on October 16 for the purpose of laying the foundation for the association, which they named *Militia Immaculatae*, in short, M.I., or the Troops or Knights of the Immaculata. Besides Friar Maximilian, the following participated in the meeting: Father Joseph Pal, a young priest from the Romanian Province: Friar Jerome Biasi from the Province of Padua; Friar Quirico Pignalberi from the Province of Rome; Friar An-

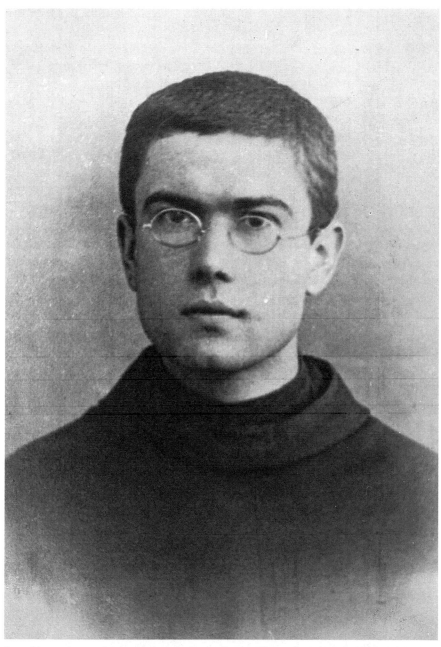

Friar Maximilian as he looked when he and six confreres founded the *Militia Immaculatae*, or *Knights of the Immaculata* movement in Rome in 1917.

thony Mansi of the Neapolitan Province; and Friar Henry Granata, also from the Neapolitan Province.

The meeting took place secretly in the evening behind locked doors. A statuette of the Immaculata stood between two burning candles at the head of the discussion table. Friar Jerome acted as secretary. The purpose of this first meeting was to formulate the program or bylaws of the *Militia Immaculatae*. Their activities at that time did not extend beyond private prayer and the distribution of the miraculous medal of the Immaculata. During its first year in existence, the society failed to develop. One of its members even tried to convince the others that the whole *Militia Immaculatae* was not necessary at all. Others accepted this in silence. Friar Kolbe, however, did not easily resign. He wrote to the Vicar-General of his Community, Father Dominic Tavani, and presented the by laws of the *Militia Immaculatae*. . . requesting his blessing for the association. The Vicar gave his blessing in writing and expressed the wish that there were at least twelve members. He also expressed the desire that the *Militia Immaculatae* be spread universally among young members of the Order.

Meanwhile. Friar Maximilian was rapidly approaching his ordination to the priesthood. On October 8, 1917, he had been ordained Deacon.

On April 28, 1918, Maximilian Kolbe was ordained to the priesthood by Cardinal Basil Pompilii in St. Andrew's della Valle Church. The young priest described this great event in a letter to his mother:

"We were more than a hundred, both religious and secular clerics of various nationalities; there was even a black man among those who had been ordained, while another acted as a servant to the cardinal during the ordination.

It was a moving scene: despite their differences, they were all united in the bond of the Catholic faith and in brotherly love in Jesus" (KW Vol. 1, #19 p. 370, para. 1).

After concluding the description of the ordination, he wrote:

"I gratefully understand that this whole affair was a gift obtained through the intercession of the Immaculata, our common Mother" (KW Vol. 1, #19 p. 370, para. 4).

"Glory, therefore, to the most Sacred Heart of Jesus through her who

was conceived without sin, who is the instrument of God's mercy for the distribution of graces. In her, I place all my confidence for the future"
(KW Vol. 1, #19 p. 370 also para. 4).

The day after ordination Father Maximilian celebrated his first holy Mass before the same altar where the Immaculata appeared to Alphonse Ratisbonne.

Unexpectedly, the Blessed Mother called the first members of the M.I. from this life. On October 18, Anthony Glowinski died, and on the 31st of the same month, Friar Anthony Mansi. A virus caused the death of both friars. Each died a beautiful death and Father Kolbe remarked that their unexpected death was a sacrifice for the intention of the expansion of the association.

The mind of Father Maximilian was not merely devotional in the strict sense of the word. A Doctor of Philosophy is bound to think broadly. Rather than brood over the evil in the world, he meditated on the manner in which everything that is in the world could render glory to God. A classic example of this was his view of motion pictures, an innovation at that time. The first films to be shown were cause for scandal. Thus, during a walk, one of the Brothers of the Order bemoaned "Satan's invention." Father Kolbe very calmly responded,

"We must convert the movies. If we give them the proper direction they will stop harming people."

"How so, Friar," the provoked cleric exclaimed.

"Do you expect the devil to reform? Don't you see that all these inventions were initiated in hell and to hell they are leading multitudes?"

"Inventions," calmly replied Father Maximilian, "in themselves are neither good nor bad. In reality, in the hands of the wicked they become Satan's weapon. For that very reason we must strive to strike that weapon from Satan's hand. By remaining on the defensive, no one has yet won a war. We must rush to attack and overtake the area assumed by the enemy, and involve the movies and all inventions in the service of God."

Often, too, his conversation with the friars touched on the matter of the press, which was often an advantage to other denominations, and not evaluated properly by the priests. He envisioned the creation of a marvelous periodical giving intelligent information about the world and pioneering in contemporary life under the guidance of the Immaculata.

He did not abandon mathematical and physical problems either. One

of his intellectual labors was designing an airplane which could be cata-
pulted into the air. His desire was to incorporate this modern technique
into his labor of spreading the Kingdom of God.

He ardently desired that the contemporary Church, similar to that of
the first century, would stand at the head of cultural and technical progress
in the twentieth century.

In November, 1918 he was overwhelmed with inexpressible happiness
rejoicing together with all the Poles in the world that Poland had regained
her independence. He was incessantly thanking God and her who had always been the Holy Queen of Poland, even in the most difficult years of its
occupation.

1914–1918
War and a Baptism of Fire:
Hoess

For Rudolph Hoess the year 1914 began, tragically. His father died, but this blow did not force him into a more serious reflection about human life. Rather, it led him to the hope of greater personal freedom.

That same year brought Europe a most terrifying war. The Manheim garrison was immediately sent to the French front. Reserve formations were organized. After only a few days the first trainload of wounded soldiers arrived from the French front.

At this time Rudolph began to attend the school of humanities known as Herere Schule in Manheim. Who could apply himself diligently to studies at a time such as this? Rudolph was no exception. His mother reluctantly permitted him to offer his services to the Red Cross. He found himself helping in the hospital where he saw blood soaked bandages on heads and arms. He saw the gray uniforms of the German soldiers and the blue and red uniforms of the French. He carried cold drinks and cigarettes to the wounded. Whenever he had any leisure from his studies, he helped anywhere he could: in the hospital, at the station, in the barracks.

In the name of the Red Cross, he distributed food and little gifts. In the hospital he was chilled with fright, affected by the painful moaning of the badly wounded soldiers and the sight of the dying who vehemently protested against the war. But even these tragic pictures were soon blotted out from the boy's memory in the presence of the humor of the slightly wounded soldiers. The sick liked the resolute boy, an untiring listener of their army experiences. They willingly related to him their real and their fictitious heroic acts, and Rudi listened to their stories with insatiable curiosity. All this, of course, aroused in him a new desire for the soldier's life.

He wanted to be a soldier by all means. He was fearful of losing this opportunity which the war presented and which demanded more and more recruits. Finally, he confided his plans to his mother.

"Son," insisted the mother, "first finish your studies, take your exams, and later decide your future. Furthermore, remember your father's advice; he desired that you become a priest and not a soldier."

He heard the same advice from his guardian and relatives. Rudi, without a word, listened to their counseling, but he did everything possible to join the army. On several occasions he ran away from home and hid himself in the army transports which were headed for the front. Nevertheless, he was always discovered and, despite his determination and pleading, sent back by the forest police because he was much too young.

Rudi, however, did not stop trying. All his thoughts and desires centered around becoming a brave soldier. At the moment, nothing else in life meant anything to him. The mother understood his feelings and desires. Yet, with the greatest kindness and patience she tried to dissuade him from his military ambitions. Relatives attempted to tear him away from all military surroundings by suggesting he be placed in a missionary seminary. The mother decidedly objected against this in the boy's favor. She did not want her son to be forced into the priesthood. Moreover, it was evident to her that he became more and more indifferent in religious matters, although he seemed to perform his religious obligations conscientiously. She felt that her son was lacking the strong guiding hand of a father.

Finally, in 1916, with the help of a certain captain with whom he became acquainted during his voluntary service in the hospital, he succeeded in getting into the regiment in which his grandfather and his father served. After brief army training, he was sent to the front. Without the permission or even the knowledge of his mother, whom he would never see alive again for she died a year later, he went to Turkey and the Iraq front. Not fully 16 years of age, the boy experienced many varied impressions during his secret army training, and subsequently during his long travels through diverse countries on his way to Turkey. He was fascinated by the exotic Constantinople. He felt self-sufficient riding a horse to the farthest front of Iraq.

Shortly after arriving at the front he and his German colleagues were assigned to one of the Turkish regiments. His cavalry regiment was divided into three divisions, as auxiliaries. Before the German soldiers were able to get into their proper ranks, they were attacked by the British army comprised of Hindus and New Zealanders. The situation was becoming critical. The Turks fled in panic. Only the newly arrived German soldiers were left at the front lines. They were scattered on a sandy desert between large rocks and ruins. They had hardly any ammunition with them, for their main supplies were left with the horses. Firing was thick and closely aimed at the group which was practically immobilized. One after another the Germans fell, either wounded or dead. The situation was becoming more and more tragic.

Rudolph looked at a friend who shortly before was fighting alongside him. He was now dead. Blood was running profusely from his head. Rudolph became terribly frightened, expecting the same fate. He thought of escaping in the tracks of the Turks. At that moment, however, he saw his captain prone behind a large stone. The captain was as calm and undisturbed here as he had been during marksmanship training. He was shooting carefully from a carbine belonging to a fallen friend. His calmness melted the frozen terror in young Rudolph. Up to this time he had not shot his weapon. Now, directing his carbine he was ready to shoot the oncoming Hindus. Just then one of them jumped from behind a mound of rocks, a tall, heavy man with a black, protruding beard. A moment of hesitation, one quick glance at his dead friend, and Rudolph shot. At that moment he shook with fear seeing how the Hindu slumped in midair and did not move again.

"My first kill," said the excited Rudolph. He felt that the chains were broken and continued to shoot just as he was taught in army training. Thoughts about his personal danger left him. From time to time he heard the captain's encouraging words:

"Bravo, Rudi! Bravo! Just continue! Excellent! One enemy less! Cheer up!"

Under the German fire, the Hindus were defeated in the attack. Meanwhile, the Turks overcame their panic, reorganized and then threw themselves into a counter-attack. That day they regained a large part of what they had just lost.

Returning from the battlefield, Rudolph again looked at his dead friend. Again, dulled perhaps by the blustering battle earlier, his feeling for humanity was aroused at this time.

After the battle, the captain expressed his admiration for Rudi for having conducted himself gallantly and calmly in his baptism of fire.

"But Captain," replied the boy modestly, "I was frightened at first. Only later, it somehow worked out."

"Every soldier lives through an experience like that," answered the captain with a laugh.

A hearty friendship developed, a relationship more cordial than that with his own father. The captain kept a watchful eye over the boy, and although he never became indulgent with him, was as fatherly and solicitous about him as he would be over his own son.

At the beginning of the year 1917, Rudolph's regiment was transported to the Palestinian front, to the Holy Land. The names well known to him from his studies of religious history and the Bible were revived in his mind. How different everything seemed from the scenes conjured up by his imagination in his youthful years through the illustrations and descriptions of books.

At first the German detachments were positioned on a camouflaged railroad track, but were later used at the front near Jerusalem. During the attack, Rudi was wounded in the knee, and malaria seized him. He was transferred to a hospital at Wilhelm in a settlement of the German Colony between Jerusalem and Jaffa. In his delirious attacks, the young patient caused much concern. One nurse in particular became very anxious about him.

In time, Rudi became aware that she was prompted not by maternal feelings but by a tender love for him. Up to this time sexual love for a woman was unknown to Rudi. At times he had heard his colleagues speak of erotic things; nevertheless, it was all strange to him. Now, for the first time, he became infatuated.

After leaving the hospital, he visited places made holy 1914–1918 centuries ago through the presence of Christ. During one such tour, he was accosted by merchants selling religious articles, and this he greatly resented. To a certain extent this, too, was a cause of his eventual departure from his Catholic faith which had already then been greatly eroded.

Each month of the war transformed Rudolph more and more. The shaky, frightened student and runaway from his mother was becoming a hard rough soldier. At 17, he was the youngest noncommissioned officer in the German army distinguished with an Iron Cross of the First Class. He spent hours gazing at it full of pride and joy. Now, as a recognized hero he was sent afar on important intelligence commissions and other diverse activities. He gave orders with uncompassionate calmness in the most difficult fighting situations to soldiers who were older than he.

Armistice Day found Rudolph in Damascus. He applied to the Corps authority for further orders.

"With your cavalry platoon, you must be interned."

"And if, on my own responsibility, I'll risk getting through to Germany with my platoon?"

The old General looked at Rudolph with forbearance.

"How old are you, young man?"

"Eighteen," Rudi responded.

"I thought so. Only such a young man is capable of dreaming such unrealistic plans. But to the courageous belongs the world. Do so at your own risk, but under the condition that only volunteers will accompany you."

Rudi uneasily faced the platoon. All the soldiers of this platoon were in their thirties while he was still in his teens.

After presenting his plan of getting through to Germany on horses and with weapons, all agreed to this seemingly mad journey.

First the platoon rode through Anatolia, then they took to the Black Sea on a crude barge to Warna and continued their ride through Bulgaria and Romania. They crossed through the Transylvanian Alps in the deepest snow; then persisted through Sevengrad, Hungary and Austria. After traveling almost three months, without maps and relying on their school boy knowledge of geography, demanding food for the men and horses, hammering through Romania which was now controlled by their enemies' coalition government, they finally reached their fatherland. No other army formation from that theater of action returned to Germany except Rudi's platoon.

Returning to Manheim, Rudolph did not find his family home. For the first time now he realized the loss of his mother. With her death he had lost all support, both spiritual and material. His sisters were students in a convent school. Moreover, the relatives had divided among themselves all the familiar furnishings, everything that made his home pleasant and dear, completely confident that, if Rudolph returned alive and whole from the war, he would at once enter the seminary, and his sisters would remain in the convent.

Full of wrath and indignation at the audacity of the relatives, he was furious about the loss of his family belongings. The very same day Rudi went to his uncle who was his legal guardian.

"Uncle," Rudi said angrily, "what happened to the property that belonged to my sisters and me?"

"Why are you so concerned about the property? Why, you were to become a priest. The money to cover your seminary expenses is put aside."

"I shall not become a priest," replied Rudi with determination.

"Are you resolving this contrary to the holy will of your parents? Didn't your mother warn you in her last letter not to forget your father's wishes?"

"Of course, she wrote. But parents have no right to force their child contrary to his will into the priesthood. Once again I reaffirm the fact that I shall not be a priest. Furthermore, I have no obligation to reveal my reasons for it."

"In spite of what you say, as your legal guardian until you are of age, I shall not give you the money for education in any other vocation because your parents chose the vocation of the priesthood for you. I cannot act contrary to their will."

Exasperated, Rudolph legally resigned his share of the money to his sisters the following day, resolutely rejecting further meddling by his relatives. Without any good-byes, he left Manheim and rode to East Prussia where he applied to the Baltic Corps of Volunteers.

1919–1923
Beginning the Battle for Souls:
Kolbe

On July 22, 1919, Father Maximilian Kolbe received a doctor's degree in theology. On the 23rd day of the same month, he took the Red Cross train, and with two well earned doctorates, he left Rome for Poland. With the new school year, he began his lectures on Church history in the Franciscan Seminary at Cracow. He was determined during this time to recruit clerics into the *Militia Immaculatae*.

The second meeting of the *Militia Immaculatae* (M.I.) took place on November 15, 1919. Father Maximilian gave a conference on the entire program of the M.I. This program became the ideological basis of all the activities of Father Kolbe, as well as of the Association. The gist of what he spoke follows:

> *"The very existence of the Militia Immaculatae depends on the fact that one is wholly dedicated to the Immaculata: unreservedly, irrevocably, without limitations, and under all circumstances. Anyone joining the M.I. becomes her absolute possession. At the same time he becomes the possession of Jesus—as she is the property of Jesus. The more perfectly one belongs to her, the more perfectly one belongs to Jesus. Becoming more and more the property and possession of the Immaculata is the essence of the M.I."*

But in what way can we become the sole possession of the Immaculata?

> *"We are instruments in the most loving hands of the Immaculata, and that is the only way we can possibly achieve our ultimate goal: the glory*

of God, not only a greater glory, but the greatest possible glory. All of our concern, therefore, ought to consist in this: to let ourselves be led, so that nothing is done except what she wants and how she wants it" (KW Vol. 2, #1248, p. 2162 segment III, para. 1).

But how will we know the will of our Queen-Leader?

"On this earth, there is only one safe way: holy obedience to the representative of God, whose will is all the Immaculata desires.".... "Also, at times we may know her intentions even by means of inner inspirations, but on our own we are hardly ever able to be sure that they do indeed come from her and not from our self-love, or from Satan." ... "Even if the Most Blessed Virgin Mary were to appear to us in person and entrust us with the most sublime of tasks, how could we possibly be sure that it is actually she who speaks to us and not some illusion or a trick of the devil?"... "So, in that case too, our surest proof is obedience, that is, confiding what we feel in our internal or external 'forum' to our Superior and doing what he commands without question" (KW Vol. 2, #1248, p. 2162-3 segment III, para. 2, 3, 4).

Father Maximilian did not tolerate ephemeral sentimentality which relied only on tender words of prayers and hymns in Marian devotion, for this was alien to the spirit of the Gospel. He remembered well the words of Jesus: "If you love me, you will keep my commandments." [Jn. 14, 15].

Thus, he observed, transposing the words of Christ, those who truly love the Holy Mother are those who fulfill her will since she wholly conforms to the will of God. Father Kolbe desired that this devotion be supported by a mind open to the truth, including God's revelation, and by a strong will essential to the attainment of natural and supernatural good.

In preparing his first *Knights of the Immaculata* for hardship and struggle Father Maximilian said:

"Trouble and adversity will come, but they must be conquered. You must be prepared for them from all sides. I do not refer here to the difficulties we will experience in every type of work or even the war in which we shall fight for salvation. At times, our best intentions and purposes will be misinterpreted, and vicious calumnies will be cast upon us as Voltaire proclaimed, 'Lie, tell falsehoods; some profit will come from it.' I

especially have in mind the persecution which we might have to face from persons who are sensible, prudent, possibly pious, holy and the best of intentions. Truly, the most searing torment comes when even those enrolled in the M.I. when someone zealously obstructs our paths to destroy what we have built for the greater glory of God. In such a case, what kind of a foundation will support us?

"*It certainly must be something stable and unchangeable, something God-like. Solely and undeniably, it is holy, blind obedience to the Immaculata manifested to us through our superiors. Whoever supports himself on this rock need not fear any storm. Let all the wicked turn against him through word and action, let the sluggish flesh be slothful, let the mind darken, let the will waver, let everyone around him testify against him, let hell go mad, let the world turn up-side-down and let everything in him rage! He nevertheless scorns everything, and does not trust himself. But he is assured of an omnipotent God through the Immaculata and so acts through her powerful hands. In truth, that, and that only is the granite rock against which all the foamy breakers of the sea dash. Supporting ourselves on that rock, we too can be immovable like God, since we are assured of his will through the Immaculata. Even though today obedience would dictate 'yes,' and tomorrow 'no,' we nonetheless would never say we were mistaken. What we did was good before, and is good now. Just as God is unchangeable even when he lets it rain today and not tomorrow. All these adversities and trials are very profitable, necessary and indispensable; they harden the will, and become a source of merit. In this manner many things were clarified for me in Rome during my trial of fire, particularly the foundation of the whole Militia. Similarly, heresies are stimuli in the Church to develop and clarify truths. Through them the will becomes aware of the strength and unchangeableness of the troth, inducing us to hold on to it until adversities disappear. The will is then encouraged and enlivened after a test by suffering, and finds it easier to cope with even greater difficulties.*"

And what reward awaits the children of Mary for that obedience?

"*God in his infinite goodness,*" continues Father Maximilian, "*gives us a taste of some of the Joy which will be our crown, so as to draw us more toward himself and enkindle in us a spirit of fervor. If we strive with all our strength to cooperate with the grace of God to spread his kingdom through the Immaculata in ourselves and in others, we shall also often-times experience that blissful peace of a child who gives himself without limit into the hands of his mother; he does not worry about anything nor is he afraid of anything. All around us the tempest will rage, thunder will strike, yet, we who are dedicated entirely to the Immaculata shall be protected. We shall be working for the salvation of souls and then rest with perfect confidence.*

"And again crosses will befall us. Besides, the grace of God inflaming our hearts will stir up in us a real thirst for unlimited sufferings; to be humiliated, despised, and forgotten, in order that through these sufferings we may testify as to how much we love our Father in heaven, our best Friend and his most loving Mother Immaculata. Suffering is the school of love, expansion and strength-seemingly sad, yet always rejoicing. This is the ideal of life. And then, although there be a whole legion of the most bitter foes against us, we shall find true friends who, united by sincere love and a common ideal, will console us in our sorrow and support us in our weaknesses so that we may never despair, but steadfastly and bravely trust only in God through the Immaculata and fight unto death. All this is only a part of our reward. We must not, however, expect consolation to accompany each of our crosses, but only when our loving Mother Immaculata, seeing our weakness in carrying the cross, will come to our aid and lighten the burden. With heartfelt gratitude and humility we must accept her loving help as an incentive to pray more fervently for strength and zeal to draw souls to God through her."

"What if the Immaculata refuses that sweet aid," Father Kolbe was gradually leading his listeners into the secrets of suffering:

"Oh, we shall merit many more graces if we are plunged into exterior and interior darkness, filled with sorrow, exhausted, unconsoled, persecuted at each step, surrounded by continual failures, abandoned by all, ridiculed, scoffed at as was Jesus on the Cross. We must, however, pray with all our strength for those who persecute us; we must strive to draw them to God through the Immaculata, and unite them with him as closely as possible.

. . . The grace of God will then inflame our hearts with such love that we will be burning with the desire of suffering-suffering without limit—humiliations, mockery, anxieties, forgetfulness, so that through all this

we may show how we love our best Father and Friend and his dearest Mother Immaculata. Suffering is definitely a school of love, of strength. . .

"There is no need to grieve when we do not see the fruits of our work on this earth.

Perhaps, it is the will of God that we reap them after death; in this world someone else may enjoy them. After death, the Immaculata will complete her work by making use of us, and then we shall labor much more than on this poor earth, where in holding out our hand to others, we must be very cautious not to fall ourselves."

Father Maximilian obtained the wisdom expressed in this conference not in the Roman universities, but on his knees in prayer. Understanding the Gospel, the teachings of St. Paul and the doctrine of the little theologian in a Carmelite habit, Therese of the Infant Jesus, this was the theology of the 26-year old Father Maximilian.

The *Militia Immaculatae* began to flourish with new recruits: Franciscan Friars and many lay people. Father Kolbe enrolled them in the "Italian hall", near the Church of the Franciscan Fathers in Cracow. The number of candidates increased daily, He preached to them on the theme of the Immaculata and interior life.

Unfortunately, an advanced stage of tuberculosis forced his superiors to send the ardent young Marian promoter to a sanatorium for therapy at Zakopane, Poland, in the early part of August, 1920. His Father Provincial forbade him to organize any more projects or to carry on the M.I. work. Father Kolbe conformed to this precisely. He not only theorized beautifully on the theme of obedience, but he also practiced it.

On August 11, he wrote to his mother:

"Now let it be an increase, or a decrease, or let the illness entirely go away according to the will of God."

The illness, however, did not impede Father Maximilian in his apostolate. The sanatorium became an academy for his Immaculata. He wrote about this in his letter to his brother Joseph, whose religious name was Alphonse:

"The Immaculata has allowed me to approach the university students who are staying in their nursing home, Bratnia Pomoc. They have a reputation as unbelievers, and not without reason. The management is socialist (so they say) and is composed of who knows whom. They (meaning

a restricted circle of patients, university students) have invited me with much insistence, to discuss religious issues with them. So I organize a short series of apologetic conversations, during which everyone had a chance to speak freely. We began with the existence of God and have got as far as the divinity of Jesus Christ. They even bought the New Testament of Szczepanski, 'Wieczore nad Lemanem' (Evenings on Lake Lemano, by Marian Morawski, SJ) and the 'apologetics' by Bartynowski" (KW Vol. 1, #52, p. 428, para.1).

Many of the students asked for confession. A good number of them began to reflect seriously on the value of human life. Among the most zealous listeners was a seriously ill Jew, a student of medicine. Father Kolbe, with most tender love and kindness, presented to him the beauty of the Christian faith. When his condition became critical, he asked Father Kolbe to baptize him; he then received Holy Viaticum and the Sacrament of the Sick. Father Kolbe placed a medal of the Immaculata around his neck.

"How happy I am now!" The grateful and happy man exclaimed. "I didn't become a Catholic sooner because I feared my family. They are adamantly attached to the faith of Moses. And even now I am afraid. What will happen when my mother comes?"

"Don't be afraid. Set your mind at ease," Father Kolbe was consoling him. "Before that happens you will be in heaven."

As it did happen, the sick boy died peacefully at 11 o'clock and his mother came at 12 o'clock. When she learned of her son's conversion, she tore the miraculous medal from his neck with a shriek. Her screams resounded throughout the sanatorium.

"You have killed my son! You have stolen my son from me!"

The case rested with the resolutely anticlerical director of the sanatorium. He called Father Maximilian and declared to him,

"I forbid you to come to the sanatorium."

"I beg your pardon, sir," replied Father Kolbe with dignity. "I come during visiting hours like other guests of the students. I'm sorry, but you have no right to make exceptions."

The director had no arguments. Father Maximilian continued his apostolate.

In February he made his retreat during which he formulated certain principles according to which he resolved to live. Here are some of the distinctive excerpts:

"I must be a saint, the greatest saint possible. The greatest possible glory of God through salvation and the most perfect sanctification of oneself and of all those who live now and shall live in the future, by way of the Immaculata.... Serenity about the past. Make up for wasted time with fervor. I shall not let through; a) any evil without reparation (destroying it) and b) any good that I may do, increase or contribute to in any measure.... the Will of God through the Immaculata. You are an instrument. Do what you are doing; and pay heed to no other things, either good or bad....Remember always that you are absolute, unconditional, unlimited, irrevocable possession and property of the Immaculata.... You are an instrument in her hands, therefore do solely what she wants; accept each thing from her hands. Have recourse to her in all things, like a child to his mother, entrust all things to her....Acknowledge that you received everything from her and that nothing comes from yourself. The whole fruit of your work depends on your union with her, just as she is the instrument of God's mercy. My life (each of its instants), my death (where, when, and how), and my eternity, all that is yours, O Immaculata. Do with all that whatever you please" (KW Vol. 2, #971, excerpts from p. 1583-4).

The following year Fr. Kolbe's doctor advised his superior that the sick friar be transferred to a peaceful village for the summer.

He was, therefore, placed in Nieszawa, a small town situated on the Vistula River. Here, too, he was forbidden to engage in the work of the M.I. In a letter to his friends in Cracow, he confessed that at times he had a strong temptation to work. He, however, remained faithful to his principle: the best is holy obedience. In reality, the M.I. expanded beyond the gates of Cracow. His Father Provincial informed him that the M.I. was developing strongly among the students in the Franciscan Order and the secondary school in Lwow, which he had attended years before.

In October Father Maximilian's health improved to the point that he could resume the work of which he was most fond. On Nov. 3 he returned to Cracow to further the development of his beloved M.I. To his great joy, the *Militia Immaculatae* received the approval of the Church authorities in Rome. On January 2, 1922, the Vicar for the Archdiocese of Rome, Cardinal Basil Pompilii, issued a decree which declared:

"Desiring that the devotion to the Blessed Virgin be spread, with our au-

thority, we canonically establish this pious association named 'The Pious Union of the Militia Immaculatae' in the oratory of the Seraphic College of the Friars Minor Conventual in Rome and as established, we sanction and approve it."

Father Kolbe resumed his work with greater zeal and ardor. The Italian hall could not accommodate those desiring to hear personally the apostle of the Immaculata. For various reasons many were unable to come to the Franciscan Friary, especially those who lived in the suburbs. Therefore a centralized meeting place had to be obtained as soon as possible. Furthermore, there was a need for a bulletin or a circular dedicated to the cause of the Immaculata, which would be the organ of the M.I.

As usual, Father Maximilian turned to his superior for permission. He resolved to do nothing, not even for the Immaculata, without obedience. The Provincial, Father Aloysius Karwacki, gave him permission with one reservation, "Neither the provincialate nor the friary shall be expected to assume the expense." The work of the Immaculata and of Father Maximilian was to start at point zero. There was no other way for Father Maximilian except to obtain the funds by begging. Imagine Kolbe, a man with two doctoral degrees, going out into the streets of Cracow seeking funds. He himself recalled this incident:

"I remember how I went out into the streets of Cracow to beg a little money for the publication of the first issue. It was drizzling, and, although I walked down several streets, I was still ashamed to stop anywhere and ask for alms.

The second day this came to my mind: 'This begging is not for you; it is for the cause of the Immaculata.' I then ventured to stop at the rectory of a priest friend, Pastor Tobasiewicz. He accepted me most cordially and gave me a donation for the new periodical. He then took me to his vicar for the same purpose and supplied me with several other addresses."

From these first offerings, the first issue of the *Knight of the Immaculata* appeared in the early part of January, 1922. This paper was very modest, without any special cover and with the cheerful warning: "Owing to the lack of funds, we cannot assure our readers of the regular publication of the *Knight of the Immaculata*. This will depend on the amount of money we receive to print the next issue."

The first publication numbered 5,000 copies. Many people received the *Knight of the Immaculata* with great enthusiasm. Some received it with curiosity, while others would not accept it at all, not even gratis. This, however, did not matter to Father Maximilian. He still went out into the streets and distributed his bulletin free to passers-by.

But the financial situation for the publication seemed catastrophic. Father Kolbe was penniless to pay the remainder of the bill for the first issue. In desperation he asked the Guardian of the friary for help, although he remembered the reservation made by the Provincial. The Guardian replied courteously but negatively.

"This is what happens, my son, when you try to attack the sun with a spade," quoting a Polish proverb. "It is now your affair to clear yourself—without jeopardizing the friary."

After holy Mass, Father Maximilian was kneeling before the Blessed Virgin's altar; much distressed, he confided his troubles to the Immaculata. Suddenly, he noticed a small package on the altar with some writing on it: "For You, Immaculata." He opened it, and to his great amazement, it contained the exact sum of money needed to pay for the rest of the first issue.

Without delay, he ran joyfully with the money to the Superior who saw the direct finger of God in this and permitted him to use the whole sum for the *Knight of the Immaculata*. After that, the bulletin was published regularly, and was read more and more. Thanks to Father Maximilian, the ranks of the M.I. were steadily increasing. At the same the Immaculata showered many graces upon her readers.

In the meantime another serious relapse later that month put Father Maximilian in bed. He was nursed directly by his own blood brother, Father Alphonse, who reported his brother's illness as follows:

"It seemed at times that the patient would not survive due to his high fever and frequent hemorrhages. These were critical moments announcing his approaching end. In those most difficult moments Father Maximilian was much concerned about his *Knight of the Immaculata*. He begged me to read him the incoming correspondence, and to correct articles ready for publication. As I was doing these things he requested, the patient seemed to revivify and to grow stronger somewhat At times, when his pain became acute he did not utter a word of complaint, but continuously repeated ejaculatory prayers. During his delirium, you could hear him recite ejaculations in several different languages. Once as I watched at his bedside, he called me:

"Alphonse! Alphonse!"

"What is it you want?" I asked him.

"Take this watch and place it by the statuette of the Immaculata."

I thought to myself, "You must submit to a sick patient and fulfill his request." I laid the watch before the statuette.

"Alphonse! Alphonse!" he called again.

"Here I am to help you."

"Take my spectacles and put them by the statuette of the Immaculata." I did as he requested and then I asked what all that meant.

Father Maximilian responded slowly and clearly.

"The watch is a symbol of time. I give it to the Immaculata. Henceforth, not one moment belongs to me; everything is her possession. The glasses are a symbol of the eyes: I want to behold her and only her incessantly. To her I dedicate myself that she may do with me as she pleases."

In August the superiors sent the sickly Father Kolbe to Mszana Dolna. He returned to Cracow a month later with only one lung and that in a weakened condition. The astonished doctors only shook their heads wondering how he could still be alive with only one faltering lung. There was an order awaiting him that he must transfer to the friary at Grodno together with his editorial office. "What would be the reason for this move?" he wondered. Grodno is located apart from the cultural life of Poland, and the friary was three kilometers from the railroad station and two from the post office.

Father Maximilian's Provincial soon explained, "In our friary at Grodno you will have more room, more time to work, and greater ease in dealing with the printers. Later, perhaps, others can help you set up your own print shop."

His Provincial had remembered that he wanted his own print shop! Father Kolbe transferred the editor's office and the administration of the *Knight* to Grodno. There was no cash box because there was absolutely no money. Father Maximilian nonetheless took with him his greatest treasure, confidence in Divine Providence and the protection of the Immaculata.

At Grodno, he came to the conclusion that the best solution for the problem would be to buy a printing press. Again he went to the Provincial for permission. The Provincial consulted with some of the other Fathers. But many of them objected, arguing that it was against the Franciscan vow of poverty, that St. Francis had no printery nor did he engage in publications, yet, he became a great saint. To this Father Maximilian, with utmost dignity, gave a most splendid reply:

"That's true, but is it a reason for reclining on the thirteenth century as if in an arm chair, banishing our modern technical progress, our economic and social structures? Whoever wants to imitate St. Francis formally, should never ride trains or read newspapers, and never, never smoke cigarettes! Holy poverty does not depend on form but on content or substance. An editor of a mass-circulation publication can be poor in spirit, if his sole purpose is the glory of God and the good of souls. Let us not be afraid of progress, but let us sanctify it!"

This convinced the Father Provincial and he readily gave his permission for the purchase of the printing machine, even lending him money for the press. Father Kolbe again stormed the heavens through prayer to the Immaculata for money needed for other expenses. His prayer was answered through the help of Father Lawrence Cyman who came from America to visit Poland. He met Father Kolbe who happened to be at Cracow at that time, at the community's recreation. There a certain friar who was trying to entertain the guest began to make fun of Father Maximilian and his work.

"Father, if you only knew," he said, "the low level of his periodical, the *Knight of the Immaculata*. People don't want it—not even for nothing. And here Father Kolbe is trying to conquer the whole world. And what's more, the editor even wants a star from heaven: he's dreaming about his own printing machines, even though his pockets are empty. What a dreamer!"

Father Maximilian was silent; he did not defend himself. He bowed his head and covered his lips with his hand.

The guest responded to the mockery of the critic. He expressed his opinion frankly:

"If the office of the *Knight* is sustaining a loss, then to a great degree you Fathers are responsible, because instead of cooperating with Father Maximilian, you are only criticizing him. Regarding the establishment of a print shop, not only should Father Maximilian strive for it, but also all the friaries of the Province ought to take upon themselves the obligation of payment for it."

A piercing stillness now prevailed in the hall. Facial expressions changed on those present who knew only how to cut and criticize, but who did nothing to help the cause. Father Lawrence turned directly to Father Maximilian.

"In order to help you, Father, I'll be the first to donate a check of $100 for this purpose."

Encouraged by this, the Provincial immediately made a loan of 1,500,000 marks for the printing press. This sum was not large because at that time in Poland there was a devaluation of money. After two months the Provincial requested that the loan be treated as a gift. The Franciscan Fathers from Wilno hastened with their aid to Father Maximilian, lending the remainder of the necessary money.

Father Kolbe did not wait long. Immediately, he began his search for a printing press. He found one at the Magdalene Sisters in Lagiewniki near Cracow. He bought the printing press with the money appropriated for this purpose through Divine Providence and the Immaculata.

In October 1922, the *Knight of the Immaculata* began its publication in Grodno. The personnel consisted of three persons: Father Maximilian Kolbe, Brother Albert Olszakowski, type-setter, and an aspirant, Gawel, a binder. Priest members of the M.I. in Cracow continued to help him by writing articles.

The four rooms allotted to the print shop contained a few chairs and tables and one chest of drawers. More importantly there was also the long-dreamed-of printing press called "Grandmother," And above all these natural things, reigned a statuette of the Immaculata.

Owing to the lack of electricity, the printing machine had to be operated by turning a crank. It took a great deal of energy to operate it. Sixty thousand turns were required to print 5,000 copies containing 16 pages including the cover of the *Knight*. The printing required from eight to ten days of work.

Father Maximilian not only prepared the contents of the particular number, but also turned the crank, despite his diseased lungs. His fever, too, never left him. He also found strength to be both the type-setter and the bookbinder. He himself frequently carried the heavy packages of the *Knight* to the post office. The local superior, unwilling to have the printing shop in the friary, did not exempt Father Maximilian from normal pastoral duties either. He worked as the other Fathers, hearing confessions in church and making sick calls. Owing to his illness, he was exempt only from preaching and singing High Masses. For that reason Father Maximilian had little time for sleep and rest. One day his brother colleagues noticed a big bruise on his forehead.

"And whom were you fighting with, Father?" the Brothers teased him.

"Nothing spectacular," replied Father Kolbe nonchalantly. "While I was walking and reciting my rosary, I must have fallen asleep. I awoke when I struck my head against the door."

In 1923 the printing press crew increased by one member, Brother Gabriel Siemienski. The Provincial himself had told him as he was leaving Poznan, "Brother, you are going to help Father Maximilian. He is a holy priest, but also a great bore."

This disturbed and frightened Brother Gabriel.

"No, he isn't bad enough to give you an ulcer."

Brother Gabriel's journey from Poznan to Grodno was most unenthusiastic. Years later he related this touching memory of his initiation at Grodno:

"The day following my arrival at the friary, I went to the print shop. After a brief explanation I was invited to turn the crank to warm up. I took hold of the handle with such energy and enthusiasm, thinking there is nothing to this. I began to turn the crank at a faster speed than did the aspirant before me. It seemed quite easy in the beginning, and I was even astonished that the aspirant became so exhausted. After some time, I, too, began experiencing great exertion. Each minute seemed like a quarter of an hour. I perspired as profusely as if I had taken at least three aspirins. 'Good Lord!' I thought to myself, 'All this time and energy and just a part of the job is finished!' What was I to do? I scratched my head a couple of times and continued to turn the crank.

"In spite of all the perspiration from the hard work, we all felt an internal joy, knowing that we were doing our best for the greater glory of God and for the Immaculata."

1919–1923
The Lure of Hitler and Nazism:
Hoess

The Volunteer Corps in the years 1918-1922 was a peculiar phenomenon in Germany. It was customary for the German government to use volunteers at the borders or in the interior of the German Confederation when danger was imminent. They were no longer used when the danger was over or when allied countries demanded an explanation. The corps was provisionally established so that if needed it could without delay be recalled secretly. This Volunteer Corps was comprised of officers and soldiers from World War I who could not adjust to peaceful conditions. This group also consisted of adventurers, some criminal elements, and some unemployed. Young enthusiasts who felt they could best serve their country in these divisions also applied.

Rudolph Hoess found himself in the Rosebach Volunteer Corps. Again, he felt like a real soldier. At the beginning of his new career, he participated in battles of the Baltic countries. The combat was very difficult, for in reality there was no front because the enemy was everywhere. Each skirmish became a massacre, and no one was taken prisoner. For the first time Rudolph experienced total war in which civilians were not spared. He repeatedly saw startling scenes of burned cottages and charred bodies of women and children. Revenge was taken on the compatriots who helped the German divisions in battle. Crime is contagious, and the German Volunteer Corps did not differ from the avengers in its cruelty toward civilians.

Hoess was distinguished with the Baltic Cross. He and his regiment were thrown into battle in Meklemburg, in the deep Ruhr, and in Upper Silesia. Between periods of active service he completed agricultural training in East Prussia and was employed as an administrator of agricultural property.

In November of 1922, the Corps members to which Rudolph belonged arranged a meeting in Monachium. A new figure was making his appearance on the German political scene in the person of Adolph Hitler, and he was the invited speaker. This slender man with a nervous countenance and glistening eyes made a strange impression on Rudolph. He evoked great enthusiastic applause when he began to speak, and to weave before the eyes of the listeners a magnificent future for the new German Empire.

Hitler did not simply speak—he virtually threw each of his words into the receptive minds of the young, adventurous soldiers who felt prepared for anything.

"We demand that the German nation be equal to other nations, that the peace treaties made at Versailles and St. Germain be abolished.

"We demand that all Germans unite into one great German Empire, a nation of self-determination.

"We demand new territories and colonies to assure food and raw materials for our people and land for settling.

"We demand the formation of a national army.

"We demand unconditional combat against all those who through their actions, harm the interest of the totality.

"Whoever is in favor of this program, let him sign up as a member of the National Socialist German Labor Party [Nazionalsozialistische Deutsche Arbeiterpartei, briefly, NSDAP]."

Rudolph and his colleagues were frantic with joy at hearing Hitler speak. Finally someone had been found who defied the world in the name of a great Germany. They had fought secretly for the same things and were concerned about the same political program.

It did not take Rudolph long to make up his mind. He signed up in Hitler's party; he was given the number 3240.

He was no less active in the Volunteer Corps of Rosebach; as one of its members, he participated in the murder of the captured teacher, Walter Kadow, in the Parchin Woods during the night of May 31 to June 1, 1923. Probably Kadow intended to betray Albert Leo Schlageter, who directed the anti-French sabotage action in the deep Ruhr, into the hands of the French. After a drinking spree, Hoess and his colleagues, among them Martin Bormann, took Kadow into the woods. There, they beat him with clubs and branches; they cut his throat and finished him off with two shots. Rudolph's accomplice, Bernard Jurisch, informed German authorities about this murder. During the trial the Tribunal concluded that he participated to protect himself, fearing that the same fate would befall him.

Hoess was arrested June 28, 1923.

1924–1928
A Spiritual Army Grows and Bears Fruit:
Kolbe

From month to month the *Knight of the Immaculata* grew in popularity in Poland. Father Maximilian was forced to increase the printings practically every month. The following statistics show the circulation in 1924:

January	6,000 copies
March	7,000 copies
June	7,500 copies
July	10,000 copies
September	10,500 copies
October	11,500 copies
December	12,000 copies

In September of that year Father Maximilian with his staff resolved to publish 12,000 copies of the *Knight of the Immaculata Calendar* for the following year. They were lacking practically everything, but chiefly time. The editorial team of four, as a result, decided to make better use not only of their free time during the day but also to sacrifice several nights. All this was done for the honor of the Immaculata. Through this particular calendar, Father Maximilian gained a great number of sympathizers for the cause of the M.I.

In the introduction to the calendar he wrote frankly that his calendar was modest and left much to be desired. He, however, mentioned nothing about payment.

He remarked that he was only concerned with the honor of the Blessed Mother, and if his calendar could contribute at least a small spark of love toward the Immaculata, that would suffice to him.

The first part of the calendar was dedicated to the Blessed Mother. The second, was entitled, "How the Knight of the Immaculata Began." This was a report of its publication. In reaction to the pictures it contained, one of Father Kolbe's coworkers wrote:

"Up to this time the readers were accustomed to see pictures of religious kneeling in prayer and sometimes nursing the sick. Now, however, it was entirely different, something new, namely: friars at heavy manual labor. From the correspondence received later, we learned that through our physical labor and our efforts, the relationship with our readers became closer and more cordial. At this time, too, there were many readers whose great interest prompted them to question us about our growing progress. The Knight of the Immaculata *intensified the readers' interest to such an extent that they considered the publication as something belonging to them."*

From then on, Father Maximilian included snapshots in the *Knight* with articles and news happenings in their printing shop. There was actually a family tie between the editors and readers; everybody felt they were children of one Mother, the Immaculata.

The year 1925 witnessed a spiraling increase in the circulation of the *Knight of the Immaculata*. The January circulation of 15,000 copies grew to 30,000 in December. At the same time the periodical was enlarged to thirty-two pages, thanks to increased donations. Father Kolbe was able to purchase the most modern machines for his printery. One especially was appreciated, the addressograph which he called a 'Dream.' A few weeks later a pedal machine arrived. It was considered very practical because it could be operated by one person. He arranged to have stereotyped printing which radically reduced costs. Most important of all was an electric generator which greatly reduced both labor and costs.

In various ways, Father Kolbe was helped with the publication work by many persons. There was also heartfelt gratitude expressed in one of the issues to the administration and the clerks at the post office at Grodno. One of the co-workers of Father Kolbe wrote as follows:

"We feel deeply grateful to the administration and to the personnel of the post office in Grodno. During the course of time that we have been operating our printing of the periodical at Grodno, we have experienced

many favors and kindnesses from you. We realize how patient you all have been with us when so often we were late with our mail and had many incorrect addresses that caused you a great deal of extra work involving overtime labor. We were pleasantly surprised to find out that although many of you are of a different denomination you showed us such great courtesy. One of your workers has a special devotion to the Immaculata, for he never fails in sending us a monthly offering of 20 zl. for the Knight of the Immaculata. Likewise, many favors were shown to us by the railroad workers of Grodno. Their advice and helpful information have decreased our cost of mailing."

Father Maximilian felt a need to increase his staff for the publication. He turned to the Provincial, pleading for permission to receive candidates as Brothers of the Order who wished to dedicate themselves to the work of the publication in order to give honor to the Blessed Mother and through her gain souls for God. After receiving the permission, he announced it in the *Knight of the Immaculata*: the call for zealous young men who would like to join his team dedicated to the publication.

That call drew many candidates. One of these applicants after joining Father Kolbe's team wrote as follows:

"It seems to me that 99% of the Brothers in Niepokolanow (The City of the Immaculata) and also a great number of Fathers are indebted for their vocation first to God, and then to the Knight of the Immaculata. *Briefly, I shall describe my experience: In the early part of 1927 a copy of the* Knight: of the Immaculata *fell into my hands by chance. It was addressed to our pastor. The introductory article, 'Penance, Penance,' made a deep impression on my soul. I decided immediately to subscribe to it. There really was nothing extraordinary in it, yet, I looked forward to it from day to day as I would for my best friend. The periodical contained something so magnetic that at times I was unable to describe it. Today, I understand it. The grace of the Immaculata accompanied every issue through the prayer and sacrifice of the editor. I had been receiving the* Knight *for several months, and with each issue something in my heart began to germinate, something that I couldn't describe or call by name. 1 was overjoyed when I learned that all Brothers work on the publication. There were even photographs of these Brothers in long black habits girded with white cords, working with motors, in the administration, expediting*

the publication, packing, . . . but one noticed at once a little statuette of the Immaculata, as the executive of the printery. The seed germinated in my heart. Suddenly, I felt a determined willingness to be among those Brothers. I felt that the Immaculata herself was drawing me closer to her. Most secretly, I wrote to the editor confiding my desires. After a few days I received a reply as follows:

Dear Michael,
From your letter radiates such a sincere and fervent willingness to dedicate yourself to the service of Jesus Christ that we would accept you almost immediately. However, there are two requirements:
   Are you entirely well?
   Did you reflect on the matter of the many difficulties involved?
   Concerning the first, a health certificate from the doctor is necessary. As to the second, remember above all that with us things will not happen the way you want them, but as the superior orders you. In short, you must submit your will entirely to holy obedience in the Order. Another thing you should know is that the superiors surely will do you no harm. They will, no doubt, love you as your parents. But you must be prepared for everything. It sometimes happens that an applicant arrives, and leaves almost immediately because he wants to govern, and here they tell you to obey.

After this letter, I was sure to be accepted. I received it at the post office myself. As I rode through the woods, I sang in full force from joy as though heaven was in my soul. On October 18, 1927, I stood in Grodno before Father Maximilian whom I loved at first sight with all my heart. He was slender, of medium height, round faced, with beautiful eyes. Those eyes beamed with goodness, love, resoluteness and penetration. They seemed to be looking right into your soul; they could read the secrets of your heart, for the flesh is no hindrance for such sense of seeing. He had me take a seat, then asked about my journey, etc. Finally, before leaving, he addressed me.
   'So, you want to serve the Immaculata?'
   'Yes, Father.'
   'Very well, my child,' replied Father Maximilian radiantly, 'I promise you that you will be happy.'
   He embraced me so tenderly and lovingly that all my fears vanished,

and my heart was filled with a wonderful peace that never has left me throughout my whole religious life. I loved Father Maximilian like my own father and like my mother. Well, was he not a Spiritual Father in reality? Did he not, through his prayer-saturated Knight *give me birth in the community? I am sure that almost all the Brothers had similar experiences with their vocation."*

The ever-growing publication pleaded for more hands to work and more new machines. Father Kolbe now made a purchase of a 4-horsepower gasoline motor, and he imported a large printing press from Germany.

At this opportune time the Provincial made a visit. He was amazed at the gigantic progress of the *Knight*. Into the Visitors' Book on June 4, 1924 the Provincial wrote: "The printery is developing and growing at a great pace, and the *Knight of the Immaculata* is becoming more powerful! The administration and the editorship is conducted by Father Maximilian Kolbe who obviously is blessed by the Immaculata."

The year 1926 began quite fortunately for the publication. The circulation of the first issue that year leaped to 10,000 copies. Father Maximilian introduced into the review several innovations, namely, illustrations with actual happenings from the Catholic world. This greatly enlivened the *Knight*.

From August 28 to August 30, 1926, the first General Polish Congress of Catholics met in Warsaw. This Congress was opened most solemnly by Cardinal Kakowski in the presence of the President of the Republic himself. The general theme of the speeches and discussions concerned the Catholic Press. Addresses were delivered by prelates, by learned, well-dressed men. Then a friar in a worn habit appeared to address the audience. This friar, of course, was Fr. Maximilian Kolbe, the editor of the *Knight of the Immaculata*. He spoke on the role of an editor of a Catholic paper, and he concluded with these distinctive words:

"An editor molds an opinion and has a dynamic influence on society. He, therefore, has a great responsibility before God. To make his work productive, he must live as a good Catholic. Before writing an article, he will pray to the Holy Spirit for light and guidance. In order to give something to anyone, one must first possess the thing himself."

After Father Maximilian's discourse, in place of applause, dead silence followed. Some were scandalized at the moral tone of the friar, others were deeply moved.

The results of this Congress were written up in verbose reports and moral directives, most of which remained untouched and filed away.

Beautiful words in themselves were valueless according to Father Kolbe. His own vigorous approach to his enterprise brought results. The *Knight* grew from thirty-two to forty-four pages in length. Since he anticipated printing 50,000 copies of the calendar, he purchased an additional printing machine.

Father Maximilian's health began to fail again. In September the Provincial sent him again to the health resort at Zakopane for eight months and assigned his brother, Father Alphonse, to substitute for him at Grodno. In the beginning, Father Maximilian was permitted to give directives concerning the enterprise to Father Alphonse.

Father Maximilian was most generous in sharing not only his ideas and encouragement with his brother and the staff, but also in offering them the theoretical principles upon which the project of the Immaculata might be supported.

One urgent problem was that some of the Fathers of the Province were unsympathetic to the bold risks of the printery. They disapproved of the mass production which to them seemed a foolhardy waste. They felt it would be more practical to limit the publication in order to save money to finance the project as well as to provide some income for the friary's expenses. On November 2, 1926 the gist of what Father Maximilian wrote to his brother is as follows:

The purpose of our publication is conquering the world for Christ, winning all the world, but not for financial profit. According to some practical minds the enterprise should not be developed further. "There are enough machines to take care of the publication; from now on we'll have an income for the friary." And so in this way they have turned the means into the end, and the end into the means. The first consequence is: "develop no further," let souls be lost and let the devil's press develop frightfully, sowing unbelief and immorality, but "we will have an income!" Inevitably, then, the curse of our Holy Father Saint Francis would have to fall upon this type of workshop which assures the friars peaceful prosperity as happened to the large landed estates of "lord" friars, as we were called long ago in Rome. It would be a blessing for such a workshop to disintegrate or be confiscated by a dishonorable government, in order that the "lord" friars would truly become poor Friars Minor. They would then get to work for the salvation of souls, or else there would be nothing to live on. If the ideal of the love of God and salvation of the greatest number of souls through the Immaculata should become extinguished, then this is what the loss of the purpose of the enterprise would lead to in the end.

Father Maximilian could bear this no longer. He defended the rights and privileges of holy poverty very tenaciously. His poverty had a very modern aspect which can be summed up in two phrases: nothing for us, all for God and the Immaculata. For us, the worst of everything; patched habit, plain food and miserable cold huts. For God and for the Immaculata, a modern workshop, the latest machines, all the products of modern techniques, the fastest means of transportation, the whole of culture and civilization.

It was obvious that these practices and principles bewildered the contemporary religious who were literal-minded. Once a certain prelate visiting the printing shop of the *Knight* had remarked tauntingly:

"What would Saint Francis do if he could see these expensive machines?"

"He would roll up his sleeves, Your Excellency, and begin to work with us."

The worldly minded could not comprehend these truths, but the simple and humble, whole-heartedly supported the poor friars who were using "deluxe" tools for the glory of God, the Immaculata, and the salvation of souls.

On January 14 the following year, after a thorough examination the doctor declared that Father Maximilian might return to Grodno and recuperate there. Father Kolbe informed his Provincial of the doctor's decision, but the Provincial disagreed and forbade Father Maximilian to travel without his permission or to do any work.

Father Maximilian who knew how to teach obedience so convincingly did not hesitate now to practice it himself. On the 1st of February, he wrote to his brothers:

"Let the Immaculata do as she pleases. My health, my illness, and I myself are her possession and are, therefore, left to her free disposition."

Father Alphonse found himself in a difficult situation. He, therefore, turned to Father Maximilian with assorted difficulties concerning the review. The latter, mindful of the Provincial's orders that he may do absolutely no work, replied thus,

"You must try your best to do the job as well as you can. Let the Immaculata guide you!"

Another time his brother asked him for criticism of a new issue. Again Father Maximilian declined.

"I am sorry, but I may not even offer my criticism."

He was, indeed, faithful to obedience.

During his prolonged treatments at Zakopane, Father Maximilian began to realize more and more that he was not the creator of the M.I. project and its publication, but rather he was only an instrument of the Immaculata. Therefore, he wrote sincerely to his brother,

> *"I don't know what the Immaculata wishes, but at times it seems to me that for the sake of the Knight and the M.I., it would be better if I would not live. When I had many anxieties and troubles with the publication, a thought came to my mind: 'You're foolish; why are you troubled? Is that your publication? If everything belongs to the Immaculata, she herself will settle everything for the best. Let her guide you.' After this, I regained peace and serenity of soul."*

In April, 1927 the Provincial permitted Father Maximilian to resume his work at Grodno even though he was not totally cured. The doctors recommended that he limit his activities, sleep ten hours every night, walk out in the fresh air for four hours daily, have sunny and dry living quarters, eat good nourishing food, and avoid lifting and carrying anything heavy, especially with the right arm. Disregarding the doctor's advice, he immediately rolled up his sleeves and zealously assumed the leadership of the ever progressing project of the Immaculata. His brother, Father Alphonse, was at this time already transferred to Poznan (Posen).

Father Maximilian's stay in the solitude of Zakopane had seemed to be time lost without any benefit to the M.I. and the publication. However, what appears as idleness is frequently great internal ferment. It was just that in the case of Father Maximilian. As a result of his reflections, he resolved to found a new friary which would serve only the publication of the *Knight* and the National Center of the M.I., and which would conform exactly to this purpose.

On Holy Saturday, April 16, 1927, when he revealed his intentions to the staff members in Grodno, they received them with overwhelming enthusiasm. Father Maximilian recommended that all of them together and

L. to r.: Prince Drucki-Lubecki, Polish nobleman who gave Father Maximilian over six acres of land from his Teresin estate about 26 miles west of Warsaw in 1927; Count Bninski, voivode or governor of the Poznan district; Father Maximilian, who with his confreres built the huge Polish friary and evangelism center known as Niepokalanow, on the six acres and subsequent donations of land given him by Prince Drucki-Lubecki (1938 photo).

each one individually search for projects and plans for the realization of the dreamed-of friary and center.

Two months elapsed and nothing materialized. On June 13, however, something began to happen.

Father Thaddeus Ciborowski, pastor of a near-by parish of Adamowicz arrived at the Franciscan friary in Grodno for the Feast of St. Anthony. During their table-talk, Father Kolbe learned that Prince John Drucki-Lubecki was parceling his land in Teresin around Warsaw and that the surveyor in charge of this work lived near Grodno in Poniemum. Father Maximilian revealed his plans to his guest and asked him to intercede for him to obtain a tract of land for the friary. Father Ciborowski hopefully brought Father Maximilian's request to the attention of the surveyor, who was favorable to the request and introduced Father Kolbe to the prince.

Drucki-Lubecki was charmed by the simplicity of Father Maximilian and his plans to conquer the world for the Immaculata. He most gladly offered him five acres of land with the privilege of choosing the most suitable spot for his future project, stipulating however that 24 Masses would be offered yearly in perpetuity in the chapel of the new friary and two Masses in the palace chapel of Prince Lubecki for the members of his family, living and deceased.

Father Kolbe referred this matter to his Father Provincial. In the meantime he placed a statue of the Immaculata on a stand in the middle of his chosen spot so that she would take this site into her- possession.

The Provincial Council did not accept the stipulation presented by the prince for good reasons. It would be impossible to burden future generations with such responsibilities perpetually.

This was a great blow to Father Maximilian. It seemed to him that all his plans had been defeated. No one, however, heard any complaint, criticism, or grumbling coming from his lips. Full of resignation he went to the prince with the sad news.

"What about the statue the Fathers placed on my land?" inquired Prince Drucki-Lubecki.

"Your gift, Prince, had been given into the possession of the Immaculata. Therefore, please decide what should be done," replied Father Kolbe in a low tone, and he sadly bowed his head.

After a tense moment, the prince said calmly, "Very well, I am offering you the land without any obligation on the part of the friary."

This time the Provincial with the Council agreed to the new foundation without any restriction.

Father Kolbe was overjoyed at this good fortune. When he read this announcement over the racket of the printing machines, he called to the Brother workers,

"Let us fall on our knees, dear children, to thank the Immaculata for her victory."

Father Maximilian began immediately to build a new town for Mary which was called Niepokalanow (City of the Immaculata). Father Cornelius Czupryk, the Provincial, was greatly encouraging and promoted the project through correspondence.

"It is well, Father, that you intend to build barracks for the duration of winter. May God bless your enterprise, and may the Immaculata take that en tire project under her special protection. May the glory of Mary radiate' from it not only over our fatherland, but also over the whole world."

Together with Brother Zeno Zebrowski, Father Maximilian laid out plans for three barracks of hazel wood. Under the smiling eyes of the Immaculata they began to build rough barracks with the help of other Brothers. The peasants of the surrounding country, seeing the heroic labor of the Brothers, gladly hastened to lend a hand in the building of the new project for the glory of God and the honor of Mary. Some brought building materials, others leveled the land and still others smoothed the walls. Charmed by the Brothers, not only men but women and children worked unselfishly for hours. They called the new project "Our Niepokalanow."

Early each morning Father Maximilian walked with the Brothers to the church at Szymanow, five kilometers away from the new building, to celebrate Mass and to distribute Holy Communion to his co-workers. This involved great sacrifice and hardship for all of them. He, therefore, hastened the work on the chapel so that it might be ready for use as soon as possible. After its completion, Father Kolbe went to the Curia of Warsaw for permission to celebrate Mass and to preserve the Blessed Sacrament there. The Chancellor of the Curia replied with bureaucratic iciness:

"Please present your request formally in writing. The Curia will consider the matter."

"Can't this be done through my verbal request?" Father Kolbe asked.

"That can be done only by His Eminence, the Cardinal."

"Then, please, permit me to have an audience with His Eminence." The Chancellor studied the figure of Father Kolbe from head to foot.

"Father, you're coming to visit His Eminence, the Cardinal. Your habit is so soiled and your shoes are pitiable!"

Father Maximilian stretched out his worn hands toward the Chancellor and said,

"Father Chancellor, I came here right from work."

The Chancellor, moved by his simplicity, introduced him into the presence of the Cardinal. Father Kolbe apologized to the high prelate for appearing before him soiled from work, and explained the urgency of the matter. The Cardinal complied most graciously and wished him success in his demanding work for God.

Father Maximilian celebrated his first Mass in the new chapel on November 17, 1927. The Brothers, together with God's people, knelt on bare ground in tribute to the birth of Christ on the altar, just as the shepherds did in the stable at Bethlehem.

As soon as the principal buildings were up, Father Maximilian went to Grodno to supervise the moving of the printery and to say goodbye to the friary which had helped him and his enterprise. The last Sunday before departure, Father Kolbe went to Wilno with his staff and workers to ask the blessing of Our Lady of Ostrobrama (Our Lady of Wilnius) upon their new friary at Niepokalanow. There, in the wonderful chapel, Father Maximilian celebrated Mass and distributed Holy Communion to his co-workers. Later they went to the Mount of the Three Crosses where, years back, the first Franciscans of Wilno died as martyrs. It was here that for the first time, Father Maximilian revealed his mission plans.

November, was the day of departure from Grodno. After some prayer in the friary choir, Father Maximilian addressed his co-workers:

"Niepokalanow [the City of the Immaculata], to which we shall go in a few hours, is a place chosen by the Immaculata exclusively to spread her honor.

Everything, whatever is and will be in Niepokalanow is her possession. We, likewise, were chosen by the Immaculata and through this we became her property. Tomorrow is the Feast of the Presentation of the Blessed Virgin Mary. She, the Immaculata, was wholly dedicated to God. Let us, on the Vigil of her feast, make an offering of ourselves entirely into her hands as instruments unreservedly, forever.

"In this friary our dedication must be whole and entire. Community life must bloom fully; above all, we will practice obedience. We need to remain poor, according to the Poverello. There will be a great deal of work, much suffering, and many inconveniences. We shall observe our holy Constitutions and all community regulations with austerity because

Niepokalanow should and must be a model of religious community living. If any of you feel a lack of strength, or if you are not willing to go there, let me know today, sincerely and openly, and I shall obtain permission for you from the Provincial to remain here in Grodno or to be transferred elsewhere."

This message was delivered without any compromise. When two of the co-workers withdrew, requesting to remain in Grodno, Father Maximilian fulfilled his promise.

The group of eighteen Brothers and one priest, together with Father Maximilian, knelt down before the superior of the friary and begged for his blessing upon their journey.

On the frosty morning of November 21st, this group of Franciscan Friars alighted from the train at Szymanow Station and turned northward where in a large field stood three poor, lonely barracks called Niepokalanow. Upon arrival they visited the chapel and adored Jesus in the Blessed Sacrament. Then a number of friars returned to the station to unpack the printing machines while the others prepared places for the printing presses.

Father Maximilian resolved to begin a new life at Niepokalanow, not with work on the printing machines only, but with work on the interior life. For that reason on the last day of November he and all his co-workers began an eight day retreat in absolute silence.

The dedication of the new friary took place on the vigil of the Immaculate Conception, December 7, 1927. The blessing was performed by the Minister Provincial, Father Cornelius Czupryk, who was assisted by neighboring pastors. Among the many guests present were the Governor, the Captain from Sochaczew and others.

New life in Niepokalanow was begun by two priests and eighteen Brothers.

Toward the end of January in 1928, the press run of the *Knight* printed at Niepokalanow numbered 65,000 copies. There were clear indications the *Knight* would continue to grow rapidly.

Since there were too few hands to do the work, Father Maximilian again made an appeal for candidates in the May issue of the *Knight*. He called for young men to the religious life who were willing to work for the honor of the Immaculata in the avocation of a printing shop. Individuals of good will began to apply. One of the candidates related his reception as follows:

As I got off the train, I looked around.

"Where is the friary?" I asked a passerby.

"Oh, over there," he pointed as he answered. Straining my eyes, I saw nothing.

The man clad in a sheep-skin looked at me and laughed.

"Well, it's not a friary like the one in Warsaw. Don't you see those huts in the field?"

"Yes, I see them," I answered in a surprised manner.

"That's the friary, and that one," pointing to another, "is a chapel. It's cold in there. They have little to eat, but they are very jolly. They are always laughing and singing."

I was welcomed by Father Maximilian himself as he was just returning from work. He looked very tired and exhausted. Seeing me, he smiled affectionately.

Father Maximilian Kolbe with L. Jonczynski, administrator of Prince Drucki-Lubecki's estate, parts of which the prince donated to Father Kolbe for the establishment and expansion of Niepokalanow. Fr. Florian Koziura, left, was Father Kolbe's assistant (1940 photo).

'The original statue of the Immaculata erected by Saint Maximilian on the site of the future Niepokalanow, the first building to be constructed there, as it appeared in November, 1927.

"You must be hungry, dear child. Come with me."

He gave me plenty to eat and drink. He was as solicitous over me as a mother over her child. He was always smiling and frequently repeated to me:

"Love the Immaculata and you will always be happy!" As I looked at him, I thought in my heart that those are not merely words but real truth, for he himself lives as he says! Suddenly, I felt so light, so peaceful in spirit that I could embrace the whole world. Truly I found in him both a father and mother.

"All the candidates who were received by Father Maximilian felt as I did for they expressed themselves about it similarly. Some testimonies of the Brothers indicate his evident affection for the new applicants:

"Our real mother did not love us as he did. We felt that he would sacrifice his life for each one of us. We, likewise, were ready even to jump into fire at his command."

"At his sight, all anxieties, doubts and sadness disappeared. It sufficed for him just to cast a glance with those kindly eyes in our direction and immediately our hearts were filled with confidence, and tranquility flowed into our souls."

And another: "I felt myself as near to him as a little child near to the heart of his mother."

With the addition of these new candidates, Niepokalanow was growing vigorously!

1924-1928
A Prison Sentence for Murder:
Hoess

On March 15, 1924, Rudolph Hoess was convicted by the State Tribunal for the Protection of the Republic to a ten-year term of imprisonment for being a leader and participant in the murder at Parchim. The sentence did not faze him or his accomplices who also were sentenced to imprisonment. Jubilantly they sang their old battle songs as they were driven to prison, expecting that at any moment the sentence would be reversed and they would be freed from prison as heroes.

A very painful disenchantment followed soon after they were transferred to the penal institution. Rudolph now faced a world unknown to him up to this time.

The Prussian prison was not an abode of rest. Prison life was regulated by military discipline in the minutest details. Greatest pressure was placed on the most accurate and diligent fulfillment of daily work. Every transgression was severely punished.

As a political convict (politischer Uberzeugungstaeter) Rudolph had the privilege of a single cell. He was independent insofar as he could do what he wanted after he performed his assigned duties. Since he was alone in his cell, he was spared the unpleasantness of listening to the grievances of other colleagues. He also avoided the terrors of the marauding groups prevalent in most communal halls.

Since his earliest years he had been accustomed to absolute obedience, punctilious order, and cleanliness; he found no difficulty in adjusting to hard prison life. He performed all his obligations and work conscientiously, to the satisfaction of his overseers; he always kept his cell in exemplary order, and the most vengeful eye could find nothing deserving a reprimand.

Contrary to his vagabond nature and mode of life, he even grew accustomed to the routine of each day which seldom was interrupted by any incident whatever.

A particular occurrence which did interrupt the boring life of the prison was the arrival of the letters permitted every three months. One interested him days before it arrived, reflecting on the contents that it might contain. The letter was from his "fiancée," a sister of a colleague. He never saw her and had heard nothing about her before. Since prisoners were permitted to write only to relatives and receive letters only from them, his colleague made the fiancée arrangement for him. This strange girl corresponded with him throughout his prison years. She complied with his wishes in every respect and informed him accurately of all happenings among his acquaintances.

Hoess could not cope with the narrowness and fraudulence of the minor officials of the prison. When these were deliberately vindictive and malicious it invariably disturbed him deeply. He felt these psychic insults as more degrading and oppressive than any physical maltreatment. He tried to be insensitive to them but he never succeeded.

He outwardly acquiesced to the sharp, rough tongue of the minor functionaries. The lower their rank the more they delighted in acting arbitrarily. When complying, he endeavored to perform even the most preposterous orders willingly and even with a smile. His manner of speaking, however, was no different from that of most other prisoners: uncouth and vulgar.

Ordinarily, Rudolph took no interest in books. However, in the solitude of his cell, books became everything to him, particularly during the first two years of his prison life. Books were now his recreation for they turned his mind away from prison.

It had seemed to Hoess that nothing that was human could be strange to him because he traveled in many different and far off countries where he'd had the opportunity to meet people of various types, customs, and morality. From the inmates of the Brandenberg prison he learned that he actually knew little about life. Although he spent much time alone in his cell, he came in contact with other prisoners during their outdoor walks, while bathing, or when working together. At his windows he heard their evening conversation from which he learned a great deal about the manner of their thinking and motivations. An abyss of human faults, crime, and passions was opening up before him.

One evening at the beginning of his confinement he overheard one of the convicts in an adjacent cell relate to his colleagues an assault he had made on a forest ranger's home. He said that at first he had to convince himself that the master of the house was not at home. Then, with a hatchet he murdered the house-maid, next the master's pregnant wife, and finally four little children who were screaming for help and mercy. He beat their little heads against the wall until they stopped 'crowing'—as he expressed it. The convict told this in a mean and boastful manner. That night a shocked Rudolph could not fall asleep.

"How could anyone kill helpless innocent children? How could anyone kill a pregnant woman?" Rudolph asked himself. "Doesn't human crime know any limits?"

Various types of characters could be found from the 'elite' to the worst scum of Berlin—from international pickpockets to well known forgers, modish embezzlers, gamblers and sexual perverts.

Nevertheless, in his early days of imprisonment, Hoess clearly realized his situation and this brought him to his senses. He had to take into account that he would spend ten years of his life in prison. A letter from one of the lawyers convinced him of this. Psychologically he prepared himself for the term of imprisonment. Thus far he lived from one day to another, took life as it came without giving any serious thought to his future. He now had ample leisure time to concentrate on his entire life, to become acquainted with his faults and weaknesses, and to prepare himself for richer satisfaction in life. As a member of the volunteer Corps he had learned agriculture. Although he boasted of his success in that area, yet he felt dissatisfied because of a lack of meaning in his life. He began to reflect:

"What does human life hold? Where am I going?"

Meanwhile, long weeks and months of monotonous living were spent in prison. After two years he suddenly fell into a strange state of depression. He became excited and nervous; he felt a resentment for his work, which at the time was tailoring. He could not eat well, or retain food. Wildly he paced back and forth in his cell and suffered from insomnia. When he became exhausted, he would throw himself on his bed and finally fall asleep. After a short time he would awaken drenched in perspiration resulting from distorted, disturbing dreams in which he was always being pursued, murdered or thrown into an abyss. The nights were becoming a real torture to him. Hour after hour he heard the striking of the clock in the steeple.

He tried to restrain himself but nothing helped. He wanted to pray but could not produce anything except a sorry stammering of fear.

"Of course, God will not help me," he reflected, "for I myself abandoned him when I formally left the Catholic Church in 1922. Why didn't I obey my parents in directing my steps from the army to the seminary?"

His unrest was increasing from day to day and from hour to hour; he was nearing insanity. Physically he was deteriorating more and more. The supervisor under whose charge Hoess worked was dismayed at this strange distraction. The simplest things Hoess did were peculiar and his performance was substandard.

Seeing the strange conduct of the prisoner and his physical exhaustion, the functionaries took Hoess to the doctor. The senior Doctor, who had been working for decades in the prison, calmly heard out the patient, examined his papers, and than said very quietly,

"It's prison psychosis. It isn't too bad; it will pass."

Rudolph was taken to the hospital where he was given an injection to quiet him down, and cold compresses were applied to his head, after which he fell into a deep sleep. During the next several days he received continued treatments and suitable food. After some time his general state of tension decreased so much that he was able to return to his cell.

Meanwhile, the director of the prison told him that because of his good conduct and his productive work, he was promoted to the group of prisoners of the second degree, and hence, additional privileges would be given to him. He was permitted to write letters every month and to receive all letters sent to him. He was allowed to keep flowers on the window sill and to burn lights until ten in the evening. On Sundays and holidays he was permitted to mingle with the other prisoners for a few hours.

All these conveniences helped him overcome his prison depression much sooner than all medical tranquilizers. In spite of this, signs of the state of depression continued for a long time. He am used himself as an observer of other prisoners similarly afflicted. Many cases of prison psychosis terminated in a madman's cell; other prisoners were led to complete spiritual despair and intellectual disorder. Some of the prisoners known to Hoess overcame the psychosis, but they remained timid, dejected and pessimistic for a long time. Most suicides at the prison were due directly to this psychosis.

After this depression, Rudolph's prison life flowed smoothly without any particular events. He was becoming more and more peaceful and well balanced. In his leisure time he studied the English language which helped him maintain internal discipline. He received books from his colleagues and friends. He read historical and scientific books avidly; he was also interested in pseudo-scientific books about race and heredity. On Sundays he played chess with his colleagues.

In his fourth year of prison life, Hoess was admitted to the third degree of privileged prisoners. He had the privilege of writing letters on his own stationery every fourteen days. He was also released from forced labor. If he worked, it was voluntary, and he could choose the type of work most suited to him, for which he received a higher compensation. He could listen to the radio and smoke cigarettes at specified hours.

At that time there was a vacancy in the position of a writer in the storehouse, and Rudolph applied for it. As a result his work was varied throughout the whole day; he saw much and heard much from the newcomers, and from the departing prisoners, and from prisoners of all ranks who came to the warehouse dally for a change of clothing, linens, etc. The storehouse became a place of obtaining varied information as well as gossip. Hoess learned how this gossip and rumors of all kinds began and spread quickly, how news and lies spread farthest through secretive channels as the elixir of prison life. The more isolated a prisoner was, the more effective the gossip; the more uneducated he was, the more credulous.

One of the prisoners who, like Rudolph, was employed in the storehouse, found a treacherous pleasure in making up lies and sowing gossip. He whispered these to others and then watched them spread and the consequences resulting from them. He proceeded very cunningly; it was, indeed, difficult to unmask him. At one time Hoess became a victim of that type of gossip. Rumors spread that prison functionaries had made it possible for him to accept women visitors into his cell at night. Some prisoner, through the mediation of a certain officer, forwarded this information in the form of a complaint to higher prison authority. Suddenly, one night the director of the prison department with some other officers appeared in his cell to convince themselves about the truth of this gossip. In spite of a prolonged investigation, it was impossible to discover either the informer or the creator of the tale. After being released from prison, Hoess' co-worker in the warehouse told him that it was he who contrived that tale about him to spite the director who had rejected his request for pardon.

After all that he saw and heard, Rudolph willingly returned to his solitary cell and there peacefully reflected on the happenings of the day. He then engaged in reading books and answering letters. Gradually, in his fifth year of prison life, he became resigned to making his cell his life. Many requests for his amnesty came from influential people but they were rejected for political reasons. He did not expect to be released from prison before his term of ten years.

A surprise awaited him one night. The Reichstag, the German Government, comprised of extreme conservative and liberal representatives, was interested in obtaining the release of all their political prisoners. This they achieved on July 14, 1928. Rudolph Hoess with many other prisoners was liberated.

1929–1934
Implanting God's Kingdom in Japan and India:
Kolbe

In Niepokalanow, there were only two priests, Father Maximilian and his own brother, Father Alphonse, working among many Brothers. The two of them could not possibly manage all the editorial work and the pastoral work with the Brothers. When the Provincial paid them a visit in May of 1929, both priests presented their request for additional priests. Jokingly the Provincial responded,

"Open a postulancy here in Niepokalanow, and you will have many priests."

The two priests did not recognize the jest; they accepted these words seriously as the voice of the Master. How amused the Provincial was when Father Alphonse appeared before him with plans for a small seminary at Niepokalanow.

"I was not at all serious," replied the nervous Provincial. "Please return to your normal work."

The two Kolbe priests were undaunted by the reply of the superior. As usual they offered the whole encounter to the Immaculata and then gave themselves up in blind obedience. But, the Provincial was uneasy about the matter. After a prayer he sat down at his desk and wrote:

"In the name of holy obedience, for the praise of Almighty God, for the honor of Mary Immaculate and the good of our Order, I command the superior to establish a small seminary in our poor friary at Niepokalanow for the year 1929-1930."

"How wonderful!" Father Maximilian received the Provincial's letter as something completely natural. He immediately printed an announcement in the July issue of the *Knight* regarding the opening of a postulancy for young men who desired to dedicate themselves to priestly and missionary labor in the Order.

But again the Provincial began to fear Father Maximilian would take on rash and unwise obligations to achieve his purposes. He personally went to Niepokalanow to stop the printing of the announcement. It was, however, too late, for 120,000 copies of that *Knight* were already being sent out into the world. The first applicants began to flow in just when Father Maximilian was building the foundation for the new building destined for the incoming students.

On September 19, 1929, many new students who desired to prepare for the service of Jesus and his Beloved Mother entered the Order.

Niepokalanow continued to increase in new vocations and new subscriptions to the *Knight* multiplied. In December the publication reached a peak of 151,000 copies. The *Militia Immaculatae* numbered 250,000 members.

During the canonical visits at the end of that year, the Provincial wrote the following into the Immaculata Visitators' Book:

"A good religious spirit that is truly Franciscan—simplicity, humility, poverty, brotherly love sacrifice of one's 'ego' without limit, action for the Immaculata moved to heroism-these are the marks characterizing our Brothers here. Although there was work without limit, we found no madness or depression, but joy and happiness. The very thought that they are working for the Immaculata gives them strength, courage, energy and spirit. Honor to the Immaculata!"

At this time of the expansion of Niepokalanow when speaking of practicality it would seem that his presence would be indispensable, Father Kolbe, considering himself always rather as an instrument in the hands of Mary, applied to the Provincial with a plan to found a Niepokalanow in the Far East. The Provincial became a little perturbed about the request because it seemed quite absurd to him. However, how could one counter such a humble petition. Father Kolbe had simply asked, "If it is the will of the Immaculata, I would very much like to establish this mission in Japan and to begin the distribution of the *Knight* as soon as possible, in Japanese."

The Provincial then inquired, "Do you have money, Father?"

"No, Father."

"Father, do you know the Japanese language?" "I do not, but I'm going to learn it."

Niepokalanow's press room in 1930. At that time the friars were turning out 120,000 copies monthly of *The Knight of the Immaculata*, Father Kolbe's magazine dedicated to evangelism through Mary the Immaculata.

"Do you have at least some support from anyone you know or some security there at the place?"

"No, but the Immaculata will help."

"I'm sorry, but I myself cannot decide this. Father, you go to Rome to the Father General and ask him for permission."

Father Maximilian, almost immediately on January 14, 1930, departed for Rome. Father General Orlich, to the astonishment of many, immediately granted him permission to start a mission in both China and Japan and to distribute the *Knight of the Immaculata*. Father Kolbe, desiring to assure himself of help from heaven, went to Lourdes in order to dedicate" his action to the Immaculata and to Lisieux to beg protection from the patroness of Catholic Missions, St. Therese of the Child Jesus. He returned speedily to Poland to his religious Brothers.

On February 26, 1930, with small parcels of essential needs for the conquest of the Orient for the Immaculata, the first group of five missionaries excitedly departed from Niepokalanow. Humanly speaking, they were unusual missionaries. Only Father Maximilian knew a few languages, but not Oriental languages. The other four Brothers knew no other language except Polish. At the departure, the Provincial ordered Father Maximilian to return to Poland in July for the Provincial chapter. As always, Father Maximilian bowed his head in submission.

On March 7, these Polish missionaries boarded the ship "Angers" at Marseille, France, heading for places unfamiliar to them but known to God and the Immaculata.

They adorned their cabin with a statue of the Immaculata and they named their dwelling the "Immaculata's ship." Father Maximilian celebrated Mass daily and nourished his religious Brothers with the Bread of Heaven. During the journey his apostolic zeal was ever increasing. As the ship approached the shores of Asia Minor, he resolved to establish in due time, a printery in Beirut so that the *Knight of the Immaculata* might be printed in Arabic for Arabia, Syria, Egypt, Tunis, and Morocco. Since the ship made a long stop at Port Said, Father Maximilian visited the Apostolic Delegate there to discuss this matter.

He took advantage of the short time on hand and managed to speak in general about the matter with the Church authorities, promising them that on his return he would remain longer to begin realizing these plans more concretely.

On March 30, Father Maximilian applied to the Bishop of Singapore explaining his desire to publish the *Knight of the Immaculata*. The Bishop requested a few copies of the publication in Chinese.

In Saigon the ship was detained for three days. Father Kolbe took advantage of the time on hand and contacted the local clergy. He was received very warmly, particularly by the Vietnamese clergy. Father Maximilian promised that in six months he would send them two Brothers who would publish the *Knight* in the Vietnamese language.

On April 11, 1930, after thirty-five days of travel, the missionaries found themselves in Shanghai. Their first destination was the friary of the "Brown" Franciscans (O.F.M.) from whom they received a most cordial reception. Father Maximilian did not waste a minute but immediately made personal contacts with the Chinese. They very definitely accepted the plans of Father Kolbe. One of them, Lo-Pa-Hong, offered Father Maximilian a house, printing machines, and a motor and he guaranteed room and board for the friars as well as for the future candidates to the Order. Just when everything seemed to be flowing smoothly the local Bishop forbade Father Maximilian to settle there and to print the *Knight* in Shanghai, but he was allowed to print it in Poland and then distribute it in Shanghai. Father Kolbe grieved greatly at this and reported to his superior in Poland,

"I have difficulties, not from the pagans, but from the European missionaries."

Father Kolbe was not entirely dissuaded by this obstacle; he informed his superior, "Today, I am leaving for Japan."

A short time afterwards, Father Maximilian confirmed the fact that Japan, among the missionary countries, was best prepared for the reception of the Word of God in the form of the printed word.

On April 24, 1930, Father Kolbe arrived at Nagasaki. The Bishop of Nagasaki, Most Rev. Kyunosuke Hayasaka received him with open arms and proposed a professorship in philosophy in his seminary. Father Kolbe accepted the position with the stipulation that the *Knight of the Immaculata* could be immediately published in Japanese.

The bishop cautioned, "Father, you are underestimating the difficulties involved in this publication."

"The Immaculata can do everything," replied Father Kolbe very calmly.

"Yes, but do you realize the fact that in the European languages the greatest number of letters is 30, but in the Japanese language there are over 6,000 symbols? Moreover, neither you nor any of your co-workers from

Poland know the Japanese language. Even after several years you will not manage to publish your paper in Japanese."

Father Maximilian, hearing all these arguments, smiled as usual and, fully confident in the help of the Immaculata, took action immediately. He mobilized interpreters from the Bishop's Seminary and obtained an agreement for issuing the first number of the *Knight* as a supplement to the diocesan paper *Katoriko Kycho*. Only a month after his arrival in Japan he sent a cablegram to Niepokalanow with this message,

"Today we are sending out the *Knight of the Immaculata* in the Japanese language. We have a printery. Honor to the Immaculata!"

The Bishop of Nagasaki was amazed at this and so were the Brothers at Niepokalanow; only Father Maximilian was not astonished. For him all this was very natural: The Immaculata can obtain everything from God through her supplication. The *Knight* in Japanese was called *Mugenzai no Seibo no Kishi*.

Father Maximilian wrote to his friends in Poland,

"You have no idea how we are suffering from poverty."

Together with his Brothers he slept on straw and ate on the floor, for there were no tables or chairs. The building was so dilapidated that after a few days of occupancy, the ceiling caved in on the sleeping Brothers who miraculously escaped death. The only food they had was rice without meat or seasoning. Father Maximilian was fortunate to obtain a printing machine similar to the one they owned at Grodno and called it "Grandma."

Together with his Brothers he manually turned the crank 10,000 times to print one issue of the *Seibo no Kishi*. This hard labor in addition to the almost unbearable heat did not dishearten the friars.

Father Kolbe wrote, "We did not spare our strength for our aim was to print as many copies as possible and to distribute them to the pagans. Sometimes we worked long hours into the night and with half-closed eyes folded printed sheets. Hands automatically turned the paper, but heads bowed lower and lower, until noses struck the table!"

The *Kishi* aroused great interest in the Japanese who were looking for meaning in life. The austere poverty of the friars aroused great respect in the Japanese. They were even visited by the superior of a Buddhist monastery who looked around their living quarters, viewed the life of these Polish missionaries and was very much impressed with their religious poverty. Shortly after his visit he gave a lecture about them in Kyoto.

The *Knight of the Immaculata* in the Japanese language interested the

East, not because of any literary value, which it did not possess, but because of its clarity and the simplicity of its arguments. The Japanese sought in it not literature but truth. Their interest extended beyond the reading of the *Kishi*. Very frequently they visited Father Maximilian and the Brothers to discuss religion and world events. Here are some comments of the missionaries:

"A certain pagan conversed with Father Maximilian on the theme that there is no God because, he claimed, Darwin said so. Today he believes that Jesus Christ is God and that he dwells among us in the Blessed Sacrament. However, he grieves over the fact that Christ did not remain present under the appearance of rice, which is a Japanese substitute for bread."

"One evening we were visited by a certain young man. We invited him to the table for supper, during which the Father Director explained some basic religious facts, detaining him until late at night. The result was that this young man expressed a desire to enter the Order."

"Not so long ago, two young pagans came to me," one of the Brothers wrote. "They greeted us according to their custom with deep bows, and then we showed them the friary. After touring the print shop, we walked into the chapel I began to commend these poor pagan souls to God. One of them knelt down beside me, and the other stood timidly in the doorway. After a little while however, he too, walked in and knelt down. In a whispering tone, I related to them that we gather here frequently for prayer. As we were leaving the chapel, one of them grasped my hand and pressing it with all his might, said, 'Please, teach me how to adore God.'

"Slowly I knelt down before the Blessed Sacrament and both of them, following my example, genuflected profoundly. Three days later, a letter arrived in which they asked if they might come more frequently to help with the work; they also made the remark that they envied us such a life."

Frequently the Japanese offered their help for the work of the publication. Most of the articles written by Father Maximilian in Latin were translated into Japanese by the local priests.

Three months after their arrival in Japan, the missionaries had their own printing shop, their friary and the *Kishi* numbering 11,000 copies. Gathering around them the pagans begged to be baptized and after that came vocations to the Order.

Meanwhile, Father Maximilian was called to Lwow to the Provincial Chapter. He left his Japanese Niepokalanow and set out on his journey on the Trans-Siberian train to Poland.

At the chapter, opinion regarding the Japanese mission was strongly divided. At one of the concluding sessions Father Maximilian presented his information in a simple way but with great apostolic zeal; he gave an account of everything in the East. Finally he requested that the chapter endorse the establishment of a new place in Japan for the purpose of publishing the *Knight of the Immaculata* in the Japanese language.

The chapter Fathers were very careful in reaching a decision. They emphasized the fact that there was a great deal of work in Poland and the small number of priests could not manage all the pastoral work required of them in that country. They also warned about the exorbitant expenses involved in mission work.

Father Maximilian's reply to these objections was so realistic and filled with conviction that the majority of the Fathers was convinced; permission was granted to open a friary—M.I. Center in Japan similar to the Niepokalanow in Poland. Father Kolbe lamented the fact, though, that he was refused a few priests to help in the missionary work. He had come to the conclusion that the Brothers, in spite of their best efforts, could not help much in editing because of their great difficulty with the foreign language. The Provincial promised, however, that he would send Father Metody Rejentowicz, who had completed his studies in Assisi. He also had asked the Provincial for a few student friars who would go along with him to Nagasaki where they could complete their philosophical and theological studies. He argued his proposition as follows:

"Along with the sacred studies, they will be able to study the Japanese language, make observations and converse; they can study the Japanese customs, their habits, their good qualities. They can develop friendly acquaintances with the co-workers. After six years they will be prepared and equipped with theoretical and practical knowledge suitable to their assignment. They will have books in the Japanese language which they can use for study. They must necessarily begin with studying the Japanese language which will take about three years. They also need time to get to know the environment-the more you observe a Japanese the less you understand him, a Salesian religious once told me."

To that letter, he added personal reasons:

"I, too, find difficulty in studying the language. Words just escape my mind. When I apply myself assiduously, I suffer from a severe headache, nervousness and I get feverish. If seminarians would come, I would immediately have great help in editing the publication, in administering the program and in training the Brothers to submit worthwhile articles. In helping me they would soon become practical missionaries. Should I become ill, they could readily take my place so that the *Kishi* could continue to be published."

These arguments touched the heart of the superior who appointed two zealous seminarians to accompany him to Japan to do the missionary work.

On August 13, Father Maximilian boarded the train at Warsaw with these two clerics. The journey through the Radziecki Union, Manchuria, Korea, and the sea took them twelve days. At the Nagasaki station, four Brothers were waiting to meet them! After exchanging joyous greetings Father Maximilian learned about the unexpected situation facing their publication and their missionary labors. During Father Maximilian's absence the two Brothers in charge of the Chinese publication were forced to leave Shanghai. The local priests of Nagasaki withdrew from their work at the print shop, fearing its liquidation. In spite of the fact that the whole issue was written by hand and completed for the month of September, the printing was still unfinished.

Besides all this, the Japanese police demanded payment of the great sum of 500 yen for the right of publishing the *Kishi*. But this was not the worst news. Father Maximilian was also informed that the Church authorities considered him and the Brothers "adventurers" who had arrived there without permission. The Apostolic Delegate declared openly that if he were asked to endorse this venture of the Polish missionaries, he would refuse. Finally, the local Bishop forbade Father Maximilian to celebrate Mass in their modest house chapel.

Despite these set-backs, Father Kolbe did not abandon the project nor did he become discouraged. He was accustomed to adversities in Poland. Realizing that Divine Providence bestowed many graces upon him and that protection of the Immaculata was with him, he began to resolve the problems very calmly.

He and all the Brothers, after their daily morning prayers, went to the parish church to celebrate Mass. He then wrote to Rome for the necessary legal permission. In order to face these difficulties, he resolved to strengthen himself and the Brothers interiorly through a communal retreat, begging all his friends for prayer, which he believed was most necessary for labor to bear fruit.

After the retreat he approached his task. First he convinced the Church authorities that he was no "adventurer," and he begged them to wait patiently for the documents from Rome. Next the police authorities were soon convinced that they were dealing not with a private publishing firm, but with poor friars who labored only for the glory of God and the Immaculata. Finally, to the joy of the Brothers, the August-September issue was printed and distributed.

And once again with dynamic force the work continued. Already in October the number of the *Kishi* reached the 18,000 mark, and in November it increased to 20,000. In December the number of copies leaped to 25,000. Besides this, Father Maximilian bought a new printing machine, and he began to look around for a suitable house for the publication.

How wonderful! The greatest help given the Polish missionaries was by the pagans and the Protestants. A certain Protestant Japanese, a professor, translated articles for the *Kishi*. As compensation he demanded that the missionaries eat the chicken he brought for them!

Toward the end of November, Father Kolbe finally received the necessary documents from Rome. Now, at last, the local Church authority acknowledged the Polish missionaries as genuine, as the documents testified.

Just when it seemed as though an azure sky opened above their new place, Father Maximilian was thunderstruck at the news that his dear brother, Father Alphonse, who had directed the work at Niepokalanow in Poland, had died after a few days of illness on December 3. This news came on the Vigil of the Immaculate Conception.

How did this blow affect Father Maximilian? Many spiritual secrets were preserved between him and God and the Immaculata. But many things were revealed in his letters. On December 9, he wrote to Father Koziura, his religious Brother in Poland:

> *"...so on the very day of the Immaculata, I celebrated High Mass for the repose of his soul in our small chapel, but with the white vestments in honor of the Immaculate Conception, while the brothers sang hymns to the Mother of God. It was not possible to do otherwise. The clerics also have recited the Office of the Dead twice, the brothers the Rosary twice, and on the next day I celebrated another Holy Mass, for here in Japan we do not form a separate friary, independent of Niepokalanow in Poland, hence 'suffragia sicut in eodem conventu."*

Then together we reflected and talked about what may have happened in Niepokalanow" (KW Vol. 1, #299, p. 703).

St. Maximilian Kolbe at his desk in Nagasaki, Japan, about 1935. It was here that he edited the Japanese magazine he founded, prepared classes as a seminary professor, and directed the by then international Knights of the Immaculata movement he had founded in 1917.

Mugenzai no Sono (Garden of the Immaculata): friary, seminary and evangelism center founded by St. Maximilian in the 1930's in Nagasaki, Japan. Contrary to all advice, Saint Maximilian built the center on a hill outside the city. As a result the hill shielded the mission from the atomic blast that leveled the rest of the city in 1945—only a few windows were broken. (1973 photo)

To his mother he wrote:

"So...the Immaculata already took Fr. Alfons to herself: Glory to her for everything. I imagine what the funeral must have been like on the very day of the Feast of the Immaculate Conception. I am still waiting for the details about his death and his funeral. I only received the telegram on the day before the Feast of the Immaculata" (KW Vol. 1, #304, p. 713).

The year 1931 began with great hardships for Father Maximilian. First of all, there were great financial difficulties, then came the Provincial's interrogation—Would it not be better for him to fold up the Japanese publication and return to Niepokalanow to save it in its critical situation after the death of Father Alphonse? In addition to this the surgery of one of the clerics and finally his own illness came about this time. His condition seemed so critical and dangerous that the Brothers informed the Provincial about it. In all this God permitted his soul to be enveloped in darkness. with the simplicity of a child he revealed the state of his soul to the Provincial in his letter of January 30.

"How often do I perceive I no longer have either faith or hope, and do not even feel love; the devil insinuates the question: 'Why did you come so far?' and my nature feels adverse to concerns, discomfort, suffering; and it longs for an indolent and lazy serenity" (KW Vol. 1, #315, p. 370).

This sincere, humble, childlike confidence, must have prevailed upon his superior to entreat God to send forth bright rays of his sun because of this love of God and the Immaculata. Being cleansed mere and more of his "ego," he desired to become a more loyal instrument in the hands of the Immaculata. He wrote about this to Father Koziura on February 17.

"For I do not belong to myself, but thoroughly to the Immaculata; also the Most Rev. Fr Provincial writes to me that a great task is still ahead of me. ... at the Final Judgement you shall learn how many things I spoiled, how much I will have omitted or neglected that it was my duty to carry out. I think that, with the help of the Immaculata, at that time I will do everything to ensure that no weakness of mine escapes anyone's attention, so that everyone may see with what 'broom' the Immaculata was able to paint such beautiful pictures" (KW Vol. 1, #322, p. 738).

This "powerless" friar obtained a wild, mountainous plot upon which to erect his first building. The transfer from the Japanese "Grodno" to the Japanese Niepokalanow took place as early as May 16, 1931. In Japanese it was called "Mugenzai no Sono," meaning literally "in the garden of the Immaculata."

Father Maximilian was overjoyed on April 7 of that year when he invested the first Japanese with the Franciscan habit. He gave him the religious name of Marion as a sign of total dedication to the Immaculata. During that same month, the long-awaited new missionaries arrived from Poland: a newly ordained priest, two clerics, and one Brother.

Father Kolbe's publication of the *Knight* in the Japanese language leaped to 30,000 copies in May. At the same time in Poland, he was informed that 420,000 copies of the *Knight* were published. The number of residents of Niepokalanow grew to 150 members. He was also very happy that they purchased a magnificent rotary press which printed 20,000 copies of the publication in one hour.

Despite joyful rays, weighty clouds made their appearance over the Japanese Niepokalanow. A new storm approached from the quarter of Church authority. Father Maximilian was reprimanded by the Archbishop of Tokyo for the contents of the *Kishi*. Father Kolbe felt that the Archbishop's action was instigated by someone else. In response to this bitter criticism Father Maximilian replied to the Archbishop with great dignity and respect, explaining the fruits reaped from the *Kishi* in the form of many Japanese conversions to the Catholic faith. The Archbishop was effectively disarmed by this answer, and said no more.

Another more painful trial came from one who had proven to be up to that time a real friend of Father Kolbe. It was the Bishop of Nagasaki, Kyunosuke Hayasaka, who was urged by one missionary to call Father Maximilian for a personal interview.

"Father, I must tell you something very unpleasant."

"I am listening, Your Excellency," replied the astonished Father Kolbe.

"I trusted you, Father, and you tricked me and deceived me."

"Never would I dare do such a thing," replied the deeply affected priest.

"What are you saying? You are here unlawfully, Father. Japan is subject to the Congregation."

"Your Excellency! I am convinced that this matter was settled in Rome completely and in due form."

"Father, you are deceiving me by lies, and I put such great confidence in you," said the bishop, annoyed.

"Father Maximilian turned pale, and his eyes filled with tears. He spoke softly, "Your Excellency! I never told a lie in my life, and I trust that the Immaculata will never permit me to tell a lie in the future. Furthermore, I would not lie to a bishop for I respect the Church hierarchy and I desire to obey her always. Your Excellency, have a little patience, and I shall telegraph our Assistant General in Rome, and the matter will certainly be clarified."

"Provided that it be done quickly," responded the bishop coldly.

As soon as Father Maximilian entered his cell he knelt down before his statuette of the Immaculata and offered her his painful cross. Two weeks later, after his telegram to the Assistant General of the Order asking for the authentic document from Rome concerning their permission, he was handed a letter from the superior at Niepokalanow which began with the words:

"Help, help! This is beyond endurance!"

As he continued to read the message he learned that the activities of Niepokalanow in Poland were threatened with bankruptcy; other painful facts were cited.

Father Maximilian immediately replied to the superior at Niepokalanow. His serene letter encouraged the superior to reconcile himself to whatever the Immaculata had in store for them. "Let us leave it to her. If she really wants the publication to continue and prosper she will support it, undoubtedly."

Other difficulties appeared at this time in the friary. It was evident that one of their new priests who came from Poland had absolutely no missionary vocation. He felt very strange in Japan, and he had no ambition to study the Japanese language, so essential for their work.

It was painful for Father Maximilian to have to report this to his superior.

"It seems to me that, in spite of his sincere piety, I cannot see any spirit of dedication in him. Rather than dedicating his life for an ideal, the ideal must suit his life. It is best for him to return to Poland."

Unfortunately this case was not the last with which Father Maximilian had to cope. One of the first four missionaries arriving with Father Kolbe at Nagasaki came to him to announce that he wanted to leave the Order, but remain in Japan. Father Kolbe feared that the consequences would be scandalous. This would no doubt give the Japanese press an opportunity to attack the Catholic religion. There also would be the possibility that the Church authorities would remove the Polish missionaries entirely from Japan as obstacles to the Church's work of evangelization.

With great difficulty and entreaty Father Kolbe persuaded him to delay his decision. Other problems arose: one of the clerics became emotionally ill, and another Brother was afflicted with pneumonia. The chalice of suffering was overflowing. The angel of solace during this time of distress was the Provincial who, through his most warm and affectionate letters, consoled Father Maximilian and counseled him not to take those troubles to heart. Knowing Father Maximilian's sensitivity, he ordered him, under his vow of obedience, not to worry any more; Father Kolbe stopped worrying.

The Provincial sent travel money for the return of the sick and dissatisfied friars to Poland. Simultaneously, the documents issued by the Propagation of the Faith arrived from Rome.

The Procurator General wrote that the Propagation of the Faith was much astonished that the Bishop of Nagasaki was causing trouble for Father Maximilian.

Was it possible that the Bishop of Nagasaki was not aware of the congregation's procedures? The Procurator asked the Bishop not to worry about the legitimacy of these procedures.

Father Kolbe immediately delivered this letter in person to the Bishop.

"Your Excellency, I have brought the requested clarification of our presence in Japan," Father Kolbe said modestly.

After reading the contents of the letter the Bishop felt very dismayed about what had transpired. He earnestly apologized to Father Maximilian for causing such great unpleasantness. As a result their friendship revived and flourished.

To replace the sick and the dissatisfied friars who returned to Poland, ardent lovers of the Immaculata came. This was a great relief to Father Maximilian who was now ready to begin anew his long anticipated apostolate of converting the East.

A new light dawned upon the little community as the Church hierarchy and the Japanese press were becoming better disposed towards it. The new building was going up steadily but slowly. At this time Father Kolbe wrote to *The Catholic Missions*.

"We feel very fortunate because the Immaculata granted us the grace to work most ardently for her to bring about the salvation of the poor pagans. There are moments, however, when we yearn for the Niepokalanow in Poland. But when we think of our future meeting in heaven, a joyful zeal and the desire of self-denial for God fills our hearts."

With serenity and hope, as evidenced by his letter to Niepokalanow, Father Maximilian greeted the New Year of 1932.

"We are doing very well here. As soon as any adversity comes our way it disappears almost immediately. It seems as though this present stillness is a foreboding of an oncoming storm for which we must be prepared. At present all is well, and the sun shines pleasantly; however, it is rather difficult to get accustomed to such a tranquil situation."

Father Maximilian was overjoyed when he learned that in Poland the *Knight of the Immaculata* reached a peak of 500,000 issues, while in Japan it was 30,000. He also published a calendar in Japanese.

He was indeed happy when he heard that on February 11 the *Knight* began to be published in the Italian language.

But he experienced the greatest joy when the entire group of friars in Japan came to him pleading that they be permitted to make a fourth vow to go anywhere and into any circumstances for the love of the Immaculata. That was truly a noble sign of perfect missionary zeal. This step assured him that his friars were very responsive to the total sacrifice of self for a noble cause. Father Maximilian himself was burning with an ardent desire to conquer the whole world for the Immaculata:

"When shall it be, O Immaculata, that you will become the Queen of all, the Queen of every individual soul? When will everyone understand you and love you most tenderly so that their hearts will be filled to overflowing with peace and happiness? Your little *Knight*, O Immaculata, is also the result of your magnanimous heart which, together with your many fervent converts, proclaims your great goodness. You have drawn to your heart many grateful servants not only in Poland but also in Japan. But this is only the beginning. How many more souls are there who know nothing about you? When will all the souls of the entire world acknowledge your great kindness and draw closer to your loving heart? When will this happen?"

Father Maximilian did not stop at these beautiful rhetorical questions; he was not a dreamer but a realist.

On May 19, when the new missionaries arrived from Poland at the Garden of the Immaculata, Father Maximilian carried out his decision of going on a journey to India for the purpose of establishing a new center there for his publication.

He went to the Indian city of Ernakulum, to the residence of a Roman Catholic Archbishop. His aim was to obtain permission to settle there and to publish the *Knight* in the Indian language. He was received rather coldly and with suspicion. Nevertheless, as he awaited his turn for the audience, his attention was attracted by the Little Flower's statue standing in the corridor of the archbishop's house. He walked up to the little saint and spoke to her.

"Do you recall our agreement, little Sister? Many years ago I promised to pray for your beatification and canonization, and for that you were to protect my missions. I pleaded for your glory, and now it is your turn to reciprocate. We shall see if you remember."

"At that moment," he writes, "a flower fell at my feet; it was like a rose. It simply detached itself from the bouquet of flowers at the foot of the statue. This made a definite impression on me and I thought, 'We shall see what that signifies!'"

The Archbishop not only permitted the Polish Franciscan missionaries to settle there, but he proposed a large tract of land which was his personal property for the future Indian Niepokalanow. This large area was located near a railroad station in a beautiful garden where a residence and a chapel stood. The Archbishop extended a genial invitation to Father Maximilian, "Come, you are welcome here!"

Little Saint Therese kept her bargain. Any difficulties with the ecclesiastical authorities in India cleared away readily as though by a miracle. The Archbishop of Ernakulum then wrote to the General of the Order officially inviting the Polish missionaries.

Father Maximilian reported these new responsibilities to his Provincial, and also asked for permission to start a mission in Chinese territory.

With the best of intentions for his new projects, Father Maximilian returned to Nagasaki. Here he met with great disappointment in his new helper, Father Constantine, who differed from him in his views on devotion to the Immaculata. Moreover, when Father Maximilian informed the Brothers of his intention of asking Father General of the Order that the Polish and Japanese Niepokalanow be taken under his immediate jurisdiction like friaries established in new regions, Father Constantine immediately became alarmed, saying that Father Maximilian intended to separate from the Order to create a new branch of Franciscans.

The Assistant General of the Order, Father Peregrine Haczela, the same person who accepted Raymond Kolbe into the Order, requested an explanation of the matter. Father Maximilian clearly defined his stand:

"I fear what others may do but I am also afraid that through sloth or egotism I may neglect something that the Immaculata wishes me to do, regardless of the humiliations and suffering which may result."

He also wrote a letter to the Father General of the Order in Rome.

"Most Reverend Father, you know me well and know I want to be afraid of one thing only, that is, of my own will. And you know that I always tried to practice holy obedience, seeing it as the Will of the Immaculata, and in it of God. And I hope that the Immaculata will lead me along that path through all my life and through eternity. Fr. Konstanty is good, zealous, but wants to go to God directly and not by means of the Virgin Mary. He is not even willing to acknowledge the happy relationship of our Seraphic Order with the Immaculata. He does not love her, as we do, and would like to attribute our sweet victory in the proclamation of the dogma of the Immaculate Conception to the Jesuits or who knows whom, but not to our Order. So he cannot understand our special love for the Immaculata. …This would obliterate the ideal of the MI (KW Vol. 1, #487, p. 1010-11).

This letter testifies that Father Maximilian, always full of amiableness and benevolence, knew how to be a true Knight when it concerned the honor of his Queen.

In concluding his letter, he begged his Provincial to consider forming a separate jurisdiction for the Niepokalanows known as a Commissariat which in a special way would realize the ideal of service and Knighthood to the Blessed Mother. He assured him that qualified Fathers from the Polish Province as well as many Brothers would volunteer for that purpose, and who were even ready to die for the Immaculata. He pointed out that in this way there was no danger of separation from the Order. On the contrary, the Commissariat would be directly dependent on the Father General himself and it might be dissolved by him at any time. The members in that case would become members of the Polish Province. It would be advantageous for the Order if Niepokalanow were a separate unit, for it would gain in strength and development.

Not contented with these letters only, he also wrote an open letter to the youth of the Franciscan Order in which he explained his basic thought of alliance and union between the Immaculata's action and Franciscan aims.

> *"We must not think that all these things are only abstract theories, impossible to carry out in practice. For the Immaculata already deigned to set up a religious house (Niepokalanow, Poland), which in the course of the five years of its existence gave evidence that such life and such work are possible.*
>
> *We ought not to fear a shortage of vocations on account of such a strict life-style, because vocations in that house have already reached the number of 400 now.*
>
> *Nor is to be feared that perfect poverty may prevent the livelihood of the colleges, because over 120 minor seminarians consecrated to the Immaculata are currently supported at Niepokalanow...*
> *I have been to many countries, I have seen many things, I have spoken with several people, but trust me: there is no better or more suitable means to address the evils of our time than our Seraphic Order, if it furthers the spirit of our Father St. Francis with courage, alertness, speed, and steadfastness"* (KW Vol. 1, #486, p. 1009).

"I have been in many countries, I have seen much, and I have spoken with many people. But, believe me, there isn't a more suitable way to counteract the evil of today's world than our Seraphic Order, providing that it will courageously, willingly, speedily, and ceaselessly develop the spirit of our Seraphic St. Francis."

This message, however, did not suffice for Father Maximilian. For complete clarification of his state of mind, he wrote a special article for a religious periodical of the Polish Franciscan Province entitled "Why and for What all This?"

The Franciscan Fathers in Poland, observing the actions of Father Maximilian, had asked themselves those same questions. Here are the answers as given by Father Kolbe.

> *"Life is motion, directed toward an end; in the same way a religious order is alive only if it has a well-defined end and actively moves toward it.*

The past generations who descended in the tomb have already reached the ends that the Divine Providence indicated to them. Even the present generation of religious has to know its proper end, so as to move toward it and not to attract upon itself the anathemas of successive generations for not having built anything on the foundations they inherited from the ancient fathers. Or for having left nothing that could serve as the foundations on which the successive generations could build, so as to delay them on their path…From the origins of the Order, the golden thread of this cause through the ages, passing from challenges and battles until, after more than six hundred years, it arrived at a glorious victory: the recognition, of the truth of the Immaculate Conception, in the proclamation of the dogma that bids everyone… The implementation, the sowing of this truth in the hearts of each and every one individually (starting from oneself), the matter of fostering the growth and production of the fruits of conversion.

Using the language of our Order, in the apparitions at Lourdes, the Immaculata proclaimed, 'Penance, penance, penance,' to refresh the memory of the 'Order of Penance' in which and through which to halt souls in their race toward the pleasures of life, entering their hearts, taking possession of them and directing them toward true happiness, to God, by the path of self-denial. The Immaculata wants to prepare in these souls the throne for Divine Love, for the Divine Heart.…This is the second page in the history of our Order and it is starting now. In it, everything belongs to her, to the Immaculata: both the souls of religious and Niepokalanow. However, how are we to make this come true? Where is it taking us? Ask the Most holy mother" (KW Vol. 2, #1168, p. 2020-21).

These letters and proclamations resounded in the minds and hearts of the religious Brothers and Fathers in Rome as well as in Poland. After many dark clouds, the skies were blue again.

Meanwhile Father Maximilian personally set out on a journey to Rome, and from there to Poland for the Provincial Chapter. During his travels he frequently wrote letters to Nagasaki to be in contact with the religious Brothers, encouraging them to continue their apostolate for the Immaculata during his absence. These earnest letters were very touching, for Father Kolbe even dared to speak in the name of the Immaculata herself. He spoke with profound humility:

"Dearest children,
In difficulties, in darkness, in weaknesses, in dejection remember that
paradise... paradise... is approaching. Every day that passes is a whole
day less to wait. Courage, then! She awaits us there to clasp us to her
Heart. Also, pay no heed to the devil, if ever he wants to make you believe
that heaven exists, but not for you, even if you had committed all possible
sins, one single act of perfect love washes everything clean, to the point
that not even a shadow remains...

   My dear ones, a thought, almost a melancholy nostalgia, a plea, a cry
may occur to you: 'Who knows if the Immaculata still loves me?' Most
beloved Children! I am telling you all and each individually in her Name,
take note, in her Name: she loves each of you and loves you very much
and at any time without any exception. That, my dearest children, I re-
peat to you in her Name. And tell this same thing to those four who will
come soon after this letter" (KW Vol. 1, #509, p. 1036).

Contrary to expectations, he was received most courteously by the
Father General who requested him to present his petitions in writing, re-
marking at the same time that he was in agreement with them. The Father
General detained him a few days in Rome in order that he could participate
in the solemnity of the beatification of Gemma Galgani and be present at
the consecration of three bishops: an Indian, a Chinese and Vietnamese.

He finally arrived at Niepokalanow in Poland on May 29. What great
joy his presence brought to his spiritual children who longed for him! Urgency, however, compelled Father Maximilian to leave for Lwow where he
had some business to transact with the Provincial Father Cornelius Czupryk. He was quite astonished to hear from the Provincial that if he were
re-elected for the third time, he would decline it. Furthermore, Father Czupryk expressed his desire to go to Nagasaki so that he could testify by this
act how very close to his heart was the idea of the *Militia Immaculatae*.

"Since I am aged," said the Provincial, "it would be difficult for me to
study the Japanese language, but if I go with you I shall be glad to assist you
in your administrative work. I can maintain the friary and procure food
for the friars in Mugenzai no Sono and, Father, you could devote your time
exclusively to the printing and publication of the *Kishi*."

"Is this possible? It seems almost incredible to me that you, Father Provincial, are willing to undertake such a fatiguing task," answered the astonished Father Maximilian.

"Yes, Father. If I become the Guardian in Nagasaki, some will write letters to Rome about their ex-Provincial, that he wants to sever Niepokalanow from the Order, but I am sure no one will believe such letters. Your mind will be more serene and your work easier. And, or course, I shall gain a little merit with the Immaculata."

"I would have never supposed that!" said the surprised Father Kolbe.

"But, under one condition."

"Yes, Father, I am listening."

"Father, I defended you several times and on your account I have even gone to Rome. So, remember, you defend me on judgment day!"

"Perhaps my defense will not be necessary, but I accept the stipulation," replied Father Maximilian with tears in his eyes.

The Provincial Chapter of the Franciscan Friars was held in Cracow from July 17 to July 20, 1933. Before the delegate Fathers, the Warsaw Custodian gave a report of the Polish Niepokalanow: the number of inhabitants of that excellent friary was over 400; the *Knight of the Immaculata* reached a peak of 680,000 copies; the publication of the children's paper numbered 25,000.

The report of the Japanese Niepokalanow was given by Father Kolbe. In his discourse he primarily emphasized the striving for perfection in religious life, a characteristic of the members of their friary.

In spite of the predictable storms lurking about Father Maximilian, the chapter sanctioned all his projects, including the founding of a novitiate at Niepokalanow. Father Czupryk, the former Provincial, was appointed the superior of Nagasaki to the great joy of Father Maximilian. The protection of the Immaculata was obvious.

During his sojourn in Poland the mission idea obsessed Father Maximilian. He was convinced even in Poland, that the Japanese could be converted to the Catholic faith. He learned that Mrs. Kawai, the wife of the Japanese Minister Plenipotentiary in Warsaw, was Catholic and her children were baptized Catholics. Without much reflection he sent Mrs. Kawai a statuette of the Immaculata. In return for the gift she sent Father Maximilian an invitation to "Skolimowska Villa," near Warsaw, where she was spending her vacation with her children. Father Kolbe graciously accepted the invitation. During his visit, Mrs. Kawai presented him with a few requests. Her husband was critically ill at Otwock and she wanted him to receive Baptism. Besides that, the mother of the Minister's wife and her maid also desired Baptism. Father Maximilian immediately began his apostolate. As the top priority he devoted the most time to the Japanese Minister, whose state of health was becoming more grave each day. On August 14, the Minister received the Sacrament of Baptism from the hands of the Apostolic Nuncio, Archbishop Marmaggi. A few hours later, he died. Father Kolbe likewise prepared the mother and the maid of the widow, Mrs. Kawai, for Baptism, and he prepared the children for their First Holy Communion.

A solemn and family-like farewell took place on August 28 between Father Maximilian, his companions, and Father Florian, the superior at Niepokalanow. The missionaries departed on August 31st.

It was the feast of St. Francis of Assisi, October 4, when the missionaries arrived at Nagasaki. A great deal of correspondence awaited Father Maximilian from the Japanese who, thanks to the *Kishi*, felt a wonderful, heartfelt sympathy for the inhabitants of the Japanese Niepokalanow. The following are some excerpts from their letters:

> *From Osaka: "I am exceedingly happy that all of you are working hard for the glory of God and that you are promoting love for the Immaculata."*
> *From Korea: Is everyone well at Niepokalanow? I beg you, work for those who have no faith."*

> *From a student in Tokyo: "In Mayas I was walking along with my friend I met a foreigner who gave me a medal of the Immaculata and a copy of the Kishi. Since that time I receive the publication monthly and read it with great pleasure and interest. I am enclosing a yen as an offering. It isn't much, but please use it for the publication of the Kishi.*

> *From Hokkaido: "During the long period of my son's illness, you have been so very kind in sending me the Kishi. That publication brought great solace to my sick son in his sufferings. My dying son requested me to send one yen to Mugenzai no Sono which I am enclosing."*

> *A pagan writes: "I am not a Catholic, but from the time I have been receiving the Kishi, I have been overwhelmed with happiness. Please continue sending it."*

In December of 1933, Father Maximilian increased the press run of the Japanese *Knight of the Immaculata* to 60,000 copies. While he was engaged in editing and distributing the publication, the new superior expanded the friary, built a church and was slowly preparing a building for the secondary school gymnasium and a postulancy for the Japanese candidates to the religious life and to the priesthood. The friars from Poland understood well that there would be no future for their Catholic action without Japanese priests and Brothers.

Both the Polish and the Japanese Niepokalanow expanded systematically and simultaneously. Father Maximilian's plans for conquering the world for the Immaculata also developed in scope and enthusiasm.

1929–1934
From Farm to SS Candidate:
Hoess

Rudolph Hoess stood on the large stairs of the Poczdamski railroad station in Berlin, absorbed in watching the multitude of passengers. After six years of isolation in prison, this movement seemed unrealistic to him. He felt as though he were in a theatre looking at an interesting film. He stood there a long time until a certain passenger approached him.

"If there is any place that you would like to go, I'll take you."

Rudolph, however, remained silent. The inquirer, seeing the blank eyes of the stranger, left.

After walking a long time through once familiar streets, he finally reached his friend's home where he was received very sincerely by the entire family. During the first days of his freedom when he had little courage to go out on the street he was always escorted by a companion. He feared the traffic of large cities for he did not know the traffic laws. Many days elapsed before he became adjusted to his freedom. His colleagues took him along to the movies, to the theatre, and to all places of entertainment and friendly receptions. Rudolph was confused by all this; he longed for peace and quiet. He made up his mind to tear himself away from the turmoil of a large city and escape into the country.

His colleagues and their friendly families proposed various plans to create a suitable existence for him and pave the way to normal life.

"We shall help you get to East Africa," counseled his colleagues.

"And why there?" he asked with astonishment.

"You know quite well that right now there is political turmoil in Germany. You will become involved in some new adventure, and then you will be in prison again. And no one knows how soon there will be a new amnesty."

"If you don't want to go to Africa, I'll find you work in the United States, Mexico, Brazil, or Paraguay," proposed another friend.

And Rudolph was given other proposals.

"Under no circumstances can you leave Germany now," argued the passionate Hitlerites. "You have belonged to the NSDAP since 1922. Tomorrow there will be a great dispute about Hitler's Germany, and in a few years we shall go forth with our dear Fuhrer to conquer the whole world. Let's hope you won't be a coward but will teach us how to fight properly for the German idea."

At this moment Rudolph Hoess rejected all proposals. He was indeed convinced that the aims of Hitler's party were equitable, and although he agreed with them, he condemned mass propaganda, bargaining for the favors and consideration of the multitudes, playing on the lowest instincts of the masses, and haranguing the public. He considered himself a member of the party, but he did not want to perform any functions in it. Neither did he want to join any of the party's auxiliary organizations. He, likewise, had no intentions of leaving his country to seek happiness abroad. His desire was to remain in Germany to help rebuild that country destroyed by war and its aftermath. During his long years of solitary life spent in prison he came to the conclusion that the purpose of his life should be to work on a farm and to have a family of many children.

After leaving prison he made contacts with the Artaman Union to achieve his ambitions. He became acquainted with this union and its purposes while still in prison through its publication, in which he took great interest. It was an alliance of young men and women established from the youth movements of all national political groups. Its members desired principally to turn from the polluted superficiality of city life to the healthy, natural way of life in the country. They held contempt for alcohol and nicotine as well as everything else that did not serve the healthy development of the body and soul according to their opinion. Believing in the principle of returning completely to the earth from which their ancestors came, they wanted to return to the source of life of the German nation-to healthy peasant life.

The Artaman Union became the road for Hoess, for the union's purpose was his long-sought aim. He resigned his employment as an agricultural economist and he joined a community of people who had similar aspirations. He broke all relations with his colleagues, his acquaintances, and his friendly family hosts because of their traditional views. On the other hand they could not understand his decision or his ability to start a new life without any hesitation.

At first he worked in the Artaman's community in Brandenburg and later in Pomerania. At the very outset of this new life he became acquainted with his future wife, Hedwig Hensel, who motivated by similar ideals, had joined the Artaman's Union together with her brother. It was love at first sight that brought them together. They found as much mutual harmony in their confidence and understanding as though they had been friends for many years. Their views on life agreed in every respect. The dream of his long years of solitude was finally realized for he found the type of woman he always desired.

He was married on August 17, 1929. A son was born in 1930, and later two daughters: one in 1932, and another in 1933.

The life of Hoess' family during these five years was not easy. Farm work demanded great exertion, but this did not discourage them. They were happy and contented with each small success. They were about to become sole owners of the land they tilled; this contributed to their contentment.

Nonetheless, Rudolph carefully observed the political events taking place in Germany. As years passed, each day brought on newer events of which Rudolph had dreamed, but he feared them.

On January 30, 1933, Hitler became the Chancellor of Germany. Four weeks later, the Reichstag building was set on fire. Hitler's propaganda presented this as an action of the Communists. It was a brilliant pretext to liquidate all Constitutional guarantees. On February 28, 1933, Hitler induced Hindenburg, President of the German Confederation, to sign a document seething with pernicious stipulations. The following day it appeared in the German press:

"The President of the German Confederation signed statutes, immediately effective, which were formed by the government for the purpose of protection against Communist terrorists threatening the country."

The most important statute abolished the following articles of the working German Constitution:

article 114, which guaranteed personal inviolability;

article 115, which guaranteed the inviolability of each German's dwelling;

article 117, which guaranteed private correspondence, privacy of the postal service, the telegraph and the telephone;

article 118, which guaranteed freedom of speech;

article 123, which guaranteed freedom of assembly of organizing meetings;

article 124, which guaranteed the right of action of unions and societies;

article 153, which guaranteed the right of ownership.

When Rudolph read this communication aloud to his wife she gave a deep sigh.

"Actually, what is a citizen left free to do?"

"Now, the prisons will be so full they'll burst," asserted Rudi wryly. "Let's see what will happen next. At any rate, let's continue working on our land as we did until now."

At the beginning of March, 1933, an election took place at which Hitler's party obtained 288 seats out of a possible 647. Hitler was not satisfied. He did not have a majority in the Parliament and therefore he could not reinforce the decree of plenipotentiary for himself which would assure him of his legislative power. He, however, took advantage of the document of February 28th and placed most members of the Communist party under house arrest. In this manner Hitler obtained a majority of votes in the Parliament, and thus became a plenipotentiary legislator. On May 26, all activity of the Communist Party in Germany was forbidden, and its members' property was confiscated. Other parties dissolved themselves in the panic. There, finally remained only one party in the political arena in Germany: Hitler's party, known as NSDAP.

The arrests of Germany's enemies—that is the enemies of Hitler's totalitarianism—grew to tens of thousands. The prisons were filled with Communists, Social Democrats, Catholics, and Jews; concentration camps, known as "schools of patriotism for the stubborn," began to be organized.

Hitler and his party now needed people wholly dedicated to his new ideas. The old soldier's blood in Hoess' veins responded. On September 20, 1933, he joined the SS as a candidate, number 193616. Himmler's words were reiterated in his mind, "The SS must become an upper stratum which will be able to take possession of the whole of Europe for hundreds of years."

Rudolph fervently desired to conquer Europe, Asia, and Africa for Germany. How much land would then be available! How many free laborers would there be! He and his beloved Hewing would be independent-a prince and princess who would only supervise everything and enjoy the wealth of Germany. But before that would come to pass they would have to obey their genial Hitler blindly and prepare for a hard battle. No one becomes a slave willingly. No one would willingly offer the Germans infinite tracts of land.

1934–1938
An Explosion of Divine
Love and Power in Europe:
Kolbe

In 1934, Father Maximilian wrote to the Polish Niepokalanow,

"Remember that it is not enough for our current spirit to have the same intensity as the spirit of the beginnings. Every year, every day there must be progress. Therefore, Niepokalanow today must belong to the Immaculata much more than in the early days of its existence" (KW Vol. 1, #605, p. 1138).

Father Kolbe believed in the laws of progress. He knew well the principle of the interior life: to stand still on the path to sanctity means, automatically, to retreat. You must always advance on that path. These principles he applied to his activity, for he was incessantly developing his Niepokalanow in both places. He feared halting, and he was exhilarated with each success.

On August 15, 1934, a new church was dedicated in the Japanese Niepokalanow. Under the church was a hall used on Sundays by Father Maximilian to give religious instruction to children.

On April 16, 1936, Father Kolbe, with the help of a number of young Japanese, began to remodel the high school gymnasium. On June 25th of that year he received formal approval by the ministry of education to conduct a secondary school.

In the meantime, Father Kolbe was becoming affected by tuberculosis. Evidently the climate of Japan disagreed with Father Maximilian's lung condition. He had great difficulty in breathing with his one lung, which was greatly weakened by a previous illness. From the spring of 1935 Father Maximilian was bedridden. He arose from bed with great difficulty only to hear Holy Mass. Even his lectures were given from bed. He was exceedingly happy, however, when he received news of the wonderful success of the Polish Niepokalanow. His apostolate was expanding in a marvelous manner. In the year 1934, Niepokalanow numbered 530 persons; by 1936, the number had increased to 600. Fifteen new buildings were erected and filled with people and machines. It was no longer just a compound; it now was a city.

The *Knight of the Immaculata* was increasing. In 1935 it passed the mark of 700,000 copies, and the *Little Knight* numbered 149,000 copies. Besides periodicals, brochures and religious books numbering many thousands were published.

A very important event occurred on May 27, 1935, when Niepokalanow began its own little newspaper called Maly Dziennik at the price of 5 groszy (less than two cents) per copy. In March 1936, the publication rose to 115,000 copies and on Sundays 150,000 copies.

With the expansion and growth of the publication it was necessary to expand both land and buildings. Prince Drucki-Lubecki, "Noted for his magnanimous heart, donated still more acres of land for the Immaculata's expansion. A few heavy trucks necessary for transportation were purchased. Since this proved to be insufficient for the bulk of the work, the friars themselves built a special railway line for a narrow-gauge train which fortunately made a connection with the station at Szymanow. Then they built a saw-mill.

Subsequently they imported far better machines. One innovation led to another.

The Franciscan Fathers looked at the development of Niepokalanow with mixed feelings. Some were overwhelmed with amazement at the pace of the progress there; others were skeptical and asked, "Where does all this lead?"

The friars themselves at Niepokalanow were unable to answer that. Other questions poured in from all sides.

"How far can we advance in our development?" "Is such activity realistic?"

"Is all this in agreement with the religious spirit of poverty?"

The only person able to answer all these questions was Father Maximilian, the founder and organizer of Niepokalanow. Therefore the Fathers of the Polish Province decided to bring him back to Poland so that he himself could direct the actions of Niepokalanow.

During the Provincial Chapter in July of 1936, Father Kolbe was elected by an absolute majority of votes as the superior of Niepokalanow, the largest friary of the Franciscan Order. Nevertheless attention was called to certain faults which were evident in the life of the large religious community.

Father Maximilian headed the friary publications with two objectives, namely: the sanctification of the friars and the development of the publications to win all souls for the Immaculata.

Father Kolbe often gathered his religious brothers and had heart-to-heart conversations with them. He enjoyed chatting with them about nature. One day, as they were all gathered for an outing in the woods, Father Maximilian questioned them.

"Tell me, dear children, what should we do now in Niepokalanow?"

A number of responses followed:

"Increase the publication of the *Knight*."

"Purchase a new linotype machine."

"Build an airport at once."

Young friars at Niepokalanow in 1938 prepare a daily press run of the Mały Dziennik (*Little Daily*) for distribution. Niepokalanow produced five monthly publications, a daily newspaper, an annual calendar-almanac and four other smaller periodicals. In 1939 the *Little Daily* had an average weekday press run of 135,000 copies and a Sunday run of 228,000 copies. The monthly *Knight of the Immaculata* had a circulation of 800,000 at its peak. In 1981 the Polish government finally authorized the friars to begin publishing the magazine again.

"Double productivity."

"Perhaps, above all, we should sanctify ourselves," came a shy reply.

Hearing this, Father Maximilian beamed forth, "Bravo, loving child! I have just been waiting for that. It is true that we should care for the technical development, but that is not the most significant thing. If we have quality, quantity will follow."

"Father, tell us on what does the true development of Niepokalanow depend," someone asked.

Father Maximilian concentrated on the problem and then replied slowly and emphatically.

"True progress does not depend on enlarging the borders of Niepokalanow, or on importing the most modern machines and improving service. Even though we build skyscrapers and gathered the most beautiful and useful inventions of human genius, that still would not be true progress. Even if our publications doubled or grew ten-fold, spreading over the whole world, that still would not serve as evidence of progress. What really is Niepokalanow? Is it that visible enclosure, or is it our souls? Truthfully I must tell you that the real Niepokalanow is in us. True development means every soul increasing in love for our Lady, Commander-in-chief and Queen, breathing her life like air in our lungs and immersing ourselves in her like fish in the sea. Then we can boldly declare that we are progressing, and that is indeed great progress in approaching our ideal. Everything else is good, but secondary. True progress is spiritual or there is none at all. It may possibly happen that an outbreak of war may sweep us off and scatter us all over the world like those leaves in autumn. An enemy may take our machines and workshops, close our Knight *publication, and throw us out of the cloister. As long as in the soul of each of us the Immaculata will reign indivisibly, nothing is lost; on the contrary, in the most difficult circumstances the most beautiful development can exist. Remember dear children, Niepokalanow is not the barracks; we are Niepokalanow. It all depends on us whether there will be progress or regression. Therefore, I caution you: Do not absorb yourself in work, but first seek that which is the most important and which no one can take away from you. The rest will be given you in abundance. What I say here is very significant. I am an older person and I shall pass away shortly. The purpose of Niepokalanow is neither to publish nor to undertake some efficient enterprise; these are only means. Our aim is to love the Immacula-*

ta and to deepen that love continually so that with it we can inflame the whole world. For that purpose we are living, working, suffering. For that aim only we want to exist even after death. All else is superfluous. We in Niepokalanow have great difficulties, but the greatest are our internal difficulties. There is no crisis in the affairs of the Immaculata as long as we remain zealous and fervent; then even the solution will be found. The essence here is inner development."

Father Kolbe frequently repeated to his religious Brothers the following,

"Our goal is sanctification. I demand that you all become saints, and I mean very great saints."

"But, Father, aren't you expecting too much of us?"

"No, my son, sanctity is a simple duty," answered Father Kolbe. "Do you recall Christ's first principle? 'Be ye perfect as your heavenly Father is perfect.'"

"What does sanctity depend on, Father?" asked another young man.

Father Maximilian smiled with his child-like eyes and said,

"Give me a piece of chalk, my child, and I shall show you how simple it is."

They all stared at him speechlessly.

"I shall write out the formula for sanctity on the blackboard for all of you." With great deliberation he calmly wrote on the blackboard before the astonished listeners: w = W.

"Here it is, the infallible formula. Whoever conforms to it in life may be assured sanctity."

"What do those letters mean?"

"It's very simple. The small "w" stands for our human will. The capital "W" means the will of God. When opposed, they cross like this +, and then it's bad and there is no sign of sanctity. However, when they are identical to each other then, my dear children, sanctity is certain. If you desire the same thing as God, you will be a saint. It is as simple as $2 + 2 = 4$!"

"Father, it is easy to write it," asserted one of the Brothers, "but it is difficult to apply it to life."

"It would no doubt, be difficult without the Immaculata. She, however, was the first one to bridge the distance between our will and the will of God, for by her fiat [Be it done] she merited for us the grace of sanctity. If you trust her unreservedly, she will help you to bend your will to that of

God. Our sanctity is her affair, her work, and her glory!"

"But how can sinners like us even dream about sanctity?"

"You have a wrong understanding of the Immaculata's love, dear child! St. Bernard says that always in all our difficulties we should call her name. We must run to her as to the kindest of mothers. An earthly mother cannot rescue her child from all dangers, but the Blessed Mother can do everything, and she will come to your aid if you call upon her. I can say without hesitation that is the secret of speedy sanctification. If you happen to commit some transgressions, do not feel depressed about it but give yourself entirely to the Immaculata. She will understand for we belong to her! Sometimes the Immaculata permits us to fall into sin so that we may be cured of our pride. I shall not be with you always, but as long as I am with you I shall repeat continually: 'Love the Immaculata!' There will be a direct proportion between the number of souls entirely devoted to the service of the Immaculata and the number of truly heroic saints."

At this point, Father Maximilian emphatically declared, "There is not one single heroic act that we cannot accomplish with the help of the Im-

Saint Maximilian and his confreres relax at a picnic in the woods in 1938. The saint's confreres at Niepokalanow say he was habitually cheerful and knew how to lift everyone's spirits.

maculata. She is the intermediary of all graces and our sanctifier."

"Where did you read all that, Father?" interjected one of the Brothers simply.

"These are things, indeed, that one cannot learn in books! These things are learned only on one's knees."

Father Maximilian was very apprehensive about the Brothers' absorption in too much external work. He preferred to see them gain their wisdom on their knees too. In his talks and conferences he always defended the priority of prayer. He preached much more by example than by words; his life was a continuous prayer.

"Remember, children," he often repeated, "that outward activity is only an expression of what is in our souls!"

He likewise remembered the Brothers who were left behind at Nagasaki. The truths he endeavored to instill in the hearts of his Brothers in the Polish Niepokalanow he also forwarded by mail to the Brothers at the "Garden of the Immaculata" in Japan...

"Let us pray," he urged them by correspondence, "that the Immaculata becomes the Queen of the world as soon as possible, because there are still so many pagans and so many sinners all around. With her help let us repeat constantly that we are prepared for everything, for all kinds of work, suffering, humiliations, and even death by starvation. But only with her help because by ourselves we cannot do anything.

"We must become in the hands of the Immaculata like a pen in the hand of a writer, like a brush in the hand of an artist, like a chisel in the hand of a sculptor so that she may do with us according to her pleasure. We must give ourselves to her without limitations and that means to be ready to labor where she wants, to be sent out to a distant mission or to go to Madrid if the Father Provincial gives such orders. If we retain even one 'but,' we are not giving ourselves without limitations.

"Let us never say, 'I can't.' That's exactly what the Immaculata is for, so that each one can do what is ordered. Let supernatural obedience be perfected in us more and more, and then peace and happiness will deepen in us because the source of all joy and peace is not outside of us but inside of us. Through the Immaculata we can do all. Let us demonstrate that by our actions we are giving the most beautiful example of sacrifice from unbounded love."

He continually expressed himself more and more clearly; his exhortations became more and more insistent; his allusions were more and more obvious as a great catastrophe loomed closer and closer. No one in Europe cared to believe that war was certain or imminent. Father Maximilian, however, spoke of it so as to prepare his Brothers and inure them to the hardships of war. During a conference in March, 1938, he said:

"We are approaching a very serious struggle. It is difficult to predict what the consequences will be. We can expect almost anything, but whatever may happen, all will be for our good because our condition is such that no one nor anything can do us harm. For the first three centuries great persecutions of the Church persisted. The effects were such that the martyrs' blood became the seed of Christianity. One of the historians of the time wrote that for about 40 years when there was peace, many Christians became contaminated with evil, and for that reason he was glad that persecutions had again broken out. We, likewise, can be happy because in time of various difficulties we shall be spurred on to be more fervent and understand better the need of prayer and greater mortification. After all, when we dialogued with the Brothers we told ourselves that the most noble ideal would be to give up one's life for the Immaculata. We live once and we die once; let it be as the Immaculata desires."

Father Maximilian had a most interesting conversation with his closest co-workers on Sunday, January 10, 1937. Aware that his end was approaching, Father Maximilian wanted to leave his "beloved Brothers" his testament, namely a secret which he had carried in his heart for a few years. One evening during the Octave of the Epiphany, according to an old Polish custom, the Brothers at Niepokalanow were staging one of the traditional mystery plays of the Nativity, the famous *Jaselka*. All the friars were anticipating the entertainment. Father Maximilian, as superior, made an announcement after the evening meal.

"Those Brothers in solemn vows who so desire may stay behind with me in the refectory."

Several friars and Father Pius Bartosik remained with Father Maximilian. The little group surrounded the priest.

"Be seated close to me, my sons." At his right sat Father Pius and next the friars according to seniority in the Community.

"Dear children," Father Maximilian began to speak with a certain solemnity in his voice, commingled with a great sweetness, "you love me and I love you in return. However, you must realize that I will not be with you always. I will die, and you will stay. Before departing, I would like to leave you something. Desiring to do only what the Immaculata wants, I asked that only those who wished to remain do so in order that she herself might choose you.

"You call me 'Father Guardian,' and you do so rightly because I am a guardian. You call me 'Father Director,' and that is correct because I am the director of these publications. It is true that I am your Father Guardian, superior, and director of the publications. But what am I really? I am your father, really and truly, even more than your natural fathers. Through your earthly father God gave you physical life, but from me you received spiritual life, your religious vocation, which is much more sublime than your earthly life. Do I speak the truth?"

"Most certainly the truth," replied one of the friars.

"If not for you, Father, there would be no *Knight*, no Niepokalanow, and it is certain that none of us would be in the Order."

And each one in turn began to recall the ways they found their calling to the Order.

"I found out about the Order by reading about it in the *Knight*," another Brother added.

"To me the *Knight* was an inspiration and a support for my vocation," said a third.

After listening to them all with a smile, he said, "Therefore I am really your father. Moreover this is the reason I address you in familiar terms just as a father does when speaking to his children. And you, of course, are my children."

A brief silence followed. Father Maximilian looked sympathetically on the friars gathered around him, and then he resumed his talk rather shyly.

"My dear children, you are all well aware of the fact that I am very much older than you and that I will not always be here. Therefore I would like to leave you something, to tell you something. May I do so?"

"Tell us, by all means, please tell us, Father," the group almost unanimously voiced their desire.

Moved with emotion Father Maximilian continued, "I want you to know that I am radiant. My heart is overflowing with as much happiness and peace as one is able to enjoy on this earth. In spite of the daily anxieties and troubles, somewhere at the bottom of my heart there always reigns peace and happiness which cannot be expressed humanly in words."

After a brief silence, he resumed his talk.

"Dear children, love the Immaculata! Love the Immaculata and she will make you very happy. Trust her, dedicate yourself to her without limitations. Not everyone can understand the Immaculata—only that person who on his bended knees begs for that through prayer. The Immaculata is the Mother of God. Only the Holy Spirit may bestow the understanding of his Spouse to whomever and however he wills. I would still like to tell you more, but is this not sufficient?"

"No, no!" begged the Brothers. "Tell us more and don't keep anything concealed from us."

"I told you that I am very happy and full of joy. Do you know why? Because heaven has been promised to me in all certitude. Dear children love the Immaculata, love her as much as you can and in the manner you know." He spoke with such emotion that tears sprang to his eyes and ran freely down his cheeks. There followed a brief silence that no one except Father Maximilian dared to break.

"Perhaps now, that will be sufficient for you."

"It is not enough. Tell us more, Father, for we probably will not have another last supper."

"Since you really want to know, I'll just add that it happened in Japan. I can't tell you anymore, dear children, and please do not ask me."

Some of the friars were persistent in knowing more, but Father Maximilian refused to reveal any more of his secrets. However, he concluded in a fatherly manner:

"I revealed my secret to you but only for the purpose of strengthening and supporting you in life's difficulties. Greater trials and tribulations may certainly be expected. There will be sufferings, temptations, and even discouragement. Then the reminiscence of this moment will uplift you in spirit, help you to persevere in your religious vocation, and inspire you to the greater sacrifices that the Immaculata will demand of you. Dear children, do not desire extraordinary things. Have a longing only to perform the will of the Immaculata, which is the will of God."

When the friars were about to leave Father Kolbe turned to them and added,

"Please, do not mention a word of what I have confided to you. Say nothing about it to anyone, except among yourselves, as long as I live."

"We promise," replied the Brothers in unison.

Meanwhile the fame of Niepokalanow as a garden of sanctity spread throughout Poland. More and more candidates applied for admission with the desire to dedicate themselves wholly and entirely to God and the Immaculata. During the time that Father Maximilian was a superior, hundreds of candidates applied every year. The selection was relentlessly made by Father Kolbe himself. He received (about 160) from the number of applicants. The main requisite was the desire for sanctity. Father Kolbe asserted:

"Here, we are interested only in the elite From Niepokalanow will go forth only great saints or execrable persons; none will be mediocre."

When he noticed that some shook their heads at his words, he said,

"Does it astonish you that it is so? It is very simple, indeed! The Immaculata's hands pour upon us a copious rain of graces, and if we do not take advantage of them, whose fault is it? Souls dedicated to the Immaculata occupy the highest places in heaven, or the lowest in hell if they are unfaithful. There is no middle way."

The assurance of heaven he explained as follows,

"We are the possession of the Immaculata. If she holds such a high place in heaven, where will we be, not because of our merits but because we are her possession? What serene peace reigns in the soul dedicated wholly without reservation to the Immaculata!"

From the friars he demanded prayer rather than material production. He repeated constantly:

"In the spiritual life everything depends on the quality of prayer."

Above all, he himself gave an example of fervent prayer. He knelt during meditation without any support, with eyes closed, and face beaming with serenity. Thanks to his prayer no difficulty could overcome him. Many times the religious Brothers saw Father Maximilian kneeling before the statue of the Immaculata embracing her feet and praying a long time whenever Niepokalanow was in a critical situation. They were confident that all difficulties would disappear and that brighter days would follow.

Father Kolbe greatly valued the apostolate of suffering. Whenever he showed guests around Niepokalanow, he usually visited the infirmary with them where the sick Brothers lay, and he explained,

"This is the only action at Niepokalanow which brings in the most unfettered income, and this makes me feel most peaceful. Our sick are a blessing to the community. All our difficulties concerning the publications I entrust to them. Whatever they don't pray away; they suffer away."

Seeing the guests bewildered at this, he explained, "As long as a person is active, self love and the pursuit of praise is evident. But illness cleanses all these defects. A hospital is a foundry where one's 'ego' is refined away, as well as defects and weaknesses. Our sick are great capitalists."

He visited his sick daily two or three times, and he extended his most tender care to them. Once the treasury was empty and there was an urgent need of expensive medication for a sick friar, Camille. Father Maximilian told the infirmarian to take the chalice from the sacristy and sell it in Warsaw to buy the necessary medicine. When he noticed how amazed the friar was at this order, Father Maximilian said,

"A sacred vessel may be sold to save a life—a living temple where Jesus finds a loving reception daily."

Father Maximilian observed poverty conscientiously and he encouraged others to do likewise.

"The Immaculata is our aim, and poverty is our capital. From these two significant points Niepokalanow may not digress under any circumstances. Without these aims Niepokalanow could not exist. Without poverty and trust in Divine Providence all our efforts are nil."

Normally Father Maximilian was always very amiable, but concerning poverty he was severe and unyielding. To this effect he solemnly announced:

"Should it ever come to pass that the spirit of holy poverty vanish at Niepokalanow then I would rather that thunder and lightning blast it and destroy whatever is here."

After a while, with a calm voice, he said:

"If you will not comply with the call of the Immaculata, she will use others. After all, Niepokalanow arose from offerings given for this purpose, namely, to conquer the whole world for the Immaculata! If it loses this aim, deterioration will follow. Niepokalanow was not won at a lottery, nor did we receive it ready to use like other friaries through funds and donations from benefactors. We came in possession of it through hard labor, sacrifices, dedication, and the untiring efforts of our friars. Niepokalanow is the possession of the Immaculata.

"Our Lord Jesus left us this confirmation of holiness, 'By this, they will know you are my disciples if you have love one for another.'" Father Maximilian, through his relationship with his religious Brothers, evidenced that he, too, was a good disciple of Jesus.

A number of years later Brother Benedict declared, "It would not be an exaggeration to tell you that we shall never meet another such father in this life. The Immaculata gave him to us as a father and mother to warm our hearts and expand them. Practically everyone of us meeting him for the first time felt surprised by his overflowing maternal love. His love was a reflection of the love of God and the Immaculata. He was a walking proof of how much our Heavenly Father and Mother Immaculata love us."

Love and goodness radiated from Niepokalanow. No wonder then that people desiring authentic holiness sought a sensible life, understanding of God's truths, and consolation through correspondence with him. On some days Niepokalanow received as many as 5,000 letters. During 1937, it received 750,000 letters and in 1938, it received 828,872 pieces of correspondence. Father Kolbe and his staff answered all the letters. This was a splendid apostolate. The *Knight of the Immaculata* was growing incessantly until in December, 1938, it reached a peak of a million copies. The calendar at Niepokalanow numbered 440,000 copies in 1937.

Father Maximilian in his apostolic zeal also had recourse to the Polish radio. On the feast of the Immaculate Conception in 1937, Father Kolbe gave a radio address to all the Poles. He spoke of Mary, the Mother of God, and the great value of devotion to the Immaculata for one's soul as well as for the Community. He concluded his address with:

> *"When the spirit of Niepokalanow, the spirit of the MI, penetrates our fatherland and all the world, when the Immaculata becomes the Queen of every heart beating under the sun, then paradise will come on earth, but not the utopian one of the communists or the socialists, but—as much as this is possible on earth—the authentic paradise, the happiness of which is enjoyed presently by those who dwell at Niepokalanow, where a single family exists, whose father is God; the mother, the Immaculata; the eldest brother, the divine Prisoner of Love in the Eucharist, while all the others are not companions, but brother and minor brothers, who love one another"* (KW Vol. 2, #1222, p. 2110).

The Polish radio granted permission once again to Father Kolbe for a 12-minute talk on February 2, 1938. Because other requests were not granted, Father Kolbe decided to install his own radio station. On October 2, 1938 the foundation for a radio station was laid at Niepokalanow. Trial broadcasts on the amateur radio "Polish station" began on December 8. The first to speak on this station was Father Kolbe. The theme of this address was again the Immaculata. The power of the station was weak, but the reception was very good. Applications for a license to operate a regular broadcasting station were still pending when World War II broke out.

To facilitate distribution of the publications of Niepokalanow, Father Maximilian planned to build his own airport from which their own airplane would operate. For this purpose a special ministerial commission came to Niepokalanow. The transaction, however, dragged on until the war stopped everything.

Father Maximilian likewise planned to produce films dedicated to Christian ideas. Unfortunately the war did not permit anything beyond some experiments.

At the beginning of 1938 Father Maximilian published the *Knight* in the Latin language. It was called *Miles Immaculatae*. This was an important step toward the realization of conquering the whole world for the Immaculata.

Through this publication, designed mainly for the clergy of the whole world, Father Kolbe hoped to inspire the establishment of the M.I. and the *Knight* rapidly in other countries through local seminarians and clergy. *Miles Immaculatae* appeared as a quarterly, numbering 5,000 issues. It was received with great enthusiasm by priests over the whole world. Letters of acknowledgment were received from England, China, France, Germany, Hungary, Italy, Brazil, and Africa. The publication increased its press increased its press run to 15,000 in 1939.

On September 1, 1938, Father Kolbe edited and published a small paper for the children in Poland, named *Little Knight of the Immaculata*, which numbered 30,000 copies. In a short time the number of copies had to be increased to 39,000.

For Father Maximilian the most joyous Tabor preceding Golgotha was December 8, 1938. It was in Warsaw in the hall of the Catholic Home "Roma," where a festive commemorative program in honor of the Immaculata was held. Among the many guests and participants were the President of the Polish Republic, Ignatius Moscicki, Cardinal Kakowski, and numerous dignitaries of the state and Church. The introductory speech was delivered by a humble friar, Father Maximilian Kolbe. No one in all Poland could speak as beautifully as he did about the Immaculata. In the musical segment of the convocation the orchestra, comprised of members of the Polish Army and the religious Brothers from Niepokalanow, performed admirably.

However, the happiness of Tabor on this earth is short-lived. The foretaste of heaven is not the same heaven which lasts eternally.

1934-1938
Brutal Training of an SS Storm Trooper:
Hoess

On April 1, 1934, Rudolph Hoess was accepted into the 88 and on April 20, he was appointed an SS Storm trooper.

In June, Rudolph Hoess was on the estate of Sallentin, Kreis Pyritz, in Pomerania marching at the head of a detachment of SS Cavalry which he had organized himself. The march was reviewed by Heinrich Himmler, who during this time was Reichsfuehrer SS, Bavarian Chief of Police, a Commissary Chief of Political Police in Meklemburg, Lubec, Baden, Hessen-Anhalt and Bremen, and an assistant of Goering, the Chief of the Prussian Gestapo.

"I am fascinated by your posture on the horse," Himmler complimented Rudolph. "We can see at a glance that you are a splendid soldier of the old school. Your cavalry detachment has displayed itself in a fine, martial way."

"Thank you for the acknowledgement," replied Hoess most respectfully.

"Have we not met earlier in life?"

"Yes, we did, Herr Reichsfuehrer! We met once during the years 1921-1922 in the home of Ludendorff and a second time in 1930 at the Assembly of the Artaman's Union in Saxony."

"I recall it was the time when I said that we must conquer all the lands in the east. The eventful moment is approaching when our nation will join in a gigantic battle to gain a great German Confederation. Therefore we need courageous soldiers ready to march even unto death for our Fuehrer and our ideals of National Socialism. At such a decisive moment could you remain on your farm? You must put on a uniform and become a soldier just as during the war and after it."

"With your permission, I must consult my wife."

"Please tell her that you will soon be advanced to higher ranks and consequently your financial income will increase immeasurably. The Germans will not stint on money for brave men."

Rudolph's wife was grieved when he presented Himmler's proposition.

"Will the career of a soldier fulfill you? Will you get any inner satisfaction?" asked his wife. "But I don't want to divert you from your purpose. Do as you think best for your family and Germany."

Hoess received his appointment from Himmler to active service in the SS Division of Sentries at the concentration camp in Dachau. He didn't reflect much about establishing concentration camps. Since he led a rather isolated life on the farm in Pomerania, he had not heard much about concentration camps. When he joined the SS, he had in mind army service and army life.

After coming to Dachau he had to go through the Infantry Recruiting Training although he had the rank of a non-commissioned officer. During the ideological lectures he learned about the theoretical basis of concentration camps. Frequently these lectures were given by Theodore Eicke, the founder and organizer of these concentration camps and Kommandant of Dachau.

"National Socialism," Eicke tried to convince the SS Troopers, "has finally succeeded in getting into power after a long battle and heavy sacrifices. Now is the time to make the most of it by disposing of all the enemies of Germany. The prisoners are forever the enemies of the state. They must be watched and treated severely, and in case of obstinacy, they must be destroyed. Behind the wired fences of the concentration camps, enemies lie in wait and observe all our movements to take advantage of our weakness. Do not expose your weak sides, show your severity. Any of you who will in any way show compassion to these enemies must be purged from our ranks. I need SS Storm troopers who are harsh and tough and ready for everything. We have no place here for spineless men!"

To harden them, Eicke ordered at least one company of the SS to be present during the flogging of prisoners.

Hoess particularly remembered the first flogging he witnessed. The two prisoners condemned to 25 lashes were brought in after the SS Regiment, in single file, formed a square around the scaffolding where the flogging was inflicted. Both prisoners were led in by the Blockfuehrer. The Kommandant of the concentration camp appeared. The Schutzhaftlager-fuehrer and a higher ranking officer, the Company-fuehrer, gave the report and the Rapportfuehrer read the verdict.

The first prisoner, small in stature, had to lie down on the scaffolding. Two soldiers from the garrison held the prisoner's head and hands tightly while two Blockfuehrers alternately struck blow after blow upon the victim. The prisoner didn't utter a sound. It was quite different with the second one. He was a strong, broad-shouldered man who was a political prisoner. At the first blow he shrieked horribly and tried to get away. He screamed to the very last blow. Rudolph stood in the first row observing the whole course of punishment. From the first scream he felt alternately hot and cold.

Rudolph had to go through this experience several more times. He did everything possible to conceal his feelings. It seemed that he covered them with a stone mask of indifference. He remarked though that there were many Blockfuehrers who were most eager to beat the prisoners. Among his SS colleagues were many who did the flogging and treated it as an interesting spectacle and a pleasurable entertainment for the onlookers.

Eicke was without compassion even for the SS troopers. During the recruiting period Hoess was a witness to the following incident: Four members of the SS committed some abuses in the slaughterhouse with prisoners. They were convicted by the Monachian Court, sentenced to pay high fines, and deprived of their freedom. In full uniform of their minor rank they were brought before a battalion of sentinels and personally degraded by Eicke and then expelled from the SS in a most infamous way. He personally ripped off their rank distinctions from their lapels and had them led before individual divisions which were also to administer justice for the unpardonable offenses.

Finally he gave them a lengthy lecture which was a warning to his subordinates,

"I would most willingly have clothed those four in prison clothes and had them flogged; then I would have sent them to their accomplices behind the wire fence. However, the Reichsfuehrer SS disapproved of it. A similar fate awaits each one of you who becomes involved with the prisoners behind the wire fence. Your intention, whether it is a transgression or whether it is sympathy you show to our enemies who will readily take advantage of it, makes no difference. Even the smallest act of sympathy for the enemies of our government is not in compliance with a member of the SS. For people with soft an unmanly hearts there is no place in the ranks of the SS; it would be better if they entered a monastery. In the SS we need people who are hard and relentless, blindly obeying every order. They do not wear the skull and crossbones with gun emblem for show, but for a purpose. They are the only soldiers who, in war and peace, day and night must keep watch over the enemy behind the wire fence."

After a half-year service in the regiment, an order suddenly came from Eicke that all senior officers and non-commissioned officers should leave their regiments and take their posts in the camp. Hoess was among them. He was transferred as a Blockfuehrer to the concentration camp. This was an unpleasant surprise to him, and at the first opportunity he reported to Eicke.

I am a soldier of blood and bone and only the possibility of becoming a soldier again induced me to active service in the SS. Therefore, please transfer me back to a regiment."

"I am familiar with your past, dear Rudolph," answered Eicke with determination. "Yet, you also experienced this type of life. You know very well how political prisoners should be treated, and therefore I feel you are well qualified for service in the concentration camp. Furthermore, I am making no exceptions, and my order is irrevocable. You must obey because you are a soldier; that's what you wanted!"

Hoess entered the concentration camp at Dachau with mixed emotions. He had been a prisoner for six years and knew the life and regimen of prisoners, their bright and dark sides, the range of their feelings and misfortunes, but a concentration camp was something else in reality. This was something new and unknown. He studied the mandatory regulations of the concentration camps thoroughly. He read every word of the purpose and structure of a concentration camp.

But what a difference there was between theory and practice in the concentration camp! How much irresponsibility was involved in observing these regulations. How much freedom the camp functionaries used in inflicting punishment upon the enemies of the government. At times they made themselves the lords of life and death of the prisoners. It took only a short time for Rudolph Hoess to be convinced of this. He was amazed when he stood before 270 greatly disturbed prisoners gazing imploringly at his stone face which showed no feeling nor compassion.

Shortly, Hoess began to classify the prisoners into two categories: the ordinary criminals and the political prisoners. He tried to engage the latter in conversation at the very outset, and they unanimously declared that they could cope with all the camp hardships and even with the SS men or the functionary prisoners; but the uncertainty of the length of their imprisonment was too difficult to bear. This weakened even the strongest will. A criminal convict was usually imprisoned for a specified number of years, whereas a political prisoner was always imprisoned in the concentration camp for an indefinite time.

Hoess soon became convinced that the fate of a prisoner in a concentration camp depended greatly on the supervisory personnel.

In the place of detention for preliminary inquiry when a prisoner was extremely cold and begged the supervisor to turn on more heat, a spiteful functionary would shut the heat off entirely. Then he would watch the half-frozen prisoner run around the cell exercising to keep warm. When the night guard, a type of very indifferent functionary, would come in, the prisoner would again ask for some heat, the supervisor would open it full force and leave it that way, unregulated. After an hour the cell would become so overheated that the prisoner had to open a window. As a result of the cold night air, the prisoner would contract a severe cold.

In the penal prison, baths were ordered at any time of the day. A malicious functionary would lead the prisoners there. In mid-winter he would order the windows to be opened wide in the dressing room to eliminate the steam. He would shout at the prisoners to hurry in their preparation, rush them into the shower room where he opened the hot water full force so that no one could stand it. Then he would turn on the cold water and everyone had to stand under this shower for a longer time. Smiling sarcastically, he would watch the prisoners who could hardly dress themselves because of the cold.

Another time, also in winter, an indifferent functionary led the prisoners to the bath. While the prisoners were preparing for the shower, he sat down and read a paper. After some time he decided to turn on the hot water and again sat down to read a paper. No one dared to get under the hot water so they called out to him, but he just disregarded them and kept on reading. After he finished reading the paper, he rose, looked at his watch, and turned off the water. Without having taken a shower, the prisoners dressed quickly, and the functionary again looked at his watch, satisfied that the allotted time was over.

A good-natured functionary in the concentration camp showed concern about not overloading the trains on the gravel road because they must go uphill. He saw to it that the tracks were securely tightened and the wheels oiled. The day passed smoothly and the required work was done.

A malicious functionary, on the other hand, ordered the trains to be overloaded so that they had to be pushed up-hill and prodded through the entire route. He considered controlling the weight as well as oiling and reinforcing the tracks a waste of time. As a result the trains ran off the tracks and the prisoners were beaten so badly that by noon they were unfit to work. All day long shouting at the prisoners persisted. As a result when evening came, only half the required work was accomplished.

A careless functionary was not at all concerned about the work groups. He left the supervision to the guards who permitted some prisoners to do as they pleased while others had to work above their norm. The leader of the guards was always absent, and the other guards chose not to see the abuses.

Hoess concluded that the inspector and the prisoner formed two hostile worlds. The prisoner was the victim assaulted by his camp life as well as by the inspectors. If he wished to survive, he would have to defend himself. Since he could not use the same kind of defense as his adversary, he had to find other ways and means of protecting himself. He either allowed himself to be victimized or he became insidious, secretive and false, thus deceiving his adversary and alleviating his pain. He may then have been transferred to another camp where he became a block functionary. In this way he created for himself a tolerable existence at the expense of his fellow-prisoners. When things became intolerable for a prisoner he either tried to escape or resigned himself to everything, thereby failing psychically, breaking down physically, and often-times, in the end, committing suicide.

Eicke's instructions about dangerous enemies of the German government were familiar to Hoess. He, too, began to seek out those enemies in the camp and endeavored to investigate what actually made them hostile. He found a certain number of Communists and Social-Democrats who, in spite of their imprisonment in the concentration camp, would continue to fight for their ideas as soon as they were freed. They openly admitted this to Rudolph Hoess. The majority of the prisoners however, after their tortures, desired only to return to their families and to work quietly to secure their livelihood.

Being trained and educated by Eicke, the creator of the concentration camp in Germany, Rudolph Hoess occupied the position of Blockfuehrer at Dachau and later Rapportfuehrer. He performed his tasks to the satisfaction of his superiors. He was severe, hard, cold, stone-like—with no sympathy for prisoners. His superior, Loritz, was convinced that he had no need to harden him as in the case of other SS men.

Inwardly, however, Hoess felt a deep dissatisfaction and unrest. At times during his wakeful hours at night, he dialogued with his uneasy conscience:

"You are not fit for service in a concentration camp. Do you recall your suffering in the prison? How did your suffering compare with the monstrosities taking place here? How can you personally be the cause of so many tears and such suffering? Apply to Himmler or to Eicke and resign from this service. What? You don't want to? Are you a coward? No, I cannot do this! I cannot compromise, and I can't show that I am spineless. I simply cannot acknowledge my weakness to anyone, for I personally consented to leave my last position for the present service."

His conscience, however, would not concede:

"Considering all this, do you feel it is still better to continue blundering along?"

"Should I become a deserter because of this? I took an oath as an SS soldier: 'I swear before God that I shall be absolutely obedient to the Fuehrer of the German Confederation and the German nation, to Adolph Hitler, the chief commander of Wermacht; and as a valiant soldier I shall always be prepared in the name of my oath to give my life.'"

"You swore that you would be a valiant soldier, not a bandit or murderer!"

"I also took an oath as an SS man: 'I swear to you, Adolph Hitler, our Fuehrer and Chancellor of the German Confederation, that I shall be loyal to you and valiant. I vow this to you and those appointed by you to the end of my life. So help me God!'"

"God? But what kind of God? What kind of God are you calling on to help you in your barbarous actions. The true God is a God of love and brotherhood, not of pride and hate."

As an old National Socialist, Hoess reassured himself, "I am deeply convinced of the absolute necessity of the existence of concentration camps. The real enemies of the government must be interned. The social and professional transgressors ought to be deprived of their freedom in order to insure the security of the German nation from their pernicious actions. I am deeply convinced that only we, the SS men, can perform that task as a protective power of the new German Confederation. I am content with my fate which I chose deliberately. Let them call me hard, for I prefer that, rather than be a weakling."

In 1936, during the great inspection tour of the Dachau concentration camp, Himmler and Bormann became very interested in the "valiant" stance of Hoess. "Are you satisfied with your service, Herr Hoess?" asked the chief of the SS.

"Yes sir, I am."

"At first you were in great doubt and you couldn't decide so readily. How is the health of your wife and children?"

Hoess was elated at the chief's interest in his family.

Himmler, in agreement with Bormann, personally recommended Hoess for his past service to Germany to a post as an AA-Unter-sturm-fuehrer. At the same time he became a member of the SS Officers' Corps. After this promotion he supervised the administration of the camp.

On August 1, 1938, Rudolph Hoess was transferred to the concentration camp in Sachsenhausen where he was appointed the adjutant Kommandant of the camp. The residence of the inspectors, over whom Eicke presided, was near the concentration camp, in Oranienburg, established in 1933 by the Berlin SA. The concentration camp in Sachsenhausen was founded by the SS in 1935-36. The Kommandant was Hermann Baranowski who received Rudolph with open arms.

"I am very happy that I received such a perfect soldier: tough and conscientious, a man of the party."

"I tried with all my power to be worthy of such trust in the opinion of my superior officer," replied the new adjutant.

Because of his duties, Hoess could then go to Berlin more frequently. There he met many of his old colleagues from the Volunteer Corps who now held key positions. Thanks to these meetings, he began to understand the ideas and intentions of Hitler and his party. Industry and trade were flourishing in Germany. The citizens by a great majority were rejoicing that Austria was annexed to Germany; they had a premonition that Germany would soon conquer all Europe and later the whole world, for the party was in possession of the whole of Germany.

After these discourses, Hoess was convinced more and more that Hitler's party was right. Now he believed firmly in Hitler and in his goal, i.e., destruction of the enemies of the Fuehrer and his ideas. Hoess was convinced that he should remain in the concentration camp as an executioner.

1939–1940
The Nazi War Machine
Collides with Truth and Love:
Kolbe

After the Sacred Heart devotion in June 1939, Father Maximilian walked out into the garden. He was surrounded by the friars, especially the youngest, one of whom commented,

"The June devotion is so beautiful and appealing. Isn't it Father?"

"It's true, Brother, but the hymn everyone sang at the end greatly annoyed me. It ought to be forbidden to be sung in church."

"Why?" several friars asked in unison.

"Dear children, how can a hymn with such words touch you? 'Our hearts are cold as ice, and void for them your passion's toil. . .' Since when are our hearts cold? Our hearts are inflamed with love; we would like to do everything possible for Jesus. Even death does not frighten us for we would most willingly die for love of God. How can anyone say 'cold hearts'?"

A dreadful time of trial was quickly approaching for Father Maximilian and for the millions of loving hearts among the Polish people. The time was drawing close to testify not with words but with life and death that one loved God and his truths above everything else.

On September 1, 1939, an avalanche of German iron and fire fell upon Poland. The heroism of the Polish soldiers mingled with the panic of startled civilians. When the Germans were approaching Niepokalanow on September 5 Father Maximilian called the friars together in the afternoon and announced that publications as well as the observance of community religious life were being suspended. Whoever wanted to remain in Niepokalanow could do so; whoever felt apprehensive could leave the friary and report to the Red Cross for humanitarian work, or go to his family home to remain there until the horror of war passed and return when peace would be assured.

Father Maximilian, deeply touched, turned to speak to the friars: "Dear children, we now have a mission. Just as Christ, our Lord, said to his apostles, 'I shall not always be with you,' so likewise I, too, must depart from you. But, be mindful of all I taught you. Remember always to give a good example. Recall often what I told you repeatedly, namely, that Niepokalanow does not mean the buildings, the machines, the surroundings, but it means you personally as members of Niepokalanow, your souls and your hearts. Remember also your solemn promise to the Immaculata. Many of you will never return here. I, too, will not survive this war. Nevertheless, remember to love the Immaculata and in all your trials and hardships, turn to her. She will, undoubtedly, answer your prayers and sustain you through all your tribulations. I worked assiduously for that, and I ardently desire that Niepokalanow always remain faithful to its ideals and that religious discipline will continue to flourish. Therefore, I beg you, dear children, promise me that you will endeavor to keep that which I spoke of so much."

The majority of friars came to Father Kolbe that same evening requesting his blessing for their journeys.

There were, however, some friars who thought of the dangers confronting Father Maximilian. They approached him and begged him to save himself.

"What will happen to you, Father? You are facing a greater danger than we are. Please leave Niepokalanow, even on the first day of the German occupation. Father, please think about it," begged the friars.

"Dear children, I am a superior here and I must remain on duty in the friary."

"Then, we shall turn to the Provincial to order you to leave Niepokalanow."

"If that's the case I shall go to the Provincial myself," said Father Kolbe, "and let him decide."

The following day, September 6, Father Maximilian found himself in Warsaw with the Provincial.

"The friars begged me to leave Niepokalanow if only for a short time and wait in a safe place while the German army occupies Niepokalanow. What shall I do?"

"What do you think about it, Father?" asked the Provincial.

"I only fear offending God; he will take care of the rest."

"Father, are you presuming that something evil will happen?" asked the Provincial.

"I don't presume anything; I only trust God. After all, I am not here of my own accord, but I promised the friars that I would consult you and have you decide."

"That's a very serious matter," considered the Provincial. "I must consult other Fathers about this action."

"I shall most willingly comply with whatever order I receive concerning my person, for I desire to abide only by holy obedience."

The situation was actually menacing. Father Kolbe was world renowned as an ingenious organizer of religious life and as the editor and publisher of *Maly Dziennik* (a small daily newspaper) which, together with the whole Polish press, was prominent for its patriotism in confronting the activities of Hitlerite Germany. No one had any idea of what the Germans would do to Father Maximilian.

"I feel," said one of the counselors, "that we should do everything in our power to save Father Maximilian from any harm. It is advisable to use all precautions to protect him for the good of our province and for the

The arrest and deportation of Saint Maximilian and his confreres in 1939. Father Maximilian and 36 friars were interned in three consecutive camps: Lamsdorf (3 days), Amtitz (6 weeks), Ostrzesow (1 month). The other friars and students—over 700 —had been evacuated and sent back to their homes before the Germans arrived. (Painting by M. Koscielniak).

future. I suggest that Father Maximilian hide until all danger is over. He is the only one who is indispensable to our community, and we want him to live as long as possible. We know what great good he has accomplished for the community, and, if it's the will of God, he may do a great deal more. He should conceal himself. In the present circumstances any other Father can replace him as Guardian."

"I think otherwise," said another counselor. "My opinion is that a superior ought to remain in the friary, especially in its most dangerous moments. It would appear unseemly that the Guardian of Niepokalanow escape. What kind of an impression would this create among the friars who decided to remain in the friary, and what effect would this have upon the lay people when they hear that the friars, and even the Guardian, fled because their lives were endangered? Certainly I agree that we have only one Father Maximilian, and because he is the only one he should not flee; he ought to remain and continue as Guardian of Niepokalanow."

"In the face of such different opinions what am 1 to do?" asked the Provincial.

"I still firmly hold to my suggestion," declared the first counselor, "although I see merit in the contrary position. The dangers to which Father Maximilian and, above all, our province are exposed are grave; it is natural that our opinions and suggestions differ. However, I think, the Provincial himself must make the decision. It certainly will be a great relief to Father Maximilian that he be directed by obedience, which for him is the will of the Immaculata, because that is most significant to him."

When Father Kolbe came to the Provincial he received the answer he anticipated.

"Father, you remain at Niepokalanow."

"Very well. Thank you, Father Provincial," replied Father Maximilian and he immediately returned to Niepokalanow.

Upon his return to the friary Father Maximilian assembled the friars and announced,

"Father Provincial ordered me to remain at Niepokalanow; I am, therefore, remaining here. If any of you wish to leave the community, please do so; I will in no way hinder you. If, however, you decide to remain with me, you must be prepared for what comes."

One of the friars, before leaving the community, came to Father Maximilian for his blessing and asked him if they would ever meet again.

Father Kolbe, his calm eyes looking far off, replied to the friar. "Dear son, I will not survive this war. I commend you to the Immaculata."

Those who remained at Niepokalanow numbered 38 friars, Father Kolbe, and one other priest.

Polish soldiers and people in the thousands fleeing east were entrenched around the friary. Father Maximilian opened wide the gates of Niepokalanow and more importantly imbued others with a strong faith in a final victory.

On the morning of September 12, 1939, the first divisions of the German army broke into Niepokalanow and occupied a part of the friary building, but beyond that they did not interfere with the life of the friars. On September 19, 1939, at about 9 o'clock in the morning, the SS men arrived at the friary. An officer ordered Father Maximilian to call all the friars together. When they were assembled, the officer asked Father Kolbe, "Is there anyone missing?"

"No one."

The officer ordered the friars to get in line and said,

"I was ordered to lead you all to the Command." Father Maximilian turning to the officer asked, "Please, permit the friars to change from their working clothes."

"Very well," replied the officer. "They have 15 minutes time. If anyone is missing after that time, all will be shot to death."

At the specified time, all the friars were present. The officer now heard another request.

"There are some wounded in the friary without care, and they are begging for a few friars to remain with them."

Permission was granted that two stay with them.

The friars begged Father Maximilian to remain, but he calmly appointed two friars to look after the wounded. Father Maximilian then briefly declared, "I am leaving with all of you."

The friars were led to automobiles and driven in an unknown direction. To his frightened friars Father Maximilian said with a smile, "Under normal circumstances we could not afford to ride in this fashion. Who knows what plans the Immaculata has in store for us? If we ourselves were to go to a mission in Germany, how much trouble we would go through— the formality, passports, and then probably they wouldn't let us go. It's a profitable opportunity, and we must take advantage of it and endeavor to do much good. Let us offer ourselves to the Immaculata to gain as many souls as possible."

Saint Kolbe's photo on his wartime identification papers—taken late 1939 or early 1940. It's the only photo extant from his later life in which he appears without his glasses. One can discern a personality matured by intense love and great suffering in his penetrating gaze.

The journey led south. First they were interned in Lamsdorf. On September 21st, in closed freight cars now, the friars were brought to Amtitz Camp, which numbered 14,000 prisoners. The condition of this camp was nauseating. Insects and hunger were the worst plagues in this camp. The food rations were very meager, that is, 25 grams of bread (about 9 oz.) and twice a day something resembling a soup. The most painful trial was the degradation of human dignity. For the smallest mistake, internees were beaten unmercifully-sometimes only for the pleasure of the SS men. Beaten and maltreated, the friars fled to Father Maximilian for comfort and consolation. As a most tender mother toward her children, Father Maximilian most kindly and calmly said, "Dear children, pray for those who beat you."

"Father, how can God look at all this injustice done to innocent people?" the friars inquired.

Father Kolbe replied very patiently, "God is love and he gave love to all people; he desires to see it in the whole world. But man's free will is inviolable and even God does not force anyone. Unfortunately, sometimes man wants to be wicked. Therefore, we must pray that God will restrain the ill will of people."

Father Maximilian himself prayed a great deal and encouraged the friars to communal prayer during free time. The lay people were greatly edified at the friars' prayerful attitude, their compassion, and great charity in sharing their small ration of bread with the more hungry men.

Father Kolbe showed no fear of the SS men. He approached them as his equals and even as a priest, a shepherd toward poor strayed sheep. To the astonishment of all concerned he tried to convert them; he even distributed the Immaculata's medals to them, which he smuggled into the camp.

October 12 was Father Maximilian's name day, and his Brothers extended to him their congratulatory wishes and sang "Plurimcos annos." Thanking them, Father Maximilian said:

"In such circumstances as we find ourselves today we need to be particularly reconciled to the will of God. When suffering is remote we are prepared for everything. Now, however, it is near, and therefore, let us take advantage of it; offer it to the Immaculata to gain the whole world for her. I was wondering what I could give you on the occasion of my name's day. And there is one certain thing I wish you in particular—that you belong to the Immaculata even more than ever. She knows how to convert those circumstances which seem destructive into very beneficial ones for us. We

are needed here right now, and not in Niepokalanow. How infinitely kind she is! Let us try, then, to win as many souls as possible for the cause of the Immaculata. We traveled here without cost; we have bunks for sleep, and food to eat so that we might gain souls for her, the Immaculata. For many of these internees this may turn out to be a blessing, if they reconcile with God. The laymen you see here are swearing, cursing, blaspheming, but when they observe your tranquility, your prayers and your demeanor, they will change for the better."

After a brief reflection he continued,

"Today, particularly, I want to propose that we make a bargain with the Blessed Mother. Let us each say to her that through our love for her we resign ourselves to everything, even death, in this revolting camp, in abandonment, among insensitive and cold hearts, as long as she would draw all of us to her and as many souls as possible, so that all souls living today, as well as those who will live to the end of the world, would love her with their whole heart and with their whole being."

The Germans transferred the Franciscans on November 9 to Ostrzeszow where the conditions were somewhat better. On November 20, Father Maximilian told the astonished Brothers, "Have courage, Brothers! Our return to Niepokalanow will follow shortly. Our mission here is approaching its end, and therefore we must endeavor to complete it as best we can. Let us not hope for it to end any sooner nor any later, but only when the Immaculata is pleased to do so."

On the feast of the Immaculate Conception a priest from a neighboring parish brought the Holy Eucharist to the friars. What a joy and what strength of will the Holy Eucharist bestowed upon them! Their resignation to the will of God became very easy. On that very same day, what a great surprise the Immaculata had in store for them! At 2 o'clock in the afternoon, the Germans liberated them, and thus Father Maximilian's prediction was fulfilled.

After they returned from the concentration camp to Mary's enclosure, their eyes beheld a very depressing sight. It is true the buildings stood intact, but everything else had been ransacked, plundered, driven away or sealed. When Brother Simon lamented the loss of all their machines and material, Father Maximilian in a kind and serene way said, "Dear Brother, we don't have to worry about material things; it is important, however, to keep up our spirits. I'll admit that the war was necessary even for Niepo-kalanow because, many corrupting influences had crept in on account of the *Maly Dziennik*, the small newspaper, and other matters. If there is no other means, God uses a cudgel. We shall again start from scratch in such circumstances as the Immaculata has placed us."

Father Maximilian had no illusions; he was now merely waiting his turn. He, however, did not wish to lose one minute of the precious time he still had on hand.

Father Maximilian started a new life at Niepokalanow by introducing continual adoration of the Blessed Sacrament to increase his active forces of prayer. He dreamed of this long before the war, but the publications consumed all the time of the friars. Now those who lived at Niepokala-now had more time. Morning to night the friars continued their adora-tion before the simple but beautiful altar. They prayed with much fervor, as they never had before. Father Maximilian's greatest concern was for the spiritual welfare of his friars. The fruits derived from adoration, vis-its, and fervent prayer before the Blessed Sacrament were obvious and brought joy to Father Maximilian's heart. He was aware that the friars were in dire need of this renewal. Many of them were greatly weakened spiritually, their zeal much diminished, and some even suffered spiritual breakdown.

Consequently he restored a more rigorous religious life in the friary. He exhorted the friars to maintain strict silence, thereby guarding them from outward dangers.

He was solicitous not only about the friars who returned with him, but also about all those who were gradually returning from their exile. To those who were unable to return at this time, he wrote letters, just as a mother does to her distant children.

"Nothing happens without the will of God. If God permits certain tri-als, they are for our benefit as long as we are faithful to our obligations. . ."

"Permit the Immaculata to lead us as she pleases. Let us disregard our own desires, purposes, and intentions. Let the Providence of God direct us rather than we ourselves."

"Beware of illusions and do not place too much value on the fruits of outward activities. The conversion and sanctification of the soul always was and will always remain an act of God's grace. . ."

"Prayer, we are convinced, is the most powerful means to restore peace in souls and to give them the joy to draw closer to God's love. . ."

"Therefore, let us pray, let us pray fervently and well, let us pray much orally and mentally, and we shall experience in ourselves the effects of the Immaculata's possession of our souls. Our sins and faults will be decreasing as we gradually come closer to God. And the more our hearts will be inflamed with God's love, the more readily will we be able to inflame other hearts with God's love. . ."

"Let us trust the Immaculata. There are still many souls who neither know her nor love her and wander far from that source of happiness and from God. We must therefore endeavor to draw her to those hearts with her help. . ."

"The essence of mutual love is not that others may not hurt our feelings, but that we learn to forgive mutually, immediately and entirely. Then, indeed, with great confidence we can recite the Our Father, and ask him to forgive us our trespasses as we forgive those who trespass against us. This prayer was given us by our Lord himself. Even saints fell several times a day, so when we fall, we must beg God to forgive those who offend us. It is sufficient to forgive others wholly and entirely for love of God. Let us love everyone without exception, friends and enemies. . ."

As a great realist Father Maximilian concerned himself with provisions for the friars who now numbered 349 and who, after their return, had resumed their religious life. He thought not only of them but of all the fugitive Poles and Jews from Lwow and western Poland, who sought shelter at Niepokalanow. By the end of 1939, there were approximately 3,500 of these exiles. Besides, these, the Red Cross was located at Niepokalanow with a number of war casualties. All these people had been deprived of their homes, provisions, and clothing. Father Maximilian took the responsibility upon himself to provide for all their needs. He, therefore, began to convert the printery building into a friary-workshop. In this, he included a locksmith shop, a blacksmith shop, a sheet-iron forge, a carpenter's workshop, and a sawmill.

At Christmas time Father Kolbe organized a traditional Polish Christmas Eve celebration for the refugees. He spoke comforting words and encouraged everyone to, have unlimited trust in God, submitting wholeheartedly to his will. Everyone broke the traditional Christmas wafer, then sang the Polish carols so dear to them all. There were little gifts for the children. No one was left out.

For the Jewish families Father Kolbe planned a New Year's Day celebration, similar to the Christmas party for the Catholics.

By order of the German authorities, the 2,000 Polish and 1,500 Jewish refugees left Niepokalanow in February, 1940. Before the departure of the Jewish caravans, their delegates approached Father Maximilian with words of gratitude. "Tomorrow we are to leave Niepokalanow," one of them said. "We have been treated here with much loving care by the good people of the friary. We have always felt the closeness and sympathy of the friars. In Niepokalanow we have been blessed with an all-embracing kindness. For that now in the name of all the Jews here we want to express our warm and sincere thanks to Father Maximilian and all his Brothers. Words are inadequate to express what our hearts desire to say. . ."

"If God permits us to live through this war," added another delegate, "we will repay Niepokalanow a hundredfold. As for the good will and care shown here to the Jewish refugees from Poznan, we shall never forget it. . ."

In a short time he organized other types of shops: repairing watches and clocks, repairing of bicycles, baking wafers, making statuettes of the Immaculata. He also established a photography studio and a district dairy. For all the services rendered to the multitudes surrounding the friary no definite price was set. Only voluntary contributions were accepted, and these proved sufficient for the sustenance of all.

Even in such circumstances as the Germans invading Poland, Father Maximilian did not renounce the *Knight of the Immaculata*. On February 16, 1940, a letter was sent to a German occupation official requesting permission to resume its publication. Here are some excerpts from his letter:

"As for the monthly, 'Rycerz Niepokalanej', I am of the opinion that it contributes to the common good, and for the following reasons:

1.   In 100 or 200 years you and I will no longer be alive. Then all of our problems will end, including the most urgent and important, and only one shall remain: will we exist at that time? And where? Will we be happy? The same must be said of all other men. Every hour, in fact, brings us a whole hour closer (no less) to that time. The religious magazine deals with problems of that kind.

2.   The Most Holy Virgin Mary is not a fairy tale or a legend, but a living being who loves each one of us. Yet, she is not sufficiently known, and her love is not reciprocated enough. Accordingly, it is necessary to announce her loving where everywhere, and that it can be achieved quite well by means of the magazine.

Finally, let me emphasize that I do not feel hatred for anyone on this earth. The substance of my ideal is found in the enclosed printed material. What is there is mine: I want to work for that ideal always, to suffer and possibly give up my own life in sacrifice. What instead is against the ideal is not mine, but comes from outside and therefore, according to my ability, I have fought it, and will fight it forever.

To convince yourself in person as to whether there is an atmosphere of hatred toward anyone in the friary, it would be best to come to us, perhaps accompanied by the Commissioner of Police.

I apologize if this letter is too long and ask you to kindly request authorization to continue printing 'Rycerz Niepokalanej'. The Immaculata will not fail to reciprocate service done to her during life and at the point of death." (KW Vol. 1, #884, p. 1438-39).

Such a letter to a German occupation official could be written only by a person with a simple heart and a deep faith—a faith that can move mountains. To the astonishment of all, Father Maximilian was given permission for a single issue. The issue was dated December, 1940–January, 1941 and numbered 120,000 copies. For this issue Father Maximilian wrote a characteristic article entitled "Truth," which dealt with falsehood and deceit.

In it he emphasized that "truth" is one; it is powerful. No one can change truth, but we can search for it, find it, and acknowledge it so that we can apply it to our lives by following it in all affairs, particularly those concerning the end of our lives.

1939–1940
The Making of an Executioner:
Hoess

On September 1, 1939, when World War II broke out, Eicke, the ideologist of concentration camps, addressed his subordinates on the necessity and functions of the SS formation in the newly created situation.

Now, the hard war laws determined what would be demanded of them. Every SS man, regardless of his past life, was to dedicate himself entirely to his duty. Every order had to be considered sacred even though it might be the heaviest and most difficult ever encountered; it had to be carried out without hesitation. The Reichsfuehrer SS demanded from the SS officers an exemplary sense of duty and dedication to their fatherland to the point of complete self-abnegation. The main function of the SS in this war was to protect the government, Hitler, and inner Germany from all dangers. The revolution of 1918 and the strike of laborers in ammunition factories in 1917 were not to be repeated. Every antagonist of the government, every saboteur was to be destroyed. The Fuehrer demanded that the SS protect their fatherland from all underhanded dealings of the enemies. Therefore Eicke demanded that the commanders train their soldiers functioning in concentration camps in a spirit of inexorable rigor in relation to the prisoners. These commanders would be forced to perform the hardest labor and to take severe orders. That was the purpose of the existence of the SS men, and only they were capable of defending the National Socialistic state from all internal dangers, because all of the other organizations lacked this indispensable discipline.

The very same day the first execution took place in Sachsenhausen camp. Observe this: Johann Heinen, a Communist, refused to cooperate in the anti-aircraft defense in Dessau. When this was reported to the factory security guard, the Communist was arrested by the local Gestapo and transferred to the Berlin Gestapo for a court hearing. The report was communicated to Himmler who ordered that the Communist be shot to death immediately. In compliance with the order of mobilization, all executions ordered by Himmler or by the Gestapo were to be carried out in the nearest concentration camp. About 10 AM, Herr Mueller of the Gestapo telephoned the concentration camp that a messenger was on his way with an order. In a short time a car with two police officers arrived, bringing with them a civilian in manacles. The Kommandant opened the sealed writing. The contents read as follows, "Johann Heinen is to be shot by the order of the Reichsfuehrer SS. He must be informed of the order which is to be carried out an hour later."

The Kommandant communicated his order to the condemned prisoner who seemed completely calm. The prisoner was permitted to write a farewell letter to his family, and then he was given the cigarettes he requested. Hoess, as an adjutant, was the chief of the command and, according to the secret order of mobilization, had to carry out the execution. He found three other non-commissioned officers of the staff to whom he related what was about to take place and then taught them how to conduct the execution. A post was quickly dug into the courtyard, and the cars arrived immediately. The Kommandant directed the condemned prisoner to stand by the post to which Hoess led him. Then he moved back and gave the order to shoot. When the victim fell, Hoess walked up to him with a gun and shot him to death. The doctor then pronounced him dead—three bullets in his heart.

Besides Eicke, there were several other officers present at the execution. Immediately afterwards they all went to the officers' club. Somehow their conversation was disjointed, and each man quickly gulped down his drink in an oppressive silence. Each one of them had participated in World War I and proved his courage, yet, after the morning talk of Eicke and the execution just carried out, Hoess had misgivings about the war which was just beginning.

During the following days Hoess had to step out with his staff of executioners to deal with saboteurs and those individuals who shirked their army service. The reasons for the executions were known only to the police administration, who escorted the condemned prisoners to their doom.

One particular incident deeply touched Hoess, as well as all the other SS men. A certain officer of the SS, a police magistrate who frequently brought condemned prisoners to the concentration camp and sometimes very important papers to the Kommandant, was unexpectedly brought to the concentration camp one night to be immediately executed. It was only the previous day that he sat with Hoess in the officers' club discussing executions and their necessity during wartime. Now, it was Hoess' turn to carry out the order of execution. The officer who escorted the victim to the execution told Rudolph that the condemned officer of the SS was given an order to arrest a certain Communist and to escort him to the concentration camp. This SS officer knew that Communist for quite some time as a quiet and well-behaved prisoner. He therefore permitted him to go home, change his clothes, and bid farewell to his wife. While the officer and his friend were conversing with the wife of the arrested husband in an adjacent room, the prisoner fled through another room and disappeared. When the escape was confirmed, it was too late to do anything about it. The SS officer was immediately arrested in the Gestapo office when he reported the run-away prisoner. Himmler immediately ordered him court-martialed. An hour later he was sentenced to die, and his friend was sentenced to a long prison term. Himmler even rejected the mediation of Heydrich, the chief of the Gestapo, as well as that of Mueller. The first serious offense during war committed by an SS officer was definitely to be punished in a manner of utmost severity. The friend who was sentenced to a 30-year term in prison was a married man and a father of three children. Up to the time of his imprisonment he faithfully served Hitler's cause. Now, he was definitely convinced that Hitler's erroneous ideas led men to their doom—even those Germans who served him most faithfully, as he himself was about to experience.

Hoess, pointing his pistol to the head of the victim, shot him in cold blood. Eicke took advantage of this opportunity and gave the SS men new morale-building advice, saying, "One must get harder and harder. The SS man must know how to execute even his nearest relatives when they commit an offense against Germany or Hitler's ideas. There is only one thing that is very important: the order!"

In spite of everything several senior officers of the SS having high service ranks dared to comment in their club that the work of the executioners disgraces the SS black uniform. Before long this reached the ears of Eicke. He called these men together and demanded an explanation of their comment. Subsequently he assembled all the SS officers of the concentration camps under his supervision and addressed them thus:

"The remarks of the SS officers regarding the work of execution testify that although they have been SS men for quite some time, they still do not comprehend its demands and tasks. The most significant requirement is to protect Germany by all possible means. Every antagonist, depending on the degree of his danger to our country, must be properly isolated or destroyed. Both the first and the second must be performed only by SS men. Only in this manner can security be assured to Germany until new statutes are enacted, positively defending the nation. Destroying the foe of the state in the interior of the country is the same kind of duty as that of destroying him at the front, and therefore it cannot be outrageous. The declarations that have been made were laden with bourgeois sentiment, which as a result of the old Adolf Hitler's revolution is antiquated. Those declarations indicate a softness and sentimentality unworthy of an SS officer and which can become very dangerous to his office. For that reason I must report the guilty ones to Himmler for punishment. Once and for all, I absolutely will not allow such a bungling representation in my men. In my division I need people absolutely rigorous, who understand the meaning of the little skull they wear as a particular symbol of honor."

Himmler did not punish these officers directly. They were, however, warned and reprimanded, and as a result they were not promoted for the duration of the war.

In the Sachsenhausen camp Hoess met many conscientious objectors. They refused to serve in the army and therefore they were sentenced to be executed by Himmler. Two conscientious objectors greatly impressed Hoess. When they heard of their death sentence, they became overwhelmed with unrestrained joy and rapture. They longed for their execution. They folded their hands, raised them, and looked ecstatically upward as they called incessantly.

"Shortly, we shall be with Jehovah! How fortunate we are to be the chosen ones of this fate."

Several days earlier they witnessed the execution of their pacifist colleagues. It was difficult to restrain them for they too wanted to be executed with them, and only by force were they taken back to prison. For their own execution, they practically ran and refused to be tied. They raised their arms heavenward and in rapture they waited to be shot to death.

All the witnesses of this execution were deeply touched. Even the execution platoon could not refrain from being distressed. Only Hoess was unmoved, hard as stone. He became the most capable disciple of Himmler and Eicke. And those "teachers" on many occasions referred to the religious fanaticism of the conscientious objectors as an example to the SS men. Just as a conscientious objector believed in Jehovah, so were the SS men to believe in Adolf Hitler's ideas. Only when all the SS men became fanatics would the permanence of Adolf Hitler's Germany be assured. Only through fanatics who desired to renounce their "ego" completely for that idea would its goals be realized and held permanently.

Generally, the condemned who evaded army service from political motives of their own accepted their doom calmly and peacefully. However, professional criminals and the common

Individuals whom Himmler ordered to be shot defended themselves and pleaded for mercy.

Hoess gave the last blow to all with a stone heart and a calm countenance.

In the concentration camp of Sachsenhausen were many so-called "V.I.P.'s" that is, prisoners who played important roles in Germany before Hitler came to power. They were treated like political prisoners in this concentration camp, without any concessions. At the beginning of the war the number of these prisoners increased immeasurably as a result of the renewed imprisonment of all functionaries of the German Communist Party and the German Socialist Party.

At the outset of the war also there was an inflow of prisoners from countries occupied by the Germans. The concentration camps in Germany were becoming internationalized. In the beginning there was an inflow of professors and students from Czechoslovakia. In November, Hoess was an eyewitness to the arrival of 66 professors from the Jagiellonian University in Cracow, Poland.

"They taught others; now we shall be teaching them," said one of the functionaries of the camp with a sneer and a whip in his hand.

Among the so-called "special prisoners" was a Lutheran pastor, Martin Niemoller, who during World War I was the commander of a submarine. This greatly interested Hoess. Niemoller was arrested for his sermons in which he called upon the people to oppose Hitler and his totalitarian system. Hitler himself was interested in inducing this courageous pastor to renounce his opposition. With this in mind prominent personalities, such as Admiral Lans, visited Sachsenhausen, but all was in vain. Niemoller stood his ground in spite of everything and persisted in his principles declaring that no state had any right to interfere in the internal laws of the church and more so to issue such orders. The pastor's wife, in her letters to him, encouraged her husband to persevere in his convictions for the good of the church and Germany itself.

Hoess, not only from duty but from curiosity, read all the correspondence of the pastor and listened attentively to the conversations carried on during visiting hours. It was as early as 1938 that Niemoller wrote to the commander-in-chief of the navy, Admiral Raeder, that he was resigning from the right to wear a navy officer's uniform because it did not conform to the ideals with which the navy should serve.

Hoess frequently talked personally with the pastor. These talks greatly intrigued him. Niemoller declared openly that God must be obeyed first and then the people. The two agreed when it came to a discussion of many topics. When, however, their conversation came to religious and church matters, Niemoller became unyielding.

"Hopefully," said the pastor, "the present suffering of Catholic priests and Lutheran pastors will hasten the hour of uniting all Christians into one family of God."

Every escape of a prisoner was a great threat to the camp. As soon as the sirens began to blast, Eicke appeared personally from nearby Oranienburg.

He demanded information on all details of the escape and pertinaciously sought the guilty SS men who by their laxity made it possible for the prisoners to flee. Day and night the same area of the camp was searched, as well as the region around; all the SS men of the garrison were called to assist in the search. According to Eicke's judgment no escape was to be successful. If a prisoner succeeded in getting through the chain of security guards, then the gigantic police apparatus was mobilized to catch the fugitive. The whole police force was activated; vigilance was observed at all highways, byways, railroads, and bridges. People living in the surrounding areas were warned about the runaway.

When the escapee was caught, he was brought into the presence of Eicke and before rows of all the prisoners of the camp who were lined up to witness the punishment. The victim wore a large sign with the inscription "Again I am here," and he had to beat a large drum which was suspended from his neck. After this he was given 25 lashes.

Hoess distinguished himself in his pursuit of escapees with his deep-seated and implacable malice. Eicke radiated with pride at the sight of this ardent SS man.

"Herr Rudolph, you are my best disciple. Shortly, you will receive a high-ranking position, worthy of your zeal. Most certainly, you will discharge that duty to the perpetual glory of Hitler, the party, and Germany."

"Yes, sir, Herr Inspector!" answered Rudolph Hoess with assurance in his voice.

1940–1941
Love is Consummated in the Holocaust:
Kolbe

More and more often the friars heard Father Maximilian repeat:

"God is my Love. . .
Let us love him with our whole heart. . .
Let us love the Immaculata. . .
Let us love our enemies!"

One of the friars remarked to another:
"It just occurs to me that Father Maximilian will not live long."
"How do you know?"
"Reading the lives of saints I was impressed that each one of them shortly before death spoke only of love. And what does our Guardian speak of?"

In the morning hours of February 17, 1941, Father Maximilian dictated his last article on the Immaculata to Bro. Arnold Wedrowski. It contains the whole "Credo" of Father Kolbe:

Immaculate Conception
These words came forth from the lips of the Immaculata; therefore they must point out most accurately and realistically who she is.

If in general human words are not fit to express divine things, so here too, the meaning of those words must be much deeper, more beautiful and more sublime than things which they generally express, or the recognition of which, reason alone even though most penetrating, could carry into effect.

The passage, "Eye has not seen, ear has not heard, nor has it so much as dawned on man what God has prepared for those who love him," (1 Cor. 2, 9) can in this case be adapted in its entire fullness.

Nevertheless, one can and even must, at least as much as our intellect and words are able, to think and speak, write and read of the Immaculata.

Who are you, O Immaculate Conception?

Not God, of course, because he had no beginning; neither are you an angel created directly from nothing; nor Adam formed from clay or Eve taken from Adam, and not even the Incarnate Word who existed from the beginning of time and is "conceived" rather than a "conception." The children of Eve did not exist before their conceptions, therefore they can more properly be called "conceptions," but you differ from all of them because they were conceived in original sin, while you are the only Immaculate Conception.

Whatever is outside God comes forth from God and is wholly from God under every aspect. For this reason it bears on itself and within itself the likeness of the Creator, and there is nothing in creation that does not have that likeness, for everything is the result of that first cause.

The truth is that words denoting created things tell us of God's perfections in an imperfect, incomplete and analogous manner only. They are more or less a remote echo of the divine attributes as are the varied creatures which they designate.

Does conception constitute an exception? That is impossible because there are no exceptions here.

The Father begets the Son, and the Spirit proceeds from the Father and the Son. These few words encapsulate the mystery of the life of the Holy Trinity, and of all the perfections there are in creatures, which are nothing else than a varied echo, a hymn of praise in multicolored tones of that first most beautiful Mystery.

Let the words taken from the dictionary of creatures serve us because we have no others, although we must remember they are very imperfect words.

Who is the Father? What constitutes his being? .

Begetting: because he begets the Son, from eternity and for all eternity he always begets the Son.

Who is the Son? He is the one who is begotten, because always and from all eternity he is begotten by the Father.

Who is the Holy Spirit? He is the fruit of the love of the Father and the Son. The fruit of created love is a created conception. For this reason, the fruit of the love—of the prototype of this created love—is nothing else than a conception. The Spirit, therefore is an eternal, uncreated conception; he is the prototype of every conception of life in the universe.

The Father, therefore, begets; the Son is begotten; the Spirit proceeds, and that is their essence which differentiates them mutually from one another. Still, the same nature, the one divine existence essentially unites them.

Hence, the Spirit is a most blessed, infinitely holy and immaculate conception.

In all the world we meet action and the opposing but equal reaction, going out and returning, retreating and advancing, dividing and uniting. Separation always looks forward to union, which is creative. All this is nothing else but an image of the most Holy Trinity in the activity of creatures. Union means love, creative love. And in no other way does God's outward activity proceed: God creates the universe, which is like a separation. Creatures then by the natural law given them by God tend to perfection; they become like God and go back to him. Intelligent creatures experience conscious love and with that love they unite with him more and more, till finally they return to him. The creature filled completely with that love and divinity is the Immaculata, who is without any stain of sin and who never deviated from the will of God. In an effable manner she was united with the Holy Spirit and by the fact that is his spouse, but in an incomparably more perfect way than that word can be expressed in reference to creatures.

What is that union? First of all, it is interior; the union of her essence with the essence of the most Holy Spirit. The Holy Spirit dwells in her, lives in her from the first moment of her existence now and forever.
In what does his life in her consist? He himself is love in her. That is, the love of the Father and the Son; the love with which God loves himself, the love/of the most Holy Trinity—fruitful love, a conception. Among creatures made in God's image the union brought about by married love is the most intimate of all. Holy Scripture states:

"Thus they are no longer two but one flesh" (Mt. 19, 6). In a manner most intimate, most interior and most real, the Holy Spirit dwells in the soul of the Immaculata, in her being, and he makes her fruitful from the first moment of her existence for the whole of her life, that is, for eternity. This uncreated Immaculate Conception conceives the divine life in

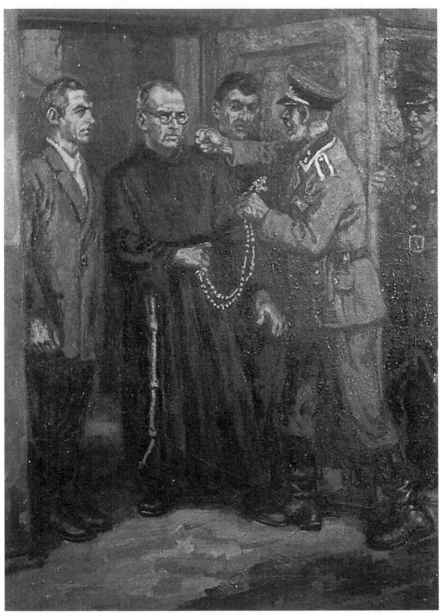

Infuriated at the sight of Father Maximilian's crucifix, a Gestapo officer in Warsaw's Pawiak prison tries to force him to renounce his faith by brutal blows to his face. (Painting by Polish artist Mieczyslaw Koscielniak, a fellow prisoner of Kolbe's at Auschwitz.)

the womb of her soul for she is his Immaculate Conception. The virginal womb of her body is also reserved for him so that in time he might conceive the divine life of the God-man. Just as everything material happens in time, this was necessary for the human life of the God-man. Thus the return to God, the equal but contrary reaction proceeds in a manner opposite to that of creation. In creation all comes from the Father through the Son and the Spirit, while here, by means of the Spirit, the Son takes on flesh in her womb, and through him love returns to the Father. . . .

The Immaculata at Lourdes is no longer merely given the title of the Immaculate Conception, but as Bernadette related:

"The Lady stood above a wild rose bush in the same pose as she appears on the Miraculous Medal. As I asked my question the third time, her countenance became serious and at the same time deeply humble... Folding her hands as in prayer, she raised them to the height of her breast... She looked up to heaven... later, slowly, unfolding her hands and leaning down toward me, she spoke in a voice which seemed slightly trembling: 'Queue soy era Immaculada Councepciou." (I am the Immaculate Conception)."

Entrance to the Auschwitz death camp through which Saint Maximilian passed the evening of May 28, 1941. The sardonic motto over the gate—"Arbeit Macht Frei" (Work Makes Free)—disguised the camp's real purpose.

Auschwitz capo "Bloody Krott" beats Father Maximilian during a work period in a field. "Capos" were criminal prisoners put in charge of the other prisoners because of their toughness and cruelty. (Painting by M. Koscielniak).

If in human society the bride receives the name of her spouse because she belongs to him, unites with him, and becomes the creator of life, then how much greater is this true of the most Holy Spirit? The Immaculate Conception is the name of the one in whom he lives in a fruitful love in the supernatural order.

About 11:00 am on February 17, 1941, the members of the death brigade with their little skulls on their cap bands appeared at Niepokalanow.

"Praised be Jesus Christ," Father Maximilian greeted them. The reply was an ominous silence. A question followed:

"Mister, is your name Maximilian Kolbe?" "Yes. Please come into my office."

The substance of their long conversation is unknown. After a time, the Nazi called four of the Fathers, namely, Father Justin Nazim, Father Urban Cieslak, Father Pius Bartosik, and Father Antonine Bajewski into the Guardian's office.

They were informed that they were all under arrest with Father Maximilian. Next, they were led into police cars and at 11:50 they were driven to the notorious Pawiak prison in Warsaw.

The remaining friars at Niepokalanow felt orphaned. They lacked the Guardian who was father and mother to them. They resolved to rescue Father Maximilian at all costs, even at the risk of their own lives. As a result, on February 26, one of the youngest friars from Niepokalanow came to the Provincial to present a written request from twenty friars, begging permission to apply to the prison and to assume all further consequences for this step in exchange for the release of Father Maximilian and the four other priests.

With deep emotion and admiration, the Provincial thought to himself, "These are worthy children of a great father." He accepted the sacrifice of the young friars. Then the friars showed the superior the written petition to the Germans in authority, asking for his approval.

"We want to explain," wrote the heroic friars to the authorities, "that no one has induced us or forced us; we have decided to take this momentous step ourselves. At the same time we are ready to willingly accept any charges and accusations as well as further consequences. . ."

The Hitlerites rejected this petition. They issued an edict affecting the whole Polish intelligentsia. This was in keeping with the attempt to exterminate all who had anything to tell their country and the world. At this time they needed only Father Maximilian, or rather, his death.

At the Pawiak prison, Father Kolbe was placed into cell No. 103, remaining fully recollected and self-possessed. He always had a smile and a friendly word for his fellow-prisoners. He uplifted them in spirit and aroused their faith in the freedom of Poland. More important, he led them to God and the Immaculata through his good word and example.

In the middle of March, a dramatic scene took place in Cell No. 103. The Scharfuehrer entered and saw Father Maximilian dressed in his habit with a cord about his waist from which was suspended a rosary with a crucifix. At the sight of the crucifix, the German became enraged.

"Do you believe in Christ?" he shouted furiously.

"Yes! I do believe!" replied Father Maximilian with dignity.

The Nazi struck the friar's face with all his might. Then with greater fury and hatred, he yelled out,

"Do you still believe?"

"Yes, I do believe," the victim affirmed a second time.

The officer struck Father Maximilian again in the face and roared, "And you still believe in that?"

"Yes, I do believe!"

For the third time the Nazi repeated his beastly act and then left abruptly, slamming the door. He could not endure the calm regard of his victim.

When one of the witnesses to this scene began to voice threats against the invaders, Father Kolbe turned to him saying, "Please do not get excited for you have plenty of troubles of your own. What happened is not important because it is all for the Immaculate Mother."

On March 13 he wrote a letter to the friars at Niepokalanow.

"Let all the Brothers pray hard and long, and work diligently. Do not worry needlessly because nothing can happen without the knowledge and will of the good God and the Immaculata."

On May 12, the Kommandant of the prison ordered Father Kolbe to take off his habit and put on civilian clothes. This was a sign that his transportation to the concentration camp would follow shortly. He took advantage of free moments and wrote his last letter from the prison to Niepokalanow,

"I cannot answer each one of you individually, because I cannot write often. . . Let us allow the Immaculata to lead us more perfectly as to how and where she wants us, so that through faithful performance of our duties souls may be saved."

On May 28, 1941, Father Maximilian Kolbe, together with other prisoners from Warsaw, crossed the gate of the concentration camp at Oswiecim. At the entrance, the newcomers had to run between rows of SS men who, with thongs, straps, or their hands, struck and tormented these prisoners. After this welcome, each prisoner received a belt and a number.

Father Kolbe's number was 16670. During the first three days, he carted stones and other building material for the fence which was to be built around the crematorium. On the last day of May, the Rapportfuehrer, Fritsch, came to block 17 where plank beds had been set up for the prisoners.

"Priests, step out," he ordered. "March after me."

He took the horror-stricken prisoners to the Babice command, which was designated for hardest labor and headed by a criminal known as "Krott, the bloody."

"Here, you may have these freeloaders and parasites of society," declared Fritsch. "Teach them to work properly!"

"I know how to take care of them quite well; I'll supervise them personally," the cruel supervisor laughed.

Saint Maximilian lifts up the spirits of his fellow prisoners with a spiritual conference on the relationship of Mary the Immaculata with the Blessed Trinity. (Painting by Polish artist and fellow prisoner M. Koscielniak).

The labor involved cutting down and carrying branches and posts needed to fence off the wet and soggy meadows. The work had to be carried out quickly.

Krott singled out one friar and ordered him to carry twice, and even three times, as many branches as the other prisoners. When other priests tried to help Father Maximilian in carrying that load, he generously declined and cautioned them not to expose themselves to beatings. "The Immaculata is helping me. I'll manage."

On a certain day, Krott decided to finish Father Maximilian. He himself began to load the heavy branches upon Father Maximilian's back, and then ordered him to run to the appointed place. During this ordeal, Father Maximilian fell under the weight. Krott found him, began kicking him in the abdomen and face, and pummelled him with heavy blows.

"You don't want to work, you blockhead! I'll show you what work means," he yelled furiously.

Father Maximilian lifted himself up with great difficulty and with serene eyes gazed at the face of the bestial criminal, whose guilt could not stand such fortitude. He told Father Maximilian to lie down upon a tree trunk and ordered one of the strongest prisoners to give him 50 lashes.

Father Kolbe fainted. The enraged Krott threw him into a mud-filled ditch, and covered him with branches.

"That is the end of this priest," thought Krott.

It was evident quite soon that this was not the end of Father Maximilian. His fellow prisoners carried him to the camp that evening and he was placed in the hospital. The prison doctor diagnosed his case as pneumonia and general exhaustion. The condition in the camp hospital was intolerable. It was not a place of cure, but agony. The three-tiered plank bunks were occupied by two or three patients apiece. Lice, flies, and nauseating stenches added to the misery of the suffering prisoner patients.

Father Maximilian then wrote his one and only letter from prison to his mother. In the most critical moments of his life, from the very depths of his suffering, he wrote these words,

"Everything is good and well with regard to me. Be peaceful and calm about me and my health, dear Mother, because the loving God is in all places, and most lovingly he thinks of all of us and of everything."

The dying and exceedingly ill people felt that this strange priest was their only life-saving consolation. They crept to his plank bed, begging for a word of comfort or priestly absolution. He consoled them most compassionately.

"Everything comes to an end; this suffering, too, will end. The road to glory is the road of the cross, the royal road. The Holy Mother of God is with us; she always helps us. . ."

However, at times one could hear a complaint from a grief-stricken heart, "Father, I can't endure this concentration camp life any longer!"

"Place yourself under the protection of Mary," counseled Father Kolbe. Just as a child trustingly holds his mother's hand, so you, too, must be calm and peaceful, for the Virgin Mary has you under her protection."

He also had to surmount the deadly hatred in human hearts, evident at the camp, saying, "Hatred is not a creative force. Love alone creates. Suffering will not prevail over us; it will only melt us down and strengthen us. Great sacrifices on our part are required in order to earn a happy and peaceful life for those who will come after us. . ."

Father Maximilian occupied the lowest bed, which was very close to the door. When someone proposed to give him a better plank bed, he replied, "Here on this low level I can more readily absolve my companions and bless the deceased who are being taken out to the crematorium."

At one time, when a very congenial attending nurse brought Father Maximilian a cup of real tea, an unusual delicacy in the concentration camp, he said, "That one needs it more than I do." He handed the tea to his sick neighbor prisoner.

"How can you do that, Father? You will become completely weakened."

"I am strong and can do everything in him who strengthens me," replied Father Kolbe, using the words of St. Paul.

When Father Kolbe was released from the hospital, he was sent to the Block for the convalescing, and finally to Block 14, and was then assigned to the command responsible for peeling potatoes. His last x-ray was taken on July 28, as the records show.

One Sunday afternoon all the Polish priests assembled secretly for communal prayer and a spiritual conference. During the second half of July, Father Maximilian delivered a never forgotten sermon on his favorite theme: the relation of the Immaculata to the most Holy Trinity.

He spoke calmly,

"The Immaculata, through the conception and birth of the Incarnate Word, became spiritually close to the Divine Persons of the Blessed Trin-

ity. In relation to the Father, she is his child, the primordial and special daughter of God. All the just are, children of God through grace, but the Immaculata is a child of God through another means and to a higher degree. So she would hold that dignity even if Christ had not extended his grace to all peoples.

"In relation to the Son of God, she is his true Mother. The dogma of the Hypostatic Union states that the human nature of Jesus Christ, from the first moment of his conception, was united with the Divine Person; without this union it could not exist. Mary, therefore, bore God and man. That infinite dignity places her above all creatures in heaven and on earth. Because of her maternity, Mary, full of grace, is favored with all privileges, takes an active part in the Redemption, and distributes an graces, thereby becoming a mediatrix to all mankind. She who gave birth to the only begotten Son of God, is full of grace and truth, and receives, as St. Thomas states, greater privileges than others.

Francis Gajowniczek, the Polish sergeant whose life Saint Maximilian saved by offering to die in his place, with his family, l. to r.: Juliusz, the youngest boy; Helena, his wife; and Bogdan, the eldest son. Both boys were killed Jan. 16, 1945, during a Russian bombardment of Rawa Mazowiecka, the small town in central Poland where they were living, before they could be reunited with their father. Helena and Francis lived together after the war until her death in his arms in November, 1982. The boys were 15 and 18 respectively when they died.

St. Maximilian Maria offers to take the place of Francis Gajowniczek, one of ten men condemned to die by hunger and dehydration in reprisal for the escape of a prisoner who had not been recaptured. (Painting by Polish artist and eye witness, M. Koscielniak).

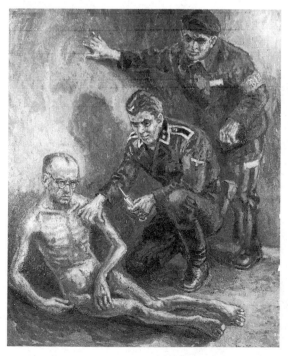

Saint Maximilian Maria receives the fatal injection of phenol in a basement cell of the "Death Block" on Aug. 14, 1941. Of the four men still alive after two weeks without food or water, Saint Maximilian was the only one still conscious. He lifted his arm to receive the shot. The orderly who came in shortly afterward to take away his body testified that it was strangely clean and radiant, not grimy and contorted as the others were.

"In relation to the Holy Spirit, she is his Spouse because she conceived through him. (She was called this by the theologians of the Middle Ages.) "Mary, likewise, gave her Son his Mystical Body with its members. There-fore, she is our true Mother and we are her children (scene at the foot of the cross—Jn. 19, 27). Is it really possible that a mother abandon her children in suffering and misfortune?

Is it possible that a mother not surround priests with her special pro-tection? After all, the union between her and the priests is so close-knit and the resemblance so great, that St. Antoninus did not hesitate to call her Virgo-Sacerdos. In a radiant vision she often appears among us, giv-ing us solace sweet as honey: 'Persevere to the end, because the Lord's day of commiseration is near.'"

Several days after that conference, the concentration camp was shaken with the news that a prisoner from block 14A had escaped. It was well known that an occurrence of this type would not pass without punish-ment, particularly for the other prisoners of that same block. The Kom-mandant of Auschwitz, Rudolph Hoess, at the very outset had announced that for every escapee, ten co-prisoners of that particular block would be doomed to die in reprisal.

Father Maximilian belonged to the unfortunate block 14A. That night no one slept. The prisoners trembled with fear and' even despair. There were some courageous ones. One, more peaceful and composed than the others, was Father Maximilian Kolbe. He accidentally overheard the whis-per of a young prisoner.

'There will be a decimation and I am frightened." Father Kolbe clasped him to his heart and said, "Do not be afraid, child. Death is not so dreadful, and in heaven the Immaculata awaits us."

The following day when all others in the command departed for work, the prisoners of block 14A remained at attention at the place for roll call while the scorching July sun unmercifully beat down upon them. They stood like condemned men, without a drop of water. . .

They stood. . .

And they stood. . .

When anyone fainted, he was not revived with water but with a taste of the lash. If this did not help, he was thrown like a log on a single pile with others like him.

Sunset stared at frightfully swollen faces and red eyes in which nothing except a monstrous fear could be perceived.

Father Maximilian, who had been doomed to die from tuberculosis twenty-five years before did not fall; he even stood erect. He stood as the Immaculate Mother at the foot of the Cross on which God, her Son, was suspended.

The prisoners of the command returned from their work. Now, they all stood at the place for roll call in order to witness the sentence of ten unfortunate victims. As Rapportfuehrer Fritsch approached the prisoners of block 14A he began to announce loudly.

"The escapee has not been found. As punishment, ten of you will perish in the starvation bunker."

Then, with a deliberately slow pace, he began to walk lengthwise along the rows of terrified prisoners, and from time to time, he pointed out a particular prisoner and uttered the horrible words, "This one!" Ten times these words were uttered. The sobbing of one Gajowniczek was heard from the group of condemned victims, "My poor wife! My poor children! I shall never see you again!"

Suddenly, someone unexpectedly stepped out of the ranks of the prisoners and walked toward Fritsch.

"Halt!" yelled the furious German. "What does this mean? What do you want?"

Before him stood Father Maximilian Kolbe, straight as the taut string of an instrument. He stated his request calmly with a controlled voice, "I want to take the place of one of the condemned prisoners."

At first Fritsch could not understand what it was all about. Could this man who now stood before him know how to overcome in himself the fear and dread of death by hunger?

"Why?" questioned Fritsch and the thousands of witnesses of this unusual event.

"Because one of these men has a wife and children. I do not."

"For whom do you want to die?"

"For this one." Father Kolbe pointed to Gajowniczek, a sergeant of the 36th regiment of the Infantry.

"Who are you?" the still astonished Fritsch asked.

"A Catholic priest."

A monstrous silence followed. Through it the consciences of the torturers and the victims might be heard screaming.

"Very well. Go!" Fritsch finally decided.

The condemned victims took off the belts they no longer needed. They went to block 11, the starvation bunker. The last one who walked in was Father Maximilian, supporting one of the victims who was about to collapse. Just before they entered the cell, even their clothing was removed. Entire deprivation prevailed. Was it complete?

Does a man know how to deprive another of everything? Yes, everything, except love! You cannot take love away from another. One's love is either preserved or lost.

Father Maximilian became great because he did not lose his love even in the starvation bunker, and he prevented others from losing it.

For two weeks no cursing was heard from the starvation bunker, but only prayer and hymns. Words became softer, weaker. . .until finally great silence prevailed. One by one the men died until four were left.

On August 14, three prisoners were dying in block 11. Father Maximilian sat on the concrete floor with eyes open, fully conscious. The concentration camp executioner came into the bunker to finish off the victims. When he came to Father Maximilian, he administered a fatal phenol injection into his left arm. After a brief moment, Father Maximilian expired. His remains were burned in the crematorium and the ashes strewn to the four winds.

At one time, Father Maximilian wrote, "I dreamed that my remains be placed as a foundation under the Japanese Niepokalanow. The Immaculata decided otherwise, but who knows where she will want my remains to be laid."

We already know that the Immaculata desired that his remains be laid in the place of utmost human bestiality, and also in the place of the greatest human heroism. We also know that the Immaculata wanted his remains laid as a foundation under the Niepokalanow which would embrace all people of good will over the entire world.

1940–1941
The Death Factory and its Architect:
Hoess

On August 22, 1939, before dismissing the higher officers of the Wer-macht from his quarters at Obersalzberg, Hitler declared:

"Our power lies in our speed and brutality. Genghis-Khan caused the deaths of millions of women and children, with total awareness and no guilt. But history sees in him only the great creator of an empire. It is no concern of mine what West European civilization thinks of me. I have issued a command and I shall sentence anyone to be shot who dares to utter one word of criticism against the principle that war has the task to destroy the adversary physically.

Therefore, I have prepared my Eastern Divisions of Elite Troops with the order to mercilessly execute all men, women, and children of Polish origin and language. Only in this way can we secure the vital space we need."

Notwithstanding the bombing of cities and towns, shooting the civilian population with automatic machine guns, causing numerous fires, and executing military and civil servants, it was impossible to destroy the 35 million people of Poland during the September, 1939 attack.

Obviously though, from the beginning of the German occupation, Hitlerism began a systematic campaign to exterminate the Polish people. The effective means were the concentration camps established on Polish soil where the Elite Troops, i.e., the SS men, were to carry out the task assigned them by Hitler: the destruction of the whole Polish nation.

The SS men trained by Himmler and Eicke, began their function. Rudolph Hoess, the most competent of the SS men, undertook the establishment of the concentration camp in Auschwitz (Oswiecim).

Toward the end of 1939, the inspector of the police and security service in Wroclaw, Arpad Wigand, initiated the creation of a concentration camp in the old army barracks in Oswiecim. In accordance with his proposal and in compliance with Himmler's order of February 1, 1940, the usefulness of this construction was investigated by a commission, under the leadership of Walter Eisfeld, which made known the results of its works in a report on February 21, 1940. During April 18 and 19, 1940, the commission, at the head of which was Rudolph Hoess, examined the location of the future concentration camp. Hoess personally gave a report of the site to Himmler:

"Oswiecim, a town of 12,000 inhabitants, lies at 50 degrees 3'3" north latitude and 19 degrees 13'30" east longitude from Greenwich. It is 50 kilometers in a straight line from Cracow, 300 km. from Warsaw, 300 km. from Wroclaw, 330 km. from Prague, 300 km. from Vienna, and 500 km. from Berlin. Oswiecim is located on the eastern border of the great communication gateway known as the Moravian Arch, and on a group of crossroads

These cell blocks and electrified fences at Auschwitz have been preserved as a museum and memorial. They were part of the original mother camp which was later expanded and divided into three camps: Auschwitz I (the mother camp), Auschwitz II (the Burkina camp), and Auschwitz III (the Monoxide camp). In addition, a network of sub-camps was created mainly at various industrial establishments in Silesia, where prisoners used as slave labor produced war materials to feed the Nazi war effort. Except for the museums and monuments, most of the once huge complex has been razed.

leading from west to east. Although it lies close to the mountains, it occupies the flat sunken places free of any slope. Therefore, the regions are swampy and humid. Already in Oswiecim are barracks into which prisoners could be confined at once. These barracks are located beyond the area of the compact city buildings, in the fork of the Vistula and Sol Rivers. It is capable of expansion in the future and it is cut off from the outer world. In locating the camp in this place, there is every indication that it will afford a convenient railroad connection with Silesia, the General Government, Czechoslovakia, and Austria."

"The area of the new camp," Himmler said with reflection, "should contain approximately 40 km. of surface. Therefore, we shall have to oust the inhabitants of the neighboring villages." Bending over the map, he continued, "Babice, Budy, Rajsko, Brzezinka, Broszkowice, Plawy, and Harmeze. This will be the extent of the camp's operation. What purpose will this camp have? Above all, it will be a place of execution for all enemies of the

1942. Here in this rare photo he is leading Reichsfuehrer SS Heinrich Himmler (first row, left) and an engineer named Faust (first row, center) on an inspection tour of a slave labor factory being erected at Auschwitz III (Monowice). Himmler, as chief of the SS and chief of all the German police, had appointed Hoess kommandant of Auschwitz, and given him the order to develop it as a death camp.

German Government. Those enemies are the Poles and the Jews. Before they are destroyed, we shall take advantage of their labor power. Oswiecim will be an experimental agriculture station."

Hoess' eyes brightened and Himmler noticed that.

"I am familiar with your interests in agriculture, and I know you hesitated about whether you should become a farmer or join the SS. Well, now you may join one with the other. I am appointing you, Herr Rudolph Hoess, the Kommandant and the originator of the new concentration camp, which will be one magnificent farmstead. Let me inform you that you may count on 10,000 free laborers, because that is the number I calculated Oswiecim will accommodate."

"Thank you very much for your trust in me," Hoess gushed.

Himmler, as though he did not hear the words of thanks, continued his reverie: "There are potentials in Germany which up to this time we did not have. Free labor will be plentiful. My subjects will not disappoint me in supplying new prisoners. We shall also have sufficient soil. Every necessary farming experiment will be carried out. Large laboratories must be established and a section for growing plants. Also, the raising of cattle of all necessary breeds and genders must be started. Milk-maids will not be lacking either," he laughed ironically. "We shall erect ponds with beautiful fish, drain lands, and build embankments for the Vistula. It will be the most beautiful European strip—one magnificent garden, and one of the best farmsteads in the world. Who will be the administrator of these miracles? I am sorry that I, myself, personally could not take charge of it, but I depend upon you and your ability to transform Oswiecim into an earthly paradise. At the earliest convenience, I shall visit you at your work."

On May 4, 1940, Hoess received the official nomination as Kommandant of the concentration camp at Oswiecim, signed by Inspector Gluck.

Hoess immediately departed for Oswiecim with several SS men. The Local occupation mayor provided him with 200 Jews for work, to arrange the camp in the suburb of Oswiecim, known as Zasole. Then Hoess demanded 30 prisoners from the Kommandant of the Sachsenhausen camp from among the professional criminals to "teach" the new prisoners camp discipline. At this time, 15 SS men from the cavalry division of the SS in Cracow came to Oswiecim.

On June 14, 1940, the first transport of prisoners arrived at the camp. It was comprised of 700 Poles.

Simultaneously, the concentration camp staff was increased by 100 SS

men, officers and noncommissioned officers, who were appointed to administer the camp. In spite of such numerous personnel, Thaddeus Wiejowski escaped as early as July 6 of that year. The irritated Hoess demanded
from one Von dem Bach who visited the camp at the beginning, in the
name of the Gestapo, an agreement to inform the Polish population who
lived in the surrounding area what the concentration camp was.

"The local people," the rabid Hoess said, "are fanatically Polish, and, as
it was ascertained during an investigation, ready to rise against the detest-
able SS garrison of the camp. Every prisoner successful in his escape can
count on all the help possible as soon as he gets to the first Polish farmhouse."

"I demand the execution of every prisoner connected with the escape
of Wiejowski," roared Von dem Bach. Shoot every strange man you meet
in the expanded area of the camp, and also clear out all suspicious persons
within 5 km. around the camp without delay."

In the meantime there was an influx of railroad transports of 1,000
new prisoners. Hoess started to lose his grip on the situation. The camp
accommodations in reality were slowly expanding, but not at the tempo required by the increase of prisoners. Scarcity of food added more difficulty.
The most unmanageable situation was with the functionaries of the camp.
They were trained in the brutal and criminal school of Eicke, and now they
had free reign to display their brutality. Their symphony of sadism had
already begun on the railroad ramp. As soon as a new transport of prisoners arrived, the SS men unbolted the cars and, with inhuman bluster and
the worst curses imaginable, ordered the newcomers to come out of the
trains. The prisoners, deathly fatigued from the journey, and stupefied by
the roar of the SS men, grabbed whatever lay nearest them, leaving the rest
of their belongings behind them, and jumped out on the platform. Before
they touched the ground, while yet in the air, everyone of them received a
blow from a fist, a stick, a gun, or a boot. Many of them immediately fell to
the ground, blocking the way for the next ones.

Now, on the double the newcomers jogged in lines, formed on a nearby path. The columns were decimated. The train ramp and the entire road
leading to the concentration camp were lined with SS men with their machine guns ready to shoot. There were also many police dogs. At the gate,
the prisoners were greeted with Hoess' favorite slogan, "Arbeit macht Frei"
(Work Makes Free). At the place of roll call, the foremen, i.e., prisoners
performing functions as overseers, took away all valuables, such as brace-

lets, wristwatches, rings and watches, pulling off chains with medals. At the same time they beat prisoners to unconsciousness.

Outside, between blocks 15 and 16, the prisoners had to strip naked, after which their hair was clipped and each received a number. From then on, they were no longer persons with a name, but only numbers. Next, they were driven into the so-called bathhouse, but there was no mention that they take a bath. They scarcely had time to splash themselves with cold water. In the next courtyard lay two piles of camp clothes with stripes for the prisoners. The prisoners had to dress quickly in these ill-fitting uniforms and get into lines. Clad in these unsized uniforms and sandals, the prisoners were caricatures. They were given neither food nor drink. Next, they were housed in barracks, theoretically accommodating only 300, but in reality jammed with 1,000 prisoners, who had to be crammed into high plank-bunks without mattresses and blankets.

During the day they were ordered to work digging ditches and draining the swamps. As a result of hunger, beatings, and other torture, the death rate rose from day to day.

Hoess felt he had no control over the situation resulting from the ever-increasing number of new prisoners. Consequently it was with great relief that he welcomed the visiting Himmler on March 1, 1941, expecting to familiarize him with the current situation and to find some help and understanding of the whole affair. Basing his explanation on his plans and maps, he showed the facts of the camp's current situation to Himmler, as well as the proposed expansion of the buildings. As they were walking through the camp, he called Himmler's attention to the overcrowding of the camp, the lack of water, personnel, and food.

But Himmler was silent. After dinner in the SS Officers' Club, he spoke suddenly,

"I promised the Fuehrer that my SS men would take over the munitions factories, which will eventually decide our victory. The production will be carried on with the labor of the prisoners. From this moment we approve only one slogan: We shall use all available prisoners in the armament industry. Armaments! Prisoners! Armaments! The Gestapo will carry into effect more and more new actions in the occupied countries in order to obtain more and more prisoners. New tasks stand before the concentration camp at Oswiecim. I intend to transfer here an important department of the munitions factories. The territory must be reserved for this purpose. As a beginning, the I.G. Farben Industry will open a branch here. Herr Hoess will prepare 10,000 prisoners for this firm's opening. Besides that, he must ready the camp for 100,000 prisoners-of-war."

When Hoess and his closest co-workers began to present the difficulties connected with these plans, Himmler dismissed them with a smile, saying,

"Gentlemen, it must be done! The reasons that bring me to this action are far more important than your objections!"

"We have no building material, there is a lack of water, the epidemic in the camp. . ." All these objections to the plan seemed useless.

"Why then," angrily replied Himmler, "was the brick industry requisitioned by the SS, and why was the cement factory? In view of this, let the camp accept these objectives under its care. Supplying water and draining the area are only technical problems which should be examined by experts and which, nevertheless, are not sufficient to cause the rejection of the project. The extension of the buildings must be rushed by all means. You must exert all your available resources. Any breakout of

The original crematory at Auschwitz in which Saint Maximilian's body was burned to ashes Aug. 15, 1941. Four huge crematoria were later built at the Birkenau camp capable of burning 7,000 to 8,000 bodies every 24 hours. These were destroyed by the SS themselves who were trying to evacuate the camp before the arrival of the allied liberation forces.

an epidemic must be controlled and positively combated. But, the transportation of prisoners to Oswiecim cannot, under any circumstances, be curtailed. Police actions directed by me must be continued. I recognize no difficulties in Oswiecim."

He turned to Hoess as Kommandant of the camp.

"Do the best you can," he directed.

Before departing, Himmler visited Mrs. Hoess and their four children. He was very pleasant and friendly.

"Rudolph," Himmler spoke in a familiar way, "expand your living quarters and furnish them adequately. The Party does not begrudge money for its faithful members. Then too, as the Kommandant, you must have a home representing your dignity. You certainly will not fall short of guests."

Hoess now began to work with renewed fervor. He spared no SS men, nor any prisoners. He rode around the whole territory looking for land on which to extend the camp, through purchase, theft or confiscation. Who would dare oppose the Kommandant of such a notorious camp?

Meanwhile, Hoess was isolating himself more and more; he was becoming unapproachable to his subject officers. With each day, he grew harder. He saw nothing beyond his work in extending the camp, the task assigned him by the Party through the lips of Himmler. His wife endeavored to pull him out of his self-confinement by inviting over his good friends. It did not help for long, however. Everywhere he suspected guile and treachery. For a time he tried to break away from his depressed feeling and disappointment by indulging in drinking. But, that too, did not help. He was cheerful for a while, and then again his state of depression overwhelmed him. His subordinate officers, Fritsch, Palitzsch, and Meier, the disciples of Eicke to whom Hoess gave much leeway in their actions, tried to surpass one another in adapting newer and better methods of discipline among the prisoners. Besides impromptu blows, full beatings were inflicted upon the prisoners by the SS men and the overseers; this was commonplace in the daily routine in Oswiecim.

Other punishments applied to the victims were flogging, penal gymnastics, labor under an overseer on Sundays and holidays, placement in penal company, standing, kneeling with arms uplifted holding stones, and finally the penalty of being confined to the hunger bunker. With particular sadism, a starvation bunker was arranged for the prisoners apprehended during their escape. On specially constructed horses or tables, a whipping was meted out publicly to them during the evening roll call. The beatings were applied with thick sticks upon the stripped body of the prisoner until he bled. If the prisoner fainted, he was quickly revived, and the beatings were continued. Hoess observed these bestial methods impassively. He livened up only when a prisoner tried to flee. Then he fell into a rage, and personally issued an order to shoot the prisoner. To him, this still was not enough. If the prisoner escaped, he had the parents of the escapee brought to the camp and had them stand in a very conspicuous place with large signs suspended from their necks, stating that they would remain in the camp until the runaway prisoner was caught. In case a prisoner was not returned, Hoess, with the co-operation of other SS men, selected hostages from among the prisoners and confined them to a bunker in block 11, where no food or drink was given them. No one came out alive from that bunker.

During the second half of August, 1941, Hoess became quite perturbed with the news, which had spread throughout the camp like lightning, that a saint had been killed.

"Herr Fritsch," he turned to the adjutant of the camp, "Whom did we make a martyr here at Auschwitz?"

'The matter concerns a priest, Maximilian Kolbe, Herr Kommandant."

"You mean the founder of that Polish Niepokalanow?"

"Yes, sir. The one who intended to 'conquer' the world for Jesus Christ."

"A competitor of our Fuehrer," Hoess declared wryly. "I recall him. Well, what happened to him?"

"He asked permission to take the place of one of the prisoners selected for the starvation bunker after the prisoner escaped at the end of July."

"Why did you let him do that?"

"Because he said he was a Catholic priest."

"You fool! You should have taken both the priest other man too. You let him put one over on you." Hoess became lost in thought. "When did he die?"

"We opened our starvation bunker on August 14, and after serving two weeks of the sentence with the group, ten in all, he was given a shot of phenol in his arm. After that he died almost immediately."

"What happened to his body?"

"It was cremated at once, and the ashes were strewn around."

"A saint without relics," answered Hoess. "How old was that man?"

"Forty-seven."

"Forty-seven," repeated Hoess, and again he fell into deep thought:

"And how many years will I live? Perhaps, I too, will live for forty-seven years. How many years am I short of forty-seven? Six. That would not be so many, in fact, it would be quite short. What could I still do during that period of time? What else?"

There was no time for further reflection. Hoess was suddenly called to Reichsfuehrer SS Himmler in Berlin. Contrary to custom, the SS chief received him without the assistance of the adjutant. He told him point-blank:

"The Fuehrer has ordered the final solution of the Jewish problem. We, the SS men, must carry out this order. The existing places of execution in the East will not be able to handle the intended action on a large scale. On account of this I have designated Oswiecim for that purpose, both for its advantageous location with regard to railroad communication and also because that large area can be easily isolated and camouflaged. Originally, I intended to assign this task to one of the higher SS officers, but I desisted, desiring at the very outset to avoid difficulty in marking boundaries of competency. Now I am entrusting this task to you, Herr Hoess. It is a heavy responsibility and difficult work, demanding absolute dedication without regard to the difficulties which may emerge from it. Further details will be given you by Sturmbannfuehrer Eichmann from RSHA, who will call upon you at his earliest convenience. The officers concerned will be notified by me in due time. You must keep this in deepest secrecy, even in regard to your superiors. After talking with Eichmann, you will immediately send me the plans for the arranged project. The Jews are everlasting enemies of the German nation, and they must be exterminated. All the Jews who fall into our hands during this war will be executed without exception. If we are not successful in destroying the strength of the Jews, then some day, the Jews will destroy the German nation."

Shortly after this, Eichmann visited Hoess and secretly confided to him the details of the planned actions. The first to be executed were the Jews from the eastern part of Upper Silesia, from the Governor General's House, from Germany, Czechoslovakia, France, Belgium, and Holland.

Then, like two experts in liquidating people and exterminating whole nations quietly, they were factually discussing the method to be carried out for the extermination. According to their reasoning, they could only consider gas as a means of liquidating such large masses of people as they expected. Shooting them seemed impossible and, in consideration of the presence of women and children, it would be too cumbersome for the SS men who would have to carry out that order.

Eichmann acquainted Hoess with the killing by means of combustion gases in trucks as had been done up to that time in the so-called "purgation" of the occupied territories of Zwiazek Radziecki (Soviet Council). Large heavy trucks were adapted for this purpose by adding a cabin provided with tightly closed doors. The outlet of the exhaust pipe of the motor led into the cabin. After starting the motor, the cabin filled with combustible gases which suffocated the people inside. The drivers of these trucks received special training. This procedure, however, could not be applied to these massive transports which were awaited at Auschwitz. Killing by spraying carbon dioxide in the baths, similar to the methods used with the mentally ill in certain places of the German Reich, would require the erection of many buildings. In this discussion they came to no decision.

"I shall be inquiring of the specialists if there is some gas which could be easily accessible and the use of which would not require special installations." Thus Eichmann concluded his talk on this theme.

Then they rode around the whole territory to select the most suitable place for the greatest crime of all times. They agreed that the ideal place for that purpose was the peasant farm located at the Northwest corner of construction section III in Brzezinka. It layout of the way, concealed by woods and brushwood, and was not too far from the railroad. The remains would be buried in the adjacent fields in deep, long pits. They calculated that they could pack 800 bodies at one time into those pits by using a suitable gas to exterminate them.

During this visit Eichmann was still unable to give the exact date on which to begin action because everything was only in a state of preparation, and Himmler had not, as yet, issued the order to start. After a few days Hoess sent Himmler a detailed plan of the situation and a particular description of the death chambers. Himmler could certainly be a proud SS chief since his subject could so speedily and efficiently arrange for the genocide.

At this time Hoess was also interested in the affairs of the Soviet Council. On the basis of Hitler's delimitations of March 30, 1941, the chief RSHA, Reinhard Heydrich, issued a command on July 1, 1941, ordering all prisoners to be murdered who were or could be perilous to National Socialism.

The order primarily was concerned with all the distinguished functionaries of the government and the party, all the people's commissaries of the Soviet Army, the Soviet intelligentsia, all Jews and all those persons labeled as agitators or "fanatic Communists."

On August 8, 1941, General Herman Reinecke, chief of the Division of the Soviet Council, issued an order comprising the following regulations: "Bolshevik soldiers lost all rights to be treated as honorable soldiers according to the Geneva Convention. Insubordination as well as active or passive resistance should be broken immediately by using a weapon. Whoever does not use a weapon in performing an order or uses it with a lack of vigor will be punished. Fugitives must be shot immediately without warning. Warning shots meant to frighten are forbidden. Using a weapon against the Soviet prisoners is, in principle, agreeable with the law."

The chief of the General Staff of the German Army, Wilhelm Keitel, confirmed these orders. "In the case of Soviet prisoners, their world outlook must be destroyed, and therefore I, Keitel, approve and ratify the orders issued and support them personally."

Hoess obtained 10,000 Soviet prisoners in 1941 who were to build a camp in Brzezinka. They were brought from the prisoner-of-war camp at Lamsdorf, which contained 200,000 prisoners in a state of complete exhaustion.

At the sight of them, Hoess fell into a rage and shouted to the officers of the convoy,

"These people are certainly fit for the hospital, but not for the camp, much less for hard labor. They can hardly stand on their feet! Himmler promised that only Russian prisoners-of-war who were especially strong would be brought to Oswiecim."

"But, Herr Kommandant," the officers trying to justify themselves said, "please believe that we selected the best human material from among the mass of prisoners-of-war at our disposal!"

"Well then in comparison to these, how do the rest of them look?"

"Like these prisoners," replied one of the officers with a certain satisfaction.

The prisoners-of-war showed willingness to work, but on account of their weakened condition they could not accomplish anything. Their wasted bodies could not accept food, and their stomachs were incapable of further functioning. They were dying en masse from general exhaustion and hunger. The one thought of these people was to eat anything to get their fill before death.

One day as Hoess was riding through the area of the camp on his beautiful horse he witnessed a whole company of prisoners numbering several hundred people suddenly, as if given an order, pounce on the nearest field of potatoes, dig them up in a flash and begin voraciously devouring them. The guards, taken by surprise, could not manage them.

"Shoot!" shouted the enraged Hoess.

The prisoners, pierced by bullets, fell, holding potatoes in their cramped hands.

The SS men reported cases of cannibalism to the camp Kommanders. Hoess himself came across a certain Russian lying between a heap of bricks. His belly had been ripped open by some dull instrument and his liver was missing.

In a short time, from the 10,000 Russian prisoners-of-war, hardly a few hundred remained.

Besides these POW'S sent there to work, the Gestapo sent Russian commissaries and the more important functionaries of the government and the party to Auschwitz for the purpose of liquidation. They were shot in gravel pits or on the outside of block 11.

During the absence of Hoess, his substitute, Fritsch, on his own, used gas to execute the Russian POW'S. He filled all the cells in the cellars with the Russians, and after putting on a gas mask, he discharged a gas, Zyklon-B, into the cells, which caused immediate death for all.

After Hoess' return, Fritsch reported to him what he did. The Kommandant of Oswiecim was radiant with joy,

"I congratulate you! Congratulations! That's just what we need. We must save the bullets for the front, and here we must use another way to kill our enemies. A gigantic task awaits us. There are so many people yet that we must kill. We shall certainly be fatigued after that task, Herr Fritsch. And now as to the thing—what gas is it?"

"Zyklon-B," calmly and expertly replied Fritsch. "In Oswiecim that gas is used by the firm Tesch and Stabenow to exterminate bugs, and for that reason the camp administration always has on hand a certain number of cans with that gas. It is a preparation of prussic acid."

During the next sojourn of Eichmann in Auschwitz, Hoess consulted him about applying Zyklon-B. They agreed that the gas would be used during the mass extermination of the Jews. Meanwhile, they continued to execute the POW's now with Zyklon-B, but not in block 11 because after each gassing it was necessary to ventilate the whole building for at least two days. The charnel house of the crematory was now used as a gas chamber. Its door was made airtight, and in the ceiling openings were made for discharging the gas into the death chamber.

This instrument of murder under the watchful eye of Hoess was becoming more and more "productive."

1942-1945
Years of Horror and Genocide; the Collapse:
Hoess

January 1942, brought the first transports of Jews from Upper Silesia. The unloading took place on the railway siding of Oswiecim-Dziedzice. Every transport numbered about 1,000 men, women and children. At the railway ramp, the camp alert received the Jews from Stapo, after which they were led to the place of extermination. Their baggage remained at the ramp, and from there it was taken to a sorting room called "Canada." Jews with children in their arms passed through the gate into the courtyard. What was to happen next, no prisoner knew. The SS escorts remained behind the gate. The sign at the gate cautioned that no strangers, even SS men from outside the camp, could trespass in that isolated place. On the outside, the Jews saw large water faucets to which they rushed and drank most greedily. Since their arrest five days prior, they had hardly anything to eat or drink. The SS men did not counteract the confusion. "Let them drink in these last moments of their lives and then go to their deaths with their thirst satisfied." They then walked about 100 meters through an alley covered with gravel, then down a few stairs underground to a concrete accommodation. Before walking down, they saw a gigantic sign with inscriptions in German, French, Greek, and Hungarian which read: "Here are bathrooms and disinfectants." This inscription calmed all, even those with the worst misgivings. Finally, they would be able to take baths and freshen up after their long, fatiguing journey.

At this point the prisoners walked into a spacious, brightly illuminated white-washed room, about 50 meters long. There were benches above which were long rows of clothes hangers with numbers.

"Please tie your clothes and your shoes together," said the SS man courteously and with a smile," and hang them on the clothes hanger. Remember your number accurately, so that after your bath there will be no confusion."

"A true German sense of order," someone remarked.

"Everybody undress!" came a sudden command.

"How, in the presence of men?" fearfully asked the women and girls.

"Just strip, without any fuss," the tone of voice did not leave any doubt about the futility of objection.

People began to be troubled. In ten minutes everybody had stripped.

Here the SS men opened a heavy double oak door. The prisoners walked into this hall where no benches nor clothes hangers were seen, but only large square tin pipes with azure sides extending through the entire middle of the room.

The SS men and Sondercommando left the bathroom. Doors slammed. Lights went out. Sobbing and cries burst forth. Groans of despair resounded throughout....

Meanwhile, an impressive Red Cross van arrived in front of the building. An officer and an SS man from the Sanitation Service Aid alighted, carrying four tin containers painted green.

They crossed the lawn and came to flat concrete slabs covering the chimney. Then they opened their containers, resembling green peas, and poured them down through the opening. The crystals fell into the green pipes extending through the room filled with people.

"That's Zyklon!" "That's death!"

Its contact with the air immediately produced a gas which flowed down through the opening over the whole hall jammed with live people. After several minutes no one survived. The electric ventilators were turned on to remove the gas. The door was then opened and, first of all, the clothes and shoes from the first room were collected and packed into trucks to be taken and disinfected.

Next, the tightly closed large double oak door was opened. Of course, the modern ventilators sucked up the gas, but there was still some left in corners and crevices. The least inhalation, even a tiny draft of it, caused a troublesome, choking cough. For that reason, Hoess wore a gas mask when he walked to the threshold of the second, now illuminated hall. He personally wanted to be assured that the task entrusted to him by Himmler with such great confidence had actually been well accomplished, and that the method of "liquidation of Germany's enemies" passed its examination. Before his eyes he beheld a most horrible sight: An appalling pyramid!

The gas emitted from the crystals poisoned the lower section of the people on the floor, and then gradually it ascended higher and higher. On that account the unfortunate victims mutually trampled one another underfoot trying to get above the gas. Those who climbed higher lived a little longer until the gas reached them. Before death a terrible struggle took place among the victims striving for a minute or two of life. The self-preservation instinct drove them to tread over their own mothers, wives, and children.

Hoess caught sight of infants at the very bottom of women, and on the very top the strongest of men. All were interlaced in a deathly embrace, with lips and noses scratched and bleeding in the struggle for a second of life. Heads were swollen and unrecognizable.

Hoess left the building, took off his mask, and observed the curious looks of the SS men. By all means, he must now show them his stone face. The plan came out remarkably well.

"Good work," he said coldly to those circled around.

The SS men, too, were satisfied. Hoess' attitude resolved their doubts about whether they still were human. Besides, there was no time for reflection. Now, the SS men had to look after the Sondercommando workers comprised solely of Jews so that they would quickly and effectively clean out the gas bunker in preparation for the next transport. They began to untangle the pyramid of human flesh. This was hard work. They tied cords on the wrists of the dead by which they pulled the corpses over the wet concrete. Now, they took one body after another. The dead women's hair was cut.

It was a valuable material used to produce bombs with a retarded ignition. The human hair does not react to dry or damp air. That peculiarity of it guarantees that the bomb will explode just on time.

Then eight people from the "Dental Command" approached the victims with two types of instruments, that is, with chisels and forceps. By means of the chisels, they opened the clamped jaws and forced out the gold bridges and gold teeth, which they threw into a pail filled with a strong acid. The acid ate away the flesh and bone, leaving only the gold. Other treasures, like pearls, gold and platinum chains, rings, etc., were put into a special coffer. The bodies were then buried in massive graves.

On July 17, 1942, Himmler arrived at Auschwitz for a two-day inspection visit. At the very outset, Hoess, as host, explained the camp as shown on a map. Then, the engineer, Dr. Kammler, explained the plans and models of the new camp buildings. First came the farm and its improvements, the construction of ramparts, the laboratories and raising of vegetables in Rajsku, the raising of cattle, one Gypsy section and one Jewish section. From the tower at the entrance, Himmler ordered Hoess to explain the disposition of the camp and its divisions, the interior arrangements providing water, the water pumps and also the proposed enlargement of the camp.

He saw the prisoners at work, examined their quarters, the kitchen and the sick rooms. At the sight of the human skeletons, the emaciated victims of epidemics and hunger, the atrocious overcrowding, and the hopeless hygienic conditions, he remained silent. Hoess did not know whether that silence meant praise or a concealed reprimand; he tried very tactfully to justify the hard circumstances of the prisoners caused by difficult material conditions. Himmler rebuffed him.

"For an SS officer, difficulties do not exist. His permanent task is immediately to confront the difficulties himself. As to how, you have to worry about that, not I. And now show me the process of the liquidation of our greatest enemy, the Jews."

He observed the whole process of extermination of the newly arrived transport of Jews. He watched everything very carefully, but made no remarks whatsoever about the effectiveness of the method used at Auschwitz. Especially during moments of a heart-wrenching sight, he closely observed the reaction of Hoess, his officers, and the noncommissioned officers. He then visited the munitions factory in which the prisoners worked.

On the evening of the first day of inspection, a reception was held for the guests and all the officers of the garrison of Oswiecim. Himmler ordered, first of all, that everyone present be introduced to him. He started to speak with the few in whom he became quite interested, inquiring about their families and the type of their service. During the reception he questioned Hoess about the officers who particularly attracted his attention. Taking advantage of this opportunity, Hoess mentioned his personal difficulties with them, their lack of ability and uselessness, requesting at the same time an exchange of these men especially in order to strengthen those on sentry duty.

"You will be surprised," replied Himmler, "with the type of officers you still will have to contend with. At the front I need every capable officer, non-commissioned officers, and SS men. For these reasons, it is impossible to grant your request. You must initiate various technical means, so as to decrease the number of guards. Use a greater number of watch dogs. My plenipotentiary of the service dogs, in the shortest possible time, will accommodate you with the newest way of benefiting from the service dogs, thereby eliminating a number of guards. The number of fugitives from Auschwitz is unusually large compared to other concentration camps. I am in accord with whatever means you use in decreasing the number of fugitives and in preventing escapes. The epidemic of escapees from Auschwitz must cease.

After the common reception, Gauleiter Bracht invited Himmler, Hoess, his wife, and a few others of the Hitlerite personalities, to his home near Katowice. Despite the fact that at times during the day Himmler was in a depressed and impulsive mood, at the evening reception, he was the most charming person. He gushed with humor and showered the ladies with compliments. He spoke on whatever topic came to his mind. He talked about the good upbringing of children, new homes, pictures, and books. He related his experiences with the SS division at the front and of his tours at the front with Hitler.

On the other hand, he did not utter one word about what he had seen that day, about how he felt at the sight of the camp horrors, or about service affairs. To the astonishment of all, Himmler, who hardly ever used alcohol, drank several glasses of red wine that evening, and he smoked, which normally he avoided. Never before had he been seen so frolicsome and amused.

The following day, in the company of Hoess, he again visited some buildings of the camp. He was particularly interested in the women's camp, and there he ordered a demonstration beating of one of the women prisoners. Permission for the punishment of the women to be whipped he reserved to his own personal decision.

After inspecting everything, he went into Hoess' office to confer with him, and there he told him:

"I examined Oswiecim very carefully. I saw everything; I saw enough and heard from you of all the deficiencies and difficulties. To change that, even I cannot help. You must somehow manage that yourself. We are carrying on a war; therefore, we must learn as we work. The police actions arranged through me cannot, under any circumstances, be withheld, and never for the reasons presented me because of a lack of accommodations, etc. Eichmann's program must continue to be carried out, and it will increase from month to month. You must expand Brzezinka faster. The Gypsies must be liquidated. You must, likewise, positively liquidate all Jews incapable of work. In a short time the munitions factories will take to their work camps the first larger contingents of Jews capable of work. Then, you will have more space.

In Oswiecim also, the munitions factory must be developed. You may prepare for it. In the area of construction, Kammler, as far as possible, will contribute further help. The farm experiments will continue to be carried out intensively. Results are very necessary to me. I saw your work and your achievements; I am satisfied, and I thank you. I appoint you Obersturmbannfuehrer."

Hoess beamed with joy and pride. He thrust out his chest. It seemed to him that for all his crimes, Hitler himself and all of Germany were thanking him. Why not be overjoyed by such unusual acknowledgement for his bloody service?

Soon after Himmler's visit came Blobel from Eichmann's Bureau, bringing an order that all the mass graves had to be emptied, and the remains burned. The ashes then had to be disposed of in such a way that in the future it would not be possible to calculate the number of dead bodies burnt. Blobel was an expert in that field because in Chelm he had already conducted various experiments in burning the dead. Eichmann therefore, directed him to initiate Hoess into his arcanum. The Kommandant of Oswiecim was very precise. He, himself, wanted to see all so that later he could perfect his trade of genocide. He personally went to Chelm where Blobel had ordered the building of various provisional stoves, which were fed with wood and benzene. Blobel had also tried to destroy the bodies by means of explosive materials, which, however, did not produce the expected results. Ashes from the incinerated bodies were strewn over the vast wooded areas, but the bones had to be ground into powder.

During his visit at Chelm, Hoess also saw appliances for destroying people, heavy trucks adapted to kill people by means of poisonous gas. The local Kommandofuehrer ascertained that this manner of killing was inefficient because it generated gas irregularly and very often in insufficient quantities to kill. Hoess was proud of his method of poisoning the people at Auschwitz. That method was fast and unfailing.

Toward the end of 1942, Hoess ordered the bodies of old victims burned so as to vacate the graves used thus about 2,000 bodies and then, later, in pits together with other already buried remains. In the beginning, the bodies were burned with crude oil, later with methanol. The burning of the bodies in the pits was continuous, day and night. At the end of November, all the mass graves were vacated. The number buried in mass graves totaled 107,000.

From the beginning of the first experiments in burning the dead in slow air, it was clear that this process could not continue permanently. During inclement weather or a strong wind, the smell polluted the air for many kilometers. The population in the surrounding areas said, "The Germans are burning the Jews."

The SS men themselves, despite the most severe orders to keep this secret, could not bear this. In their resulting talkativeness, they revealed the crimes committed at Auschwitz.

Besides, the air defense protested against the fires seen from afar during the night. Hoess did not accept this protest. He replied, "We must burn the remains at night in order to accommodate the incoming transports of the enemies of Germany. The schedule of the transports has been accurately determined at a conference of the Ministry of Communication and must be unquestionably observed in order to avoid overcrowding and confusion on the railway lines, chiefly out of consideration for the military."

Nonetheless, Hoess was forced to seek better methods of destroying the remains. As a result, he planned to build two large crematoria and later two smaller ones. Both crematoria I and II were erected during the winter of 1942–1943; in the spring of 1943 they were put to use. Each one had five stoves with three retorts, so 2,000 bodies could be burned within 24 hours. Both crematoria had underground dressing-rooms and gas chambers. The remains were conveyed by elevators to the stoves located above. The gas chambers could hold 3,000 people. The two smaller crematoria, III and IV, according to the calculation of the Topf Firm of Erfurst Construction Industries, could burn 1,500 bodies during 24 hours.

Hoess was very proud of his accomplishment of perfecting the method for speedily disposing of such a large number of bodies and of obliterating all traces of them. In this regard he surpassed all his Hitlerian colleagues.

Simultaneously, Hoess proceeded to build a sorting house for the belongings seized from the gas victims. Thirty new barracks were immediately filled to capacity on completion. Clothes and shoes were carefully searched for valuable objects which were sent to the German government. These valuables were taken over by a special division of the camp administration, where experts sorted them according to value. So, too, was the procedure with money. Valuable objects were often found: precious stones worth millions; gold and platinum watches with diamond settings; rings, earrings and necklaces. Frequently, they found hundreds of thousands of dollars in thousand dollar bank notes on individuals. Many Jews were under the impression they could bribe the SS men for their lives. Unfortunately, they were mistaken. Their lives were taken away for nothing, together with their money.

Hoess became the best supplier of gold and valuables for Hitler's Germany. For this he received a Martial Cross of Merit, Class I, and on April 20, 1942 a Cross of Merit, Class I, with swords.

The watchful eye of Hoess noticed that not all the gold and valuables found their way to the government bank. Some of the SS men kept many treasures for themselves. The heaviest penalties of loss of freedom and even of life did not deter them.

In his fervor for the destruction of Jews, Hoess was not satisfied with receiving transports of, them ready for extermination. He traveled elsewhere to seek them out. In the summer of 1943 he went to Budapest to discuss further action against Hungarian Jews with Eichmann.

"You may expect," said Eichmann, "that we will provide you, Herr Hoess, with about 3 million Jews at Oswiecim from Hungary. We're having a little difficulty with the Hungarian Government and the Hungarian Army, particularly the higher officers who are against the idea of giving up the Jews because they are deployed in units at the front,"

"When we finish the liquidation of Hungarian Jews, where do we proceed?"

"The next country will be Rumania. We will free it of 4 million Jews. Then there will be Bulgaria with presumably 2-1/2 million Jews."

"And will Italy also belong to our zone of action?" Hoess was insatiable.

"Mussolini, to be sure, promised to extradite the Italian Jews, as well as those Jews found in the parts of Greece occupied by him. Unfortunately, the Vatican, which has tremendous influence on Italian opinion, and also the Royal House are strongly opposed to it. Therefore, we cannot count much on Italy.

"And Spain?"

"Certainly, influential circles have turned to us most willingly to dispose of the Jews; however, Franco himself and the people influenced by him are against it."

"A great pity!" sighed Hoess. "Perhaps, Hitler, himself, will help."

The liquidation process of the Jews was in no way a hindrance to Hoess in simultaneously performing the normal tasks of Kommandant in a concentration camp. He had the most difficulty with the women's camp where the living conditions were definitely harder than in the men's. The women had a much smaller living space and hygienic conditions were in a hopeless state. Hoess could never implement proper order in the women's camp, due to the overcrowding which existed from the very beginning. The worst criminal elements were sent from Ravensbruck to act as functionary prisoners so that they could unleash their meanest instincts on political and Jewish prisoners.

On a certain night in the summer of 1941, Jewesses from France who had been placed in a penal company in the village of Budy, rebelled against these functionary prisoners. In a fit of despair they flung themselves upon the functionaries. The result was terrifying. Ninety French prisoners lost their lives. After being informed of that occurrence, Hoess immediately made his way to the place and, although immune by this time to the sight of horrible spectacles, shook perhaps for the first time when he saw the proof of what one woman can do to another. The French Jewesses were murdered with rods and axes, and some were decapitated. Others were strangled to death or literally torn apart. The only relief to Hoess was the fact that not one of the functionaries was lost.

Not only was Hoess in trouble with the functionaries but also with the guards. None of them wanted to come to Auschwitz from other concentration camps. Those who came were unable to control the situation. Usually at roll call, the correct number of prisoners was lacking. In their confusion, the guards flitted about like fretful hens and did not know what to do. When time permitted, Hoess hastened with help. His hate-filled glance sufficed to restore order.

Himmler expressed the wish that the women's camp, under the general supervision of Hoess, would be directed by a woman with the help of one of the SS officers. Every officer appointed there begged Hoess to be exempt from that duty. No one's nerves could bear a cruel woman's domineering conduct over other women.

Because there was a shortage of guards, Hoess decided to follow the advice of Himmler and use various divisions of guards with dogs to supervise women prisoners during work. It appeared, however, that 150 dogs were not enough. In the judgment of the Kommandant the Oswiecim "dog company" was to be the most select group that ever existed, but, in reality, it had negative consequences. When Hoess began to look for volunteers to be instructed as trainers of dogs, half a battalion applied. The candidates expected to have easier and more varied work. After their training in Oranienburg, the soldiers returned to Oswiecim and formed the "dog company." The Kommandant fell into a rage when he saw them working. They were either playing with the dogs or lying in some concealed corner sleeping, trusting the dogs to awaken them in case of emergency. To relieve boredom, they would frequently sic the dogs on the women prisoners for their own amusement.

For the first time, Hoess realized that Himmler had no gift of infallibility. He had deluded himself into thinking that dogs could be so trained that they would continually surround prisoners and control them as sheep dogs control flocks of sheep, and that in this way they would frustrate every attempted escape. He believed that one guard with several dogs could easily control 100 prisoners. Experiments proved this futile. Hoess, too, understood now that dogs were, and would remain, animals over which men endowed with understanding would rule.

But doesn't man devoid of all moral restraint become something much worse than an animal?

One winter day a group of Polish women were occupied in digging a ditch. The prisoners were clad in thin clothes during this bitterly cold day. Besides, they were all atrociously hungry. One of them especially suffered terribly, for at almost any moment she expected to deliver her child. Cold sweat covered her tortured face. She was breathing hard, as though she wanted to feed the infant in her womb with oxygen. She was about to faint. One of her companion's looked around, seeking help for the sick woman. A short distance away stood a young man in a finely tailored uniform, carrying a small gun at his side and wearing a tall, well-fitted cap. The face of the young man was composed and calm. The silver skull and crossbones on his cap band were the only things that made the woman feel uneasy. The SS man was playing with his dog throwing a stick to him and the dog retrieving it. The Polish woman finally decided to approach the young man. After walking over to him, she began speaking in a pleading voice, "Please, Sir, take a look at my friend and see the condition she is in right now. She will deliver a child in a few minutes. Please help her!"

The young man listened to her quite impassively; he glanced at the distressed woman but said nothing. He continued to play with the dog. After a time, he grew tired of playing, and walked over to the woman who was doubled over with pain. He took the spade away from her and then looked strangely at the Polish woman who had the courage to see in him a sympathetic human being. She smiled in gratitude and joy assuming she wasn't mistaken in thinking he was human! But, suddenly, that smile changed into a terror-stricken grimace. The SS man raised the spade high and struck the pregnant woman with full force directly in her abdomen. A terrible moan burst forth. At the same time, the SS man threw her spade far into the ditch and ordered the victim to go for it. This most inhuman and cruel form of play finished with the death of the mother and her unborn child.

Meanwhile, Hoess was informed by Himmler that the concentration camps were being enlisted to help in the expanding armaments industry. This task required precise management of everything. The job of the camps was to supply laborers for the munitions factories. Obedient to the directives, Hoess organized a division in Oswiecim whose duty was to obtain the most efficient labor power possible from the prisoners. This division was called Arbeitseinsatz. It organized capable working teams of prisoners and sent them to hard labor in the industrial plants and into the mines throughout Upper Silesia.

Near the camp, the Krupp firm built munitions factories, taken over later by the "Union" firm. Likewise, in the neighborhood of Oswiecim, at Monowica, the firm, I.G. Farben-Industry, built a factory for the production of synthetic gasoline, "Buna-Werke."

The Oswiecim camp supplied thousands of workers to build these factories. This slave labor drove people to extreme exhaustion. They were forced to work in absolute silence at full speed, and guards beat them without cause. Anyone who fell from exhaustion was shot on the spot. Places of work were places of torment and murder. Prisoners no longer capable of working were sent to Brzezinka (Birkenau) and gassed. In their place the camp supplied new prisoners to fill the contingent determined by contract between the SS and the firm.

From this slave labor, the SS organization derived a gigantic income. The factory paid 6 marks to the concentration camp for one day's labor of a skilled worker and four marks for an unskilled laborer. On the other' hand, to maintain one prisoner only cost the camp about 30 pfennigs (pennies) a day.

Hoess found other means of increasing income. He was selling not only the labor of the prisoners in his charge but the prisoners themselves. One day he received a proposition from a world-renowned firm, the Bayer Co., which manufactured medicine. "We shall be very grateful to you, Herr Hoess, if in connection with your intended experiments you would be willing to place a certain number of women at our disposal on whom we could test our new sleeping pills."

"Certainly, but not without charge. Would you offer 200 marks per head?" he asked.

The firm answered, "We received your reply. Two hundred marks per head for one woman seems too high a price for us. We are offering you not more that 170 marks per head. If this is satisfactory to you, we are ready to receive the women. We need about 150 women."

"One hundred and seventy marks per head." Hoess expressed his agreement.

Again, the firm wrote, "We confirm your agreement. Please prepare 150 women, if possible the healthiest. After we receive word that they are ready, we shall accept them."

The transport was sent. The Bayer firm acknowledged; "We received 150 women. In spite of their emaciated condition, we find them suitable for our purpose. We shall inform you about the course of our experiments."

After some time, Hoess received a letter, "The experiments were performed. All the women died. Shortly, we shall again communicate with you about a new supply."

The Oswiecim concentration camp itself became a monstrous medical laboratory for experiments on the prisoners. Its principal purpose was to find out methods of sterilization for the destruction of whole nations. In the first place were the Jews, and later, the Poles and the Czechs.

Then new orders came, but this time from Brandts at Himmler's headquarters.

"On July 1, 1942, the Reichsfuehrer held a conference with the SS Brigadefuehrer Prof. Gebhardt, SS Brigadefuehrer Gluecks, and SS Brigadefuehrer Prof. Clauberg from Chorzowa. The Reichsfuehrer promised Brigadefuehrer Prof. Clauberg that the concentration camp at Oswiecim was at his disposal for his experiments on people and animals. On the basis of a few major experiments, a method of sterilization had to be devised so that the persons sterilized would be unaware. The Reichsfuehrer requested that results of this experiment be made known to him for practical application for the sterilization of Jewesses. He also referred to a stabilizing method for sterilizing men with the co-operation of the German X-ray specialist, Prof. Highfelder. In the presence of all the members of the commission, the Reichsfuehrer emphasized the fact that these matters were most confidential and could be discussed only in strict privacy. Likewise, all those participating in the experiments or conferences are obliged to keep the secret."

With the permission of Himmler, various doctors applied to Hoess for the purpose of experimenting on the prisoners. In this way, Dr. Ernest Robert von Gravitz carried out experiments for the purpose of studying the causes of contagious jaundice, and Prof. Rascher carried out experiments in the camp on freezing people to death. The most horrible experiment made on the prisoners of Auschwitz was the one that used them as material in making up a collection of skeletons. In 1942, Prof. Hirt, Director of the Anatomy Department in Strassburg, received permission from Himmler to make 150 skeletons from the prisoners. In 1943, 115 prisoners were selected. Among them were 79 Jews, 30 Jewesses, 2 Poles and 4 prisoners from Central Asia. They were sent to a monstrous death.

In the presence of all these monstrosities Hoess was aware of the fact that some day he would have to render an account of his terrible responsibility for all these crimes. What was the interior aspect of this man in view of the bestiality in which he took a leading part?

Above all, he believed in, and desired, the victory of Hitler and the Germans over the whole world. He especially craved to add his share by blindly performing the orders of Hitler and Himmler. Auschwitz became the largest establishment in the world for murdering people. Himmler's order to prepare the concentration camp at Oswiecim as the place for the extermination of 12 million Jews and many millions of people of other nationalities was monstrous, yet to Hoess it seemed entirely right-for the good of Germany. While carrying out the murderous plans of Hitler and Himmler, Hoess did not permit himself to become emotionally involved in any way, so as not to oppose them. He was deliberately becoming more and more harsh, calloused, and merciless toward the prisoners. Being himself urged on to criminal activities, he gave no breathing spell to his subordinate SS men, civil functionaries, firms and doctors. For him there existed only one task, namely, to move on with the work of exterminating people speedily.

The SS men who participated in this mass slaughter questioned Hoess in moments of reflection: "Is what we are doing necessary for the German nation?" "Why are we murdering women and children?" "What do children owe Hitler and the Party?"

"First, we must obey the Fuehrer," Hoess would reply, "and not philosophize. Secondly, once and for all, we shall free the German nation of the Jews, the greatest enemy of our government."

These replies did not satisfy his subordinate officers. They observed their chief closely in order to see what impression these murderous gassing of women and children would make upon him; they were curious to see if his face would reveal some human sympathy at least once. Unfortunately, they never did see this. He always had the same stone face, the face of a cold-blooded murderer.

One time, two little children were so absorbed in their play in front of the gas bunker that even the mother could not get them away from it. The time for gassing was approaching. The mother, having misgivings as to her children's fate, looked at Hoess in desperate pleading. Absolute stillness followed. The SS men waited to see if, at least this once, their chief would show some human reaction. Meanwhile, Hoess, with a commanding move of his hand, beckoned to one of his subordinate officers who took the resisting children into his arms and carried them into the chamber over the heart-rending cries of the mother who followed them.

At another time a woman walked up to Hoess and pointed to her four children who were holding hands politely in order to lead the youngest over a rugged area. She whispered to him, "How can you have the heart to murder such beautiful and sweet children? Don't you have any heart at all?"

An old man passing near Hoess hissed, "The Germans will have to atone heavily for this mass murder of the Jews."

A beautiful young woman once attracted the attention of Hoess. She did not seem to him to be a Jewess. She helped the children and the older women undress. Tenderly, she tried to quiet them. She was one of the last to enter the gas chamber. She stopped at the door and threw a defiant look into the face of Hoess. She said, "I knew from the very beginning that we were going to Oswiecim to be exterminated. I avoided being included among those capable of work, by taking in children. I wanted to experience all this completely, with full awareness. This certainly won't last long. At any rate, be well!"

That was worse than a slap in his face. Hoess felt very small; he felt like a bandit.

Day and night Hoess was present at the gassing and burning of the bodies. For hours he observed the extraction of gold teeth and bridges from the dead bodies and the clipping of the women's hair.

From time to time, Himmler sent various dignitaries of the party to Auschwitz to observe the extermination of the Jews. It shocked all the spectators. Many times those who theoretically claimed the necessity of destroying the Jews remained silent and horrified at this sight. They often asked Hoess, "How can you look at that continually? What's more, how can you organize such an action yourself?"

"The command of the Fuehrer," he replied calmly, "must be carried out with iron discipline. In the presence of all this, weak human reactions must disappear."

Each of the dignitaries approached Hoess and sincerely admitted that he would never want to perform that task.

At every opportunity, Eichmann encouraged Hoess to crime, repeating frequently, "We must mercilessly carry out the extermination of the enemy as quickly as possible. Any kind of consideration will later lead to bitter revenge against us."

After these talks with Eichmann, all human reactions seemed to Hoess to be a betrayal of Hitler and Germany. Whenever any human doubts were awakened in him, he mounted his favorite horse and began a frenzied ride.

Often during the night he went to the stable. There, among his friendly horses, he found relief. The greatest anxiety in his heart was aroused by the sight of his own wife and children. When he observed how his own children played and how very happy his wife was in holding their youngest daughter close to her heart, a question often came to his mind, "How long, will your happiness last?"

Standing during the night by the transports, by the gas chambers, by the flames in which the dead bodies of women and children blazed, he often thought of his own wife and children. At times he heard the same reflection from married men, serving in the crematorias.

Hoess' wife and their children had an ideal life in Oswiecim. Their every wish was fulfilled. The children could romp at will, and the wife had many of her favorite flowers there. "I feel as though I'm in paradise," she confided tenderly to her husband. One day, however, she asked her husband, "Is it true, dear Rudi, that you are gassing women and children and burning their bodies on the grounds of the camp?"

"Yes," replied Hoess quietly.

The woman became deathly pale. She attempted to say something but her voice caught in her throat. She was silent when it was really necessary to scream! Silence is not always golden; sometimes, it is a crime.

In November, 1943, Hoess was recalled from the position of Kommandant at Oswiecim and transferred to the headquarters of the Economy and

Administration of the SS (WVHA) which included the inspection of the concentration camps known as Amtagruppe D. He assumed the office of a Commissary at first and later became the real Chief of the D.I. Office, otherwise known as the Division of Political Inspectors.

The departure from Oswiecim was very painful to Hoess. After all, it was the project into which he had put all his strength and work. Nevertheless, he felt comforted because the present position was also connected with the domain of concentration camps with which he was so familiar for the past nine years. He resolved to be in personal contact with the concentration camps; as chief he would be in a position to improve them more and more in carrying out the tasks placed on them by Hitler and Himmler.

In 1944, all the concentration camps were overcrowded, and there was no end to the new arrivals of prisoners. Tens of thousands of Jews were withdrawn from Oswiecim for use as slave laborers in the new munitions factories. Their housing in the new places, however, and their nourishment were hopelessly inadequate for the exacting labor. They were, therefore, dying at a rapid pace. Hoess was grieved, not with the death of the people, but with their minimal value as workers.

He suggested to Himmler in a report that he have all the weak Jews led directly to the gas chambers at Oswiecim and to select only the healthiest and the strongest for work. The availability of large numbers of capable workers could not be given in the reports, but people could be pointed out who had worked for a long time. Hoess was also aware of the fact that the Jews sent from Oswiecim, not only took up space in the camps at the factories but also deprived the capable workers of food.

Toward the end of 1944, the military situation in Germany was becoming fatal. The eastern front fell to pieces under new offensives by the Soviets.

On the west, too, the German army was retreating before Allied Army attacks. Hitler, however, was incessantly talking about victory, and Goebels, the master of Hitlerite propaganda, talked and wrote continually about the miracle that would make the Germans victorious. However, even a man like Hoess began to wonder whether Germany would win the war. He saw and heard many things, yet, against all logic, he still believed in Hitler's victory.

At the beginning of 1945 his wife asked, "How can we still win this war?"

"Right now, we are producing a terrible weapon with which we will destroy all our enemies," replied Rudolph. He, himself, however, was losing faith in the official propaganda, although it was difficult for him to believe that his whole world was tumbling down. He continued to work with an intense bitterness as though victory depended on his work.

In fact, in April of 1945, after the fall of the front on the Oder River, he made it his business with the SS to maintain the munitions factories at full speed, that is those that still remained and had not been stilled by bombing or artillery fire. If he caught anyone neglecting his work or escaping, he punished him severely.

When the Soviet offensive began in January of 1945, Himmler ordered the evacuation of concentration camps located in Eastern Germany. The order, at the same time, was a death sentence for tens of thousands of prisoners. Hoess wanted personally to see that whole concentration camps were evacuated and every thing destroyed that could possibly bring discredit to him and to Germany before the whole world. Fortunately, he failed to obliterate all evidence of the monstrous crimes. He rode as far as the Oder River near Racibor. On the opposite side, Polish and Soviet armor was readying.

On all the roads and highways of Silesia west of the Oder River, he met columns of prisoners forging their way with difficulty through deep snow. The prisoners were completely without food. The SS men leading these columns of skeletons did not know precisely where to lead the prisoners. All the groups were heading in the direction of the Sudeten.

Hoess also saw transports of prisoners loaded in open coal cars, transports composed of completely frozen people. These cars stood hopelessly on the side railways. He also noticed groups of prisoners walking without any supervision.

Deep snow covered the ground all around, the frost was making the evacuation a great tragedy. At the edge of the roads lay not only cadavers of prisoners, but also of German women and children. At the. entrance of a certain village, Hoess saw a German woman sitting on the stump of a tree, rocking her child and singing a lullaby. The child had been dead for quite some time. The mother had lost her mind.

The food situation was catastrophic. For weeks, these places had been traversed by whole units of escapees. Allied bombers were circling over the roads day and night, causing still greater panic.

Finally, Hoess understood that this was the end. There was no longer time to think of the government but only about saving himself. He took his family and a few families of other dignitaries in cars and began to flee from justice. That flight was hideous. They rode through the night without lights, on jammed roads. During the day, the autos I slipped from one wooded area to another because dive-bombers were directing fire on the main road. On the way, at some farmhouse, Hoess found out that the "immortal" Hitler was dead. "Now, it is our turn," whispered the bluish lips of Hoess' wife.

"Yes," confirmed her husband. "Together with Hitler our whole world is lost. After all, would there be any sense to continue living? We shall never find peace. We are going to be always tracked town and persecuted. I have some poison for us with me."

Rudolph looked at his two-year-old daughter. No, they could not take away their lives and deprive their children of their parents.

Like a flash, another thought came to Hoess. Perhaps, the lives of all five children should also be taken away.

The one who had sent millions of women and children to gas chambers, now could not decide on the death of one woman and five children, because they were his. Did he ever think that those women, too, had husbands? That those children, too, had fathers?

Hoess left his family in Holstein and then reported to Himmler at Flensburg. Hoess thought that in this tragic moment for Hitlerism, Himmler would order them to fight until death. But here he met a laughing, hysterical man, who in response to the question of his subordinates, gave his last command, "Tell the army to disappear!"

Hoess, with a group of dignitaries, concealed himself in the ranks of the marines under an assumed name and documents. Now, he appeared as a modest chief petty officer, Franz Lang; in the general confusion he left for the Silt Island to the Union Marine School. Since he had some knowledge of navy life, he did not draw anyone's attention. After a short time he heard that Himmler was imprisoned and that later he had committed suicide by poison. Although he always had an ampoule of poison with himself, he decided to wait.

The Marine School was transported to the zone of internment between the Canal of the North Sea and Schlei Bay.

As a professional farmer, Hoess, alias Lang, was discharged before his term was up and passed all English controls without any difficulty. Through the Employment Agency, he was directed as a laborer to a farm near Flensburg. The proprietor of that farmstead was still an American prisoner, so

Rudolph felt quite safe. He remained there for eight months keeping in contact with his wife through her brother. He knew that he was wanted by the police and that his family was closely watched.

In the meantime, the whole world was searching for the originator and Kommandant of the concentration camp at Oswiecim, looking for one of mankind's greatest criminals.

Rudolph Hoess, architect and first kommandant of Auschwitz, at the moment of his extradition to Polish authorities May 26, 1946. Few photographs of this man are available.

1946–1947
Arrest, Trial and Final Repentance:
Hoess

March 9, 1946, Hoess accidentally broke his ampoule of poison. He became uneasy about it. What sign is this, is it a good future, or is it the contrary? Two days later the answer came during the night. The English Searching Security Police woke him suddenly from sleep and immediately transported him to Heide army barracks from which the English had discharged him eight months earlier. As a welcome he received one lash with a horsewhip.

"Do you recognize this," inquired a policeman, showing him the horsewhip.

"Yes," replied Hoess meekly.

"Did you ever use this for beatings?"

"For a horse, almost never."

"But people?" shouted the police officer.

"Rarely."

After a few days he was transferred to Minder, near Weser River, where his hearings were conducted by two officers of the Investigation Unit of War Crimes of the British Army. He testified,

"I was a Kommandant at Auschwitz until December 1, 1943. The number of victims killed and liquidated in the gas chambers and in the crematoria according to my estimation was 2,500,000 people. Besides that at least a half-million died of hunger and illness, making the sum total of approximately 3,000,000. This comprised about 70-80% of all the people directed to Auschwitz as prisoners. Among the dead and burned in the crematories were about 20,000 Soviet prisoners-of-war, hunted out pre-

viously by the Gestapo from the camps of war prisoners and brought in by army transports under the escort of officers and soldiers of the Wehrmacht. The remaining part of the whole number were predominantly Jews from Holland, France, Belgium, Poland and Hungary, Czechoslovakia, Greece and other countries. During the summer of 1944, we liquidated 400,000 Hungarian Jews at Auschwitz."

After three weeks Hoess was given a shave, a haircut, and was permitted to wash up. The manacles put on his wrists at the time of the arrest were not taken off. He was transferred to Nuremberg, where he was to appear before the International Military Tribunal as a character witness in the defense of Kaltenbrunner at the request of his attorney.

On April 15, Hoess entered the Tribunal Hall with small steps and head burrowed into his shoulders. He bowed like a shy student and occupied the place indicated.

In the hall a dreadful stillness followed. All eyes were turned on the man who directly participated in putting to death 3,000,000 people. All present in the hall now realized the fact that before their very eyes they were seeing one of the greatest criminals of all times.

The questions were to be put to him by the attorney for the defense of Kaltenbrunner, Dr. Kauffman. He began with a pathetic speech.

"The confessions of the witness will be of tremendous significance. However, I want to call his attention to the fact that he is possibly the only person who could enlighten us on some unclarified matters. He could tell us what persons issued the order for the extermination of the European Jews, in what sphere of activity that order was carried out and to what degree he was successful in concealing its performance."

Judge Lawrence tapped the table with a pencil and spoke calmly but firmly through the microphone.

"Dr. Kauffman, perhaps now you could begin questioning the witness."

"Yes, Your Honor," replied the confused lawyer.

He now turned toward Hoess.

"Herr Hoess, were you the Kommandant at Oswiecim from 1940 to 1943?"

"Yes, sir," he replied in a subdued tone.

"And during that time hundreds of thousands of people were sentenced to death—is that correct?"

"Yes, sir."

"Is it true that you did not keep an accurate account of the murdered victims because you were not allowed to make any lists?"

"Yes, sir."

"Is it true that a man named Eichmann gave you instructions that 2,000,000 were to be exterminated at Oswiecim?"

"Yes, sir!"

The sharp questions thrust at him he answered quietly and colorlessly. To these questions Judge Lawrence himself added his own interrogations.

"Since various numbers were heard before our Tribunal, according to differences of opinion, as to the general number of concentration camps in Germany and the occupied countries, let the witness, as an expert on concentration camps, state this number precisely."

Hoess with his intimate knowledge ascertained that mother-concentration-camps numbered only thirteen. However, in the course of years, these camps were eventually divided into branches. Toward the end of the war the number of all the camps was 900. The servicemen and guards employed comprised a working force of not less than 330,000 as men and over 10,000 soldiers of the Wehrmacht, Luftwaffe and the Marines.

That last statement of Hoess made a great impression on all present in the hall. The soldiers of Germany were used for such criminal activities of Hitler.

In the course of the hearings, and not without a certain pride, Hoess talked of his talents in organizing and of his criminally efficient methods. He said,

"I visited the camp at Treblinka to satisfy myself on the manner in which they were liquidating the prisoners and on its practicality. From the Kommandant there I learned that during six months he exterminated 80,000 persons. The victims were put to death by means of coal carbon dioxide, and that method, to me, seemed quite ineffective. From the time I began to build the extermination pavilions in Oswiecim, I started to use Zyklon-B, i.e., a crystallized solution of prussic acid which we poured down through small openings into the death chambers. To kill the people in the gas chambers, I needed three to fifteen minutes at the most, depending on the atmospheric conditions. When all screaming ceased, it was a sign that the victims were dead. We often waited about a half hour longer to remove the bodies. The groups of our people with special assignments would take off bracelets, wristwatches, etc., from the bodies.

Gold teeth and gold bridges were removed. We surpassed Treblinka also in regard to another matter. We built gas chambers which could liquidate 3,000 persons. (At Treblinka) there were ten gas chambers, each for 200 people. In regard to other conditions, we also achieved better results than in Treblinka. There the victims were aware of the fact that they were going to their deaths, whereas we at Oswiecim tried to keep the people convinced that they were going to be disinfected. In reality it often happened that the victims guessed our intentions, and at times we faced rebellious groups and difficulties. Very often, too, the women tried to hide their children under their clothes. When we found them, it was obvious that they, too, had met their death. The extermination action was to be carried out wholly in secrecy, but nevertheless, the abominable and nauseating stench of the day-and-night burning of bodies spread all over the

Preparatory proceedings for Hoess' trial began in Cracow on August 28, 1946. The last verbal explanation of Hoess in the Preparatory proceedings took place January 11, 1947. His public trial took place between March 11 and March 29, 1947 before the highest National Tribunal in Warsaw. On April 2, 1947 a death sentence was pronounced.

surrounding territory so that all the inhabitants of the nearby villages knew that extermination was taking place in Auschwitz."

In the continuing hearings Hoess construed his actions as obedience to the orders of Hitler and Himmler.

"Did you show compassion at any time to the victims?" he was asked. But thinking of his own wife and children, he replied, "Yes."

"And in spite of that, did you not have any scruples in carrying out that action?"

"Even though certain doubts pervaded my mind, yet, since that had been an order given expressly to me, I felt it was sufficient, together with the reasons for action which were explained by Reichsfuehrer SS Himmler."

"What type of an order was it?"

"Himmler told me in the summer of 1941, that the Fuehrer issued an order for the final solution of the Jewish question. We, the SS men, had to carry out that order. If it were not carried out, the Jews would later destroy the German nation. In view of the accessibility of the railroad and the possibility of locating the camp in isolation, he chose Oswiecim. I was given this heavy task to perform. All human considerations, however, had to be forgotten, and my thoughts had to be centered on the performance of the order."

"Did you not raise any kind of objection at all?"

The countenance of Hoess revealed great astonishment.

"And what could I say? The only possible answer was 'Ja wohl.' It was actually an exceptional thing on his part that he called me personally before him to clarify all things. He could have sent his order directly to me, and I would have had to carry it out. Frequently he demanded impossible things, impracticable in normal conditions. But when such an order was received, one's whole energy had to be utilized for its realization, and thus impossible things were accomplished. The building of a dam on the Vistula River near Auschwitz is an example. Estimating the time necessary to build it, I figured it would take at least three years, but he gave us only one year, and in one year we built it."

In Hoess the Tribunal saw standing before it Hitler's ideal citizen and SS man, an unsurpassed example of Nazism. An exemplary executor of orders, he had been blindly obedient to his superior officers and wholly uncritical toward administrative authority. He himself had not reasoned, for he would see no problems but only obeyed and acted in agreement with the orders. He had become in effect a reliable and highly efficient robot. His unthinking mind-set in turn had brought about frightful results for himself, society and the whole world.

During the investigation in the Nuremberg trial, an American doctor threw Hoess a tricky question.

"How was it technically possible to kill such a large number of people?"

"Technically?" Hoess was surprised. Oh, that was not so difficult. You could exterminate an even greater number of persons. Working in three shifts, that is within 24 hours, I was able to kill 10,000 persons daily. Among the six gas chambers there were two larger ones which could accommodate 2,000 persons, and the four smaller chambers held 1,500 persons."

"Under these circumstances, should not the result have been numerically greater?" asked the doctor.

"You don't know how to visualize this. The killing itself consumed the least time. The most time was needed for burning the bodies. The killing was easy, even guards were not necessary to drive the people into the chambers. They simply walked inside expecting to take a shower, but instead of water we were dropping poisonous gas. Everything went fast. The most difficult problem was the burning of the bodies and not the killing."

Hoess' imprisonment in Nuremberg ended. Following an extradition proceeding, he was delivered into the hands of the Polish authorities.

On May 25, 1946, he was brought to the airport where he was guarded by Polish officers. In an American plane, Hoess was flown from Berlin to Poland. The criminal was now approaching the place of his crimes for retribution. In the Warsaw prison several functionaries surrounded him, showing him the tattooed numbers of Auschwitz. He could not understand what they said in anger and indignation. Yet he surmised it.

After the arrest he was kept completely isolated. On July 30, he was transferred to Cracow. At the railroad station, surrounded by the police, he had to wait for an automobile. The people quickly recognized the brutal exterminator of the Poles. No one struck him with a stone nor did anyone spit in his face. No one wanted to degrade himself with the methods of Hitler's criminals.

The preparatory proceedings began in Cracow on August 28, 1946, conducted by a judge and member of the Main Commission for the Investigation of Hitlerite Crimes in Poland, Prof. John Sehn. The proceedings were conducted in agreement with the regulations of the Criminal Section of the Polish Code, according to which Hoess was instructed regarding his inalienable rights of defense, including, according to Art. 73 of the Code, the right to remain silent.

Hoess accepted the information. Nevertheless he declared that he did not want to pass up anything in silence, or conceal anything. He did not take advantage of the right not to answer the given questions although he was reminded of this in the course of the proceedings, too; but he most willingly communicated exhaustive replies to all given questions. The hearings took place in the judge's chambers from 9:00 am to 12:00 noon without a break.

During the free hours outside the hearings, Hoess had the opportunity and favorable conditions to write. He willingly wrote his declarations and personally handed them to the interrogator. He also clarified problems which were the subjects of the hearings of the day, confirming and completing the content of the verbal explanations. At this time, too, he worked out the network of locations of over 900 concentration camps.

Hoess did not know the Polish language, and therefore the hearings were conducted in German. The minutes were also translated into German. Hoess confirmed that the contents of the minutes were faithfully reported, and in proof, he signed them all personally.

The last verbal explanation of Hoess in the course of the preparatory proceedings took place January 11, 1947. The concluding passage of the minutes of that day contains the following:

Today, in evaluating my actions on the basis of its results, also on the basis of all those facts and events which National Socialism brought with it for Germany and the whole world, I am truly convinced that I have chosen the wrong path, and moreover, by participating in the actions of the organization, as previously described, to which I belonged, I became an accomplice of that evil which encumbers those organizations. Finding myself with the SS men and trained in the discipline of that organization, I believed that every order given by the chief and also by Hitler was right, and I considered it to be a disgrace and a weakness if I were to try to shirk from the responsibility of performing their wishes and orders in any way. Having such an attitude, I persevered to the end in every position to which I was appointed, and I most ardently performed all orders and direct commands, although during my work in the concentration camps I saw that there were inhuman things going on. At times during the action of the mass killing of the Jews, I wondered if Providence really existed, and if it did, then how was it possible that such things could happen. In spite of everything, I was present everywhere—in receiving the transports, at the gas chambers, and at the burning of the bodies, desiring to be an example to my subordinate officers, so that no one could reproach me for demanding from them what I myself was unwilling to endure. As I emphasized previously, the concentration camp in Oswiecim and the other German camps were morally wrong, and that evil was demanded by the higher command of the government and the party which created the existing conditions in the camps and changed them into camps for the destruction of life. It was my fault that, in spite of everything, I worked with servile zeal in those camps, actually functioning as a martinet and finding no human approach to the prisoners in the camps. Leaving the evaluation of my activities and blame to the judges who will adjudicate the matter on the basis of the established facts and the revealed activities, I acknowledge the following:

1. *From November, 1922, up to the fall of Germany in 1945, I was a member of the National Socialist German Labor Party (NSDAP).*
2. *From June, 1933, up to the fall of the III German Reich, I was a member of the Protection Staff (SS) in which 1 attained the rank of SS Obersturmbannfuehrer.*
3. *During the time of May 1, 1940, to the end of November, 1943, I performed the functions of Kommandant at the concentration camp at Oswiecim and also chief of the garrison SS in Oswiecim.*
4. *From December 1, 1943, to the fall of Germany in 1945, 1 performed the functions of the chief of the Administration D.I. in WVHA.*
5. *From 1941, I was preparing for, and from January, 1942, I directed the mass killing of the Jews in the extermination set-up at Oswiecim.*
6. *During my activities in Oswiecim, millions of people were murdered, but I am unable to state the exact number.*
7. *The victims in Oswiecim were robbed of an enormous amount of belongings and property, the exact value of which 1 am unable at present to appraise.*
8. *According to the mandatory regulations, as Kommandant of the camp I was fully responsible for everything that took place in the camp.*

All the contents in the minutes and covered in my written account, I consider essentially complete.

Awaiting trial before the highest National tribunal during his imprisonment in Cracow, Hoess wrote his autobiography entitled, *My Soul, Life,
Formation and Experience*s. He concluded it with the following confession:

> *I am now standing at the end of my life. In the present notes I included
> only the essentials, whatever befell me in my life, what made a great im-
> pression upon me, what particularly affected me. I wrote truthfully, and,
> in reality, precisely as I saw things and experienced them. I omitted many
> insignificant points, some I have forgotten, and I recall others only very
> vaguely. As a matter of fact, I am not a writer, and I have never been too
> good at writing. I have no doubt that I repeated myself often, and pre-
> sumably 1 have frequently failed to express myself clearly. . .*
>
> *My life was colorful and varied. My fate led me through highlands and
> lowlands. Life was often hard and difficult for me, but I always managed.
> 1 never lost courage. I had two guiding stars which directed my life when
> I returned as a mature person from the war to which I set out as a boy
> in my school years: my country and, later, my family. My unlimited love
> of my Fatherland and my national awareness led me to the NSDAP and
> the SS. I considered that only the National Socialist outlook on the world
> was suitable for the German nation. In my opinion the SS was the most
> energetic champion of this idea, and it alone was capable of gradually
> leading the whole German nation to a life suitable to its nature.*
>
> *My family was my second sacred object. For me, it was a strong sup-
> port. Its future was the object of my constant concern. A farmstead was
> to be our home. My wife and I saw the purpose of life in our children. The
> task of our life was to give them a good up-bringing for the future and
> to create for them a strong family home. And even now my thoughts are
> revolving principally around my family. What will happen to it?*
>
> *That uncertainty about the fate of my family causes my present im-
> prisonment to be so difficult. I disengaged my person from the very be-
> ginning, and I am not worried about it; with that I am finished. But, my
> wife, my children?*

The public trial of Hoess took place between March 11 and March
29, 1947, before the highest National Tribunal in Warsaw with the par-
ticipation of the accused, the defense attorneys from the administration
of Thaddeus Ostaszewski and Francis Umbreit, interpreters, the press and
the radio. In the course of the trial, Hoess did not retract anything, nor did

he correct any of his verbal and written statements rendered during his inquest. He, however, referred to them in his explanations during the hearings as evidence of the office he held.

In his last testimony, Hoess said the following:

"From the first day of my sojourn under arrest, and from the first day of investigation, I always said that as a Kommandant I was fully responsible for Oswiecim. Personally, I myself did not steal, neither did I maltreat the prisoners nor kill them. Everything that happened there I did as I was ordered by my superiors, and I have not committed any wrong of my own free will. In making this statement I have no intention of shirking my responsibility."

On April 2, 1947 a death sentence was pronounced on Hoess. Its most significant parts read as follows:

Sentence Of Death

In The Name Of The Republic Of Poland, The Highest National Tribunal... [seeing that] Rudolf Franz Ferdinand Hoess, who was born November 25, 1900 in Baden-Baden... during the time from May 1, 1940 to the end of October, 1943 as Kommandant of the entire concentration camp at Oswiecim, expanded by him on the occupied territory of the Republic of Poland; afterwards, from December, 1943 to May, 1945, as Chief Administrator D.I. in the Board of Economics and SS Administration; besides, during June, July and August, 1944, as Kommandant of the SS garrison at Oswiecim; as one of the German co-creators of the Hitlerite system of tormenting and destroying nations through concentration camps and places of extermination; and as a leader putting that system into effect in the concentration camp at Oswiecim, over which he had full charge in relation to persons among Polish civilians and Jews, and also many other nationalities living in the German occupied territories of Europe, as well as Soviet prisoners-of-war, acting in this manner either personally or through his subjects, the camp personnel, intentionally:

1. *took part in executing murders among the above mentioned peoples: a) approximately 300,000 people incarcerated in the camp, according to camp evidence;*

b) an indefinite number of people amounting to at least, 2,500,000, chiefly Jews delivered to the camp in transports from various European countries for the purpose of immediate extermination, and therefore not recorded in the files of the camp;

c) at least 12,000 Soviet prisoners-of-war, contrary to the regulations of international law regarding treatment of prisoners-of-war, i.e., by suffocating them in gas chambers, burning them alive, shooting them down, giving lethal injections, performing medical experiments, exposing them to hunger, forcing them to work in those particular conditions of camp life which always brought on death, etc.;

2.   *brought harm to persons among the civilian population, to military personnel and to prisoners-of-war by:*

a) holding them in slavery connected with imprisonment in a closed camp with various kinds of physical and moral harassment, as hunger, forced labor beyond human strength, tortures, infliction of inhuman punishment, exposure to severe illness, maltreatment of human dignity, etc.;

b) participating in mass robbery of property, predominantly precious jewelry, clothing and other valuable objects taken away from persons brought into the camp, and especially those who came directly from the transports to the gas chambers for extermination, or, taken from the dead bodies in the camp, frequently connected with violation of the bodies by extracting from their jaws gold crowns, dentures and also cutting the women's hair. . .

condemns the accused RUDOLPH FRANZ FERDINAND HOESS for the above actions. . . by applying article 33, sec. 2 k.k.

During the reading of the verdict, Hoess once again displayed his stone face. A justification of the verdict was then read which certified:

After difficult war struggles, years of oppression and anguish, human justice has triumphed together with the restoration of human dignity in the name of which the Highest National Tribunal holds the accused

Rudolph Hoess responsible for all the wrongs inflicted upon this humanity, together with his accomplices in the criminal team to which he belonged, as a conspirator and planner, and dispenses justice to him, resting upon the legal verdict of the Republic and the dictates of world conscience, through the only punishment provided in the legal regulations-the death penalty.

When the reading was completed, Hoess thanked his attorneys for their work and affirmed that he did not want to appeal for pardon, since he felt that he could not be pardoned. Nevertheless the President of the Highest Tribunal immediately sent an account of the acts to the Minister of Justice for the purpose of presenting the matter before the President of the Republic who had the power to pardon. Hoess did not take advantage of it. The Procurator of the Highest National Tribunal then entrusted the execution of the verdict to the District Procurator in Wadowice.

* * *

Awaiting the execution of the verdict in Wadowice, Hoess wrote a farewell letter to his wife on April 11, 1947. In it he showed he still did not face the complete enormity of his crimes, nor accept full guilt for them. He was still blaming others to some extent. There was still denial of complete responsibility—self-pity, self-justification—by blaming the system. But he does confess:

It was here in the Polish prisons that I have learned what humanity is. As a Kommandant of Oswiecim I caused the Polish nation much pain and sorrow and did so much harm, even though it was not done personally, nor from my own initiative; yet they have shown me humane forbearance which deeply abashes me. This has come not only from the higher officers but also from the most common guards. Many of them were prisoners at Oswiecim and other camps. Now, in the last days of my life, I am experiencing humane treatment which I never expected. In spite of everything that happened, they still always see a human being in me.

Further on he relates his rejection of Nazism and his return to God:

During my long isolated sojourn in prison, I have had ample time and peace to reflect thoroughly on my whole life. I have examined thoroughly my whole course of action.

In the light of my present convictions, I see today very clearly what for me is very hard and bitter, that the whole ideology, and the whole world in which I believed so firmly, were resting upon completely false foundations and certainly had to fall into ruins some day.

My life in the service of this ideology was also absolutely false, although I acted in good faith, believing in the legitimacy of this idea. It is therefore quite logical that it awakened in me many doubts. Likewise, did not my fall from faith in God depend wholly on my false foundations? This was very difficult to overcome. Nevertheless, I have recovered my faith in God.

Hoess also wrote a tender and beautiful letter to his children giving earnest counsels to each one individually. Significantly he confesses:

"The greatest mistake in my life was that whatever came from "higher authority" I trusted blindly. I did not dare have the least doubts as to the validity of the given orders.

Go through life with an open mind. Don't be one-sided; reflect on the pros and cons of all matters. In all that you undertake, direct yourself not only with your understanding, but particularly pay attention to the voice of your heart."

* * *

Finally, on April 12, Rudolph Hoess spontaneously wrote the following declaration, indicating he had at last fully acknowledged and accepted the enormous gravity of his guilt:

"My conscience is forcing me to make also the following assertion: In the isolation prison I have reached the bitter understanding of the terrible crimes I have committed against humanity. As a Kommandant of the extermination camp at Auschwitz, I have realized my part in the monstrous genocide plans of the Third Reich. By this means I caused humanity and mankind the greatest harm, and I brought unspeakable suffering particularly to the Polish nation. For my responsibility, I am now paying with my life. Oh, that God would forgive me my deeds! People of Poland, I beg you to forgive me! Just now in the Polish prisons

have I recognized what humanity really is. In spite of everything that happened I have been treated humanely, which I had never expected, and this made me feel deeply ashamed. Would to God ... that the fact of disclosing and confirming those monstrous crimes against mankind and humanity may prevent for all ages even the premises leading to such horrible events."

This done, Hoess once again asked himself: "Is everything settled now?" At that moment he heard the sound of the convent bells of the Discalced Carmelites and he drew near to the latticed window. Through springtime's green trees he saw a red brick monastery and two steeples pointing to heaven. Again grace touched him.

Before the eyes of his soul stood Rudolph's youth: an altar boy full of faith and zeal, father and mother speaking to him of a priestly vocation, his desire to become a great person. How did it happen that from an altar boy, a model boy, he had become one of the greatest criminals of all time? Yes, he must now answer that question for himself. But what priest would have the courage to hear his confession? The prison chaplain gave him an evasive answer. Father Lohn, a Jesuit, was brought from Cracow.

The secret of the confessional now veils the mystery of the man.

The day of Hoess' doom, April 16, 1947, came swiftly. He was driven to Auschwitz.

Now he was no longer a Kommandant, but a condemned man; not a lord of life and death for millions of people, but himself a prisoner in chains. The sentence was not to be carried out on the territory of that camp, for this was not an act of revenge but of justice. The place where millions were martyred was not to be profaned.

Rudolph Hoess was hanged on a gallows enclosure of the camp. With that act he entered into history as one of the greatest criminals ever to scourge mankind, but also as one of the greatest ever to acknowledge and repent of his crimes, and be reconciled with God.

* * *

Maximilian Kolbe had prayed and had offered his life as priest and victim for all those with whom he shared the horrors of Auschwitz, including its Kommandant, Rudolph Hoess.

Kolbe had once spoken of the special recompense given to those who "burn with the desire to save souls"— namely "the possibility and the facility of 'catching' souls in the most effective way possible, even after death."

Rudolph Hoess' repentance and his reconciliation with God seem a signal from heaven that Maximilian Kolbe eternally enjoys that God-given reward.

—Editor

1948–1970
A Bright, Glorious Figure Bursts Forth:
Kolbe

As commissioned by the Sacred Congregation of Rites (decree of August 12, 1947), the information gathering phase of the beatification process of the Servant of God, Fr. Maximilian Kolbe, began in Padua May 24, 1948. Shortly afterward subsidiary processes began in Warsaw, Nagasaki and Rome; they were completed in 1952.

In 1960, the so-called *introductio causae* (introduction of the cause) followed, and a year later the apostolic process began; it was concluded in Warsaw September 18, 1962, and in Padua February 9, 1963. At the request of the Polish and German Episcopates in 1965, the Holy Father granted a dispensation from Canon 2101 of the Code of Canon Law, and thus permitted discussion on the heroism of Maximilian Kolbe's virtues to begin in the Congregation of Rites a before a lapse of 50 years from the time of his death.

The Sacred Congregation of Rites assembled January 30, 1969, at the Vatican in the presence of Pope Paul VI, and along with two other items voted to certify the heroism of the virtues of the Servant of God, Maximilian Kolbe, a priest and professed religious of the Friars Minor Conventual.

The Holy Father then addressed the dignified assembly with evident joy and pleasure. He summarized the work of the Congregation presented to him and noted that he agreed totally with their conclusions. He then immediately issued his decree which among other items declared that the Servant of God, Maximilian Kolbe, had achieved heroism in the practice of the theological and moral virtues, and that the process of beatification could therefore continue.

From that point Father Maximilian's cause for beatification moved forward rapidly. Growing numbers of enthusiastic voices and acclamations accompanied it. Some examples are the following:

> "Through the mingling of political prisoners with notorious criminals; through the continuous by the Nazis and their cohorts of one prisoner against another; through previously unheard-of filthy ideas, feelings and talk which became commonplace, man became a wolf to man. Into precisely that environment came the self-sacrifice of Father Maximilian. It sliced through that desperate atmosphere like a thunderbolt! It sent a moral shock through the whole camp."
> —Joseph Stemler, co-prisoner, Auschwitz.

> "The heroism of Father Kolbe can be compared to a powerful explosion of light in the dense, black night of the camp, which infused a regenerating, strengthening charge of optimism."
> —George Bielecki, co-prisoner, Auschwitz.

> "If the figure of Father Kolbe did not exist in reality, it would be necessary in an epoch such as ours, in an epoch of cruel selfishness, to discover it. No example will explain better to people today that not everything leads to selfishness. What is more, selfishness is the plague which poisons mankind most, and its opposite-generosity and Christian charity are an irreplaceable remedy for the world."
> —Professor Ludwig Persone, Italy.

> "Almost the whole Catholic world resounds with praises for the glory of this exceptional man. . . Whether you listen to the glorious and invincible Poland, which brought him into the world, whether you visit the respectable city of Rome, which educated the mind and heart of this man, whether you cross through the Japanese Empire where his missionary activities still produce rich fruits, whether you travel through both Americas or African countries and in all others where the Militia Immaculatae which he founded numbers 2 million members—practically everywhere over the whole world the name of Maximilian Kolbe is invoked for blessing, for good fortune and in grateful memory."
> —John Torre, Lawyer.

"Without exaggeration it may be affirmed that Father Kolbe is one of the greatest graces which God has given the Church."
— *Fr. Gabriel Roschini, O.S.M., Mariologist.*

"The beatification of Father Kolbe will become the source of salvation for a great number of souls."
— *Paul Yamaguchi, Bishop of Nagasaki.*

"The life and death of Father Kolbe operate as a powerful spiritual leaven in our wayward world. I, myself, fell rapidly into his net just as all those who have made contact with this truly unusual life. Like other giants of sanctity whom God and the Blessed Virgin commissioned with a universal message, Father Kolbe continues his so-called follies of Marian conquests."—Roger Brien, Member, French-Canadian Academy.

1948–1970
His Fatal Error:
Hoess

As a perfect instrument for crimes, Rudolph Hoess has not ceased to interest lawyers, psychologists and historians. A rich literature has sprung up concerning him. Mankind fears it may repeat the monstrous activities of Hitlerism under whatever label. Therefore it seeks an answer to the mystery of the soul of Hoess. How did this person come to form himself on the path of genocide? Investigation of these questions reveals the shocking fact that imperceptibly, from day to day, a person can gradually become a hardened criminal.

The analyses of these facts have for their purpose not only to record the facts, but also to warn all nations and each person individually to guard human values in themselves and in every individual without regard to nationality, race, political and religious convictions, and to protect the world from a horrible repetition.

One of the best psychological analyses of Hoess is the work of Professor Batavia, "Rudolph Hoess, Kommandant of the Concentration Camp at Oswiecim." The following are some significant excerpts:

Kommandant of Auschwitz: in considering certain of his individual traits, we find the embodiment of the peculiarities most characteristic of Hitler's mentality and an uncommon direct specimen of that parthenogenetic type so immensely valuable for administrators of the ill Reich, and which over the course of a long time, made the realization of Hitler's criminal plans possible.

Hoess was the embodiment of all the qualities which the National Socialistic regime could demand from SS men. He was an excellent per-

former of all orders received, blindly obeying his superiors, wholly with-
out any criticism in relation to every administrative authority. He always
believed firmly in the legitimacy of everything the Fuehrer announced,
and as a faithful believer of Hitler's ideas, immeasurably dedicated to the
cause, he never argued, he never had any reasons for questioning, but
obeyed and performed all orders. . .He represented a type of robot, rather
than a reasoning being, and at the same time, an ideal citizen of the III
Reich and SS man, as well as an unsurpassable example for all Hitlerites
as an ideal performer of every order. . . .

Rudolph Hoess deserves to be singled out because he is a unique speci-
men among war criminals. Immediately after his arrest in 1946, he felt
it was his duty to lay down truthfully exhaustive statements about the
crimes committed. He was also aware of the fact that as Kommandant
of Auschwitz he must accept responsibility for everything that took place
in the camp, and he understood that he must atone with his life for the
extermination of millions. . . .He spoke little, his formulated answers
were brief and concise, and he was immensely factual and accurate in
relating the various events. He tried to reconstruct all the details as they
really were, and the sequence of significant facts. At times he returned to
the same questions during subsequent testimony, desiring to complete his
answers by affirming that he had thought about them and that it seemed
to him they were not accurate, or that he was not sure whether he had
reproduced his experience of them exactly.

In answering questions concerning his experiences and the facts of
his personal life, Hoess never formulated his answers in a manner typi-
cal of persons endeavoring to present themselves in an advantageous
light, as a victim of fate, of special circumstances, incidental occur-
rences, etc. Besides, he was not psychologically capable of analyzing
his personal experiences, of selecting pertinent facts liable to attest to
his definite peculiarities. Obtaining declarations of the substances of
his experiences and the manner of his reactions to certain happenings
was not a simple matter because of his psychological helplessness. In
general, this man reflected little on himself; his mind was set on activity
rather than on thinking. . . .

In December 1934, Hoess began his training in the concentration camp
at Dachau. This, however, was really no different from the regular train-
ing. By using Paulian language, it may properly be defined as developing
in the SS man certain definite, dynamic stereotype characters, produc-

ing conditioned, compulsive mechanisms which in given vital situations would never fail to operate.

The purpose of the training was to make robots of the SS men and to program them for a certain stereotyped kind of behavior in response to certain stimuli, so that they would act by routine in an unchangeable manner. Thus: the possibility of critically evaluating one's goals and one's own reactions was eliminated. Definite words and symbols were used to evoke the designed stereotype for primitive psychic processes and the stereotyped manner of action. Words such as "Communist," "Jew," "criminal," etc. were to produce immediately an aggressive posture; a given order was to give rise immediately to a compulsive manner of acting.

As a result, the methods applied tended to dehumanize the individual and make him a robot programmed with the most primitive, unrestrainable and compulsive conditioned reactions. They had to cause the formation of the defined specific type of mutilated human mentality that constitutes the human psyche characteristic of the SS men in whom Hitler's Fascism found the perfect performers for its planned crimes.

Destruction of all disposition to critical thinking in the SS men had to be accompanied also by annihilation of the formerly acquired ways of effective reactions in the range of higher feelings. The degradation in the sphere of the intellect had to comport with the affective degradation. An ideal SS man could be only such an individual who both ceased to think critically and who deprived himself of adequate tender reactions, above all, compassion. . . The SS men had to be kept constantly in a tension of counter-revolution and have an object of hate incessantly before their eyes, an enemy who would not allow them to weaken in their readiness to aggressive action.

. . . The history of the Kommandant of Auschwitz has little connection with pathology.

Rudolph Hoess was not a subnormal individual or morally insane, nor an apathetic psychopath, nor a person who showed any inclination to crime or sadistic tendencies. He was an individual of average intelligence inclined from childhood, thanks to the influence of home environment, to hardly any criticism of events and to easy conformity to all authority. We meet this type of person quite frequently. He was a very reserved individual and, no doubt, had the sensitivity of a schismatic, although he did not show his reactions or feelings. A mass of such schismatics with psychopathic traits is found in every country. He was a man accustomed *from an early age to treat all his duties seriously and to perform them conscientiously and fervently; these were usually considered virtues. He was an individual described also as a very strong person with a powerful will. These qualities, however, were advantageous to Hitlerism and they revealed themselves in matters tragic to the victims of his activities.*

Following the history of his life accurately, one can be convinced that under the influence of certain historical events and the social environment with which his life was connected, there took place a gradual metamorphosis of this social, and at one time harmless, individual, into the described type of Fascist mentality. How did this happen? This change was conditioned by natural social functions. At first, by the precursors of Hitlerism, and then by the National Socialistic ideology, young Rudolph was transformed from his vital ethical feelings into a hardened criminal, who while serving faithfully the false and criminal ideology, sank into the abyss of Hitlerite crimes!

* * *

Obedience. It's a quality which found embodiment in both Hoess and Kolbe, who once observed that "obedience constitutes an unshakable foundation" for the way one must live.

It might seem to some that there's a contradiction here. Obedience brought Hoess to monstrosity and death on the gallows. Obedience guided Kolbe to heroic holiness, vast apostolic fruitfulness, and to his martyrdom of charity at Auschwitz.

The difference is that for Kolbe God's will was the ultimate good. He obeyed his legitimate superiors because he trusted God to guide him through them. His obedience therefore was really obedience to God. For the same reason he absolutely refused to obey any order that contradicted God's revelation or God's law.

Hoess' obedience was not to God. He had rejected God's will as the ultimate good. He had chosen as his ultimate good a world and an authority directly opposed to God. As he said in his last letter to his wife, he had given himself body and soul to that world. But for that fatal decision, Rudolph Hoess might have matched Maximilian Kolbe in holiness.

—Editor

1971–1982
His Victory Deepens and Spreads:
Kolbe

October 17, 1971, was Maximilian Kolbe's first day of triumph. On that day in the Basilica of St. Peter, Pope Paul VI numbered Fr. Maximilian Maria Kolbe among the Blessed of the Catholic Church.

Pilgrims from all over the world came to Rome for these solemnities. From Poland, Japan, West Germany, Italy, America and elsewhere they came—over 30,000 of them. Delegates were also present from the Polish and West German governments. Father Maximilian's confreres too were there from Niepokalanow and Mugenzai no Sono.

One hour before the ceremonies commenced, the basilica resounded with Polish hymns by the Polish people who filled the two wings of the transept and the whole apse. They sang with their whole hearts "Serdeczna Matko" (Loving Mother), "Pod Twoja Obrone" (We fly to thy protection), and other hymns to the Blessed Mother.

During the solemn High Mass, the Sistine Choir sang, alternating with the pilgrims. After the "Kyrie Eleison" the Secretary of the Sacred Congregation for the Causes of the Saints, Archbishop Ferdinand Antonelli, read the following petition for beatification:

Holy Father,
Rising today above the sad recollections of the last World War is the luminous figure of the Servant of God, Father Maximilian Maria Kolbe, son of Catholic Poland. Born in 1894, he entered the Franciscan Order of Friars Minor Conventual at an early age. After completing his theological studies in Rome, he was ordained a priest in the Roman Basilica of St. Andrew della Valle, and after receiving his doctorate in theology,

he returned to his Fatherland. The source and inspiration of his deep interior life and unusual apostolic activity was his very tender devotion to the Immaculate Virgin. His apostolate of social love deepened after World War II broke out. In February, 1941, he was arrested and deported to the well-known camp of Oswiecim (called Auschwitz). There, seeing a greatly depressed father of a family who unfortunately was among a group of victims sentenced to death, the Servant of God offered himself willingly in substitution for the family man. After days of horrible suffering, he serenely welcomed death on August 14, 1941.

News of this heroic act aroused such admiration in the whole world that very soon the Processes for his beatification were begun.

One hundred fifty-seven eyewitnesses were interrogated regarding the entire life of the Servant of God. There burst forth from this investigation the bright and glorious figure of an exemplary, indefatigable apostle, impregnated always and everywhere with faith, hope and Christian charity. After long investigations, the Cardinals of the Sacred Congregation for the Causes of the Saints came to the conclusion that Father Maximilian Maria Kolbe had practiced the Christian virtues in an heroic degree. That heroism was solemnly proclaimed by Your Holiness with a decree on January 30, 1969.

Following this proclamation was another regarding the two miracles obtained through the intercession of the Servant of God. These were discussed and recognized as signs from on high with a decree on June 14 this year (1971).

Now, nothing else remains, Holy Father, except that you grant the wishes of the Episcopate and the Polish Nation, the Franciscan Order of Friars Minor Conventual, represented here by the Postulator of his Cause, and of all the clergy and faithful of the whole world; and be pleased to list the Servant of God, Maximilian Maria Kolbe, in that book of the Blessed which the Church honors and venerates. For this, too, the Sacred Congregation for the Causes of the Saints earnestly pleads.

* * *

This text was then delivered in the Polish language by Bishop Ladislaus Rubin. Then followed the most significant moment: Pope Paul VI delivered in Latin the formula of the Beatification Proclamation:

We, fulfilling the wishes of our many Brother Bishops, the whole Order of Friars Minor Conventual, and numerous faithful, and having at hand the resolution of the Sacred Congregation for the Causes of the Saints; after serious consideration and after invoking light from above; on the strength and by virtue of our Apostolic Authority, enroll the Venerable Servant of God, Maximilian Maria Kolbe, Priest of the above mentioned Order of Friars Minor Conventual, among the Blessed, granting authorization that his Feast be observed each year on August 14, the day of his birth into Heaven, in the places and in the manner established by law. In the name of the Father and of the Son and of the Holy Spirit. Amen.

Next the Holy Father intoned the "Gloria in Excelsis Deo." During the singing of this angelic hymn, amid the thunderous applause of the faithful, the picture of the new Blessed in Bernini's "Gloria" was unveiled. The Holy Father then read the prayer in honor of Blessed Maximilian Maria.

After the Gospel the Holy Father began his homily in honor of the newly Blessed:

Maximilian Kolbe—Blessed! What does this mean? It means that the Church recognizes in him an exceptional figure, a man in whom God's grace and the soul have so interacted as to produce a stupendous life... 'Blessed,' therefore, means worthy of that veneration permitted by the Church in certain places and among certain groups, veneration which implies admiration of the one who is their object because of some unusual and magnificent reflection of the Sanctifying Spirit in him. It means 'saved and glorious.' It means 'citizen of Heaven' with all the peculiar signs of a citizen of earth; it means 'brother and friend' whom we know is still ours, more so than ever, in fact, because he is identified as an active member of the Communion of Saints, which is the Mystical Body of Christ, the Church living both in time and in eternity. It means, therefore, 'advocate and protector' in the kingdom of love, together with Christ "who is always able to save those who approach God through him, since he forever lives to make intercession for them" (Heb. 7, 25; cf. Rom. 8, 34). Finally, it means 'exemplary specimen'—a type of man to whom we can conform our way of life, since he, the Blessed, is recognized as having the Apostle Paul's privilege of being able to say to the Christian people: "I beg you, then, be imitators of me" (I Cor. 4, 16). . . .

Following the Beatification Mass, the Holy Father recited the 'Angelus' together with the 200,000 faithful who filled to overflowing, the entire piazza of St. Peter's Basilica. He took the occasion to speak again about Blessed Maximilian. It was in the concentration camp at Auschwitz that "his heroic act of love was accomplished," the Pope said. He recalled how Father Kolbe spent his last days in a starvation bunker, after choosing to offer his life for an unknown man condemned to death, an innocent father of a family.

This was not the only deliberate act of generosity recorded in the terrible history of those years. (But) Father Kolbe's case is emblematic because of the personal virtues of this meek and exemplary Franciscan, and the tragic circumstances connected with it. In some measure, it draws together all the other unknown sacrifices which were accomplished in those barbarous events.

One of Father Kolbe's bywords illuminates his sacrifice and the horrifying epic of those years like a perpetual lamp: "Love alone creates," This

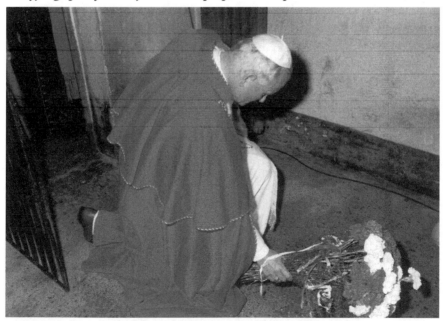

Pope John Paul II lays flowers and prays in Kolbe's death cell at Auschwitz during his visit there June 7, 1979. "I have come then to this special shrine—the birthplace, I can say—of the patron of our difficult century."

byword rises above the politics, the egoism, abuse of power, blindness and pride of people living without the Gospel; it should be engraved in our souls and in the new history of the world. This is the knowledge which Father Kolbe attained in the school of Mary, and which he continually transmits and will always transmit to the Church and to the world.

Of the many addresses and homilies delivered in Rome in the days following Father Kolbe's beatification, the one given by Cardinal Julius Doepfner, President of the West German Episcopal Conference, is especially significant. Paying tribute to the great holiness of Father Kolbe, the West German leader summoned his people to seek the forgiveness of the Polish people:

The source of Father Maximilian's indefatigable zeal, in spite of his frailty, was his ardent love of God permeated with illimitable trust. We cannot, even for a moment, disregard his especial love for the Blessed Mother. He called himself the "Knight of the Immaculata." He founded the Militia Immaculatae and his apostolic centers he named Niepokalanow, i.e., the City of the Immaculata. Because of his overwhelming love for Mary, he was called the "Fool of Mary." As a matter of fact, some of the forms and signs of his devotion are at first startling. However, the greatness of the saints is not confined within our limited structures; that which limits them inspires us with hope and admiration. A Protestant doctor who became acquainted with Father Kolbe in Auschwitz describes him in his mature perfection as follows: "I knew that Servant of God as a person of no common mind, sedate and of a wholly well-balanced character."

In many respects Blessed Maximilian directs his appeal and testimony of death to us as Germans. Surely, the concentration camp at Auschwitz was not a satanic work of the Germans directed exclusively against the Poles. Indeed, we know that a year later a Carmelite Nun, Edith Stein, a Jewess, was gassed there. Both in Auschwitz and in other concentration camps people of different nationalities, and also not a few Germans, suffered and were exterminated. We must, however, remember with regret and shame that it was precisely Germans who accomplished these crimes against Poles. Father Kolbe stands before us as a luminous sign summoning us to reconciliation, which is a superior task for both our nations. All declarations of witnesses testify that this person, naturally passionate and by no means permissive, a fervent Polish patriot up to his horrible death, radiated interior freedom and conciliatory love. Father Kolbe is a Martyr of reconciliation. That is exactly why he requests that we plead for forgiveness from our brother Poles for all the wrongs which they suffered from the Germans, and that they renounce all desires of reprisal. Political efforts for a lasting peace and order should find their source in a spirit of constructive reconciliation.

* * *

On June 7, 1979, John Paul II flew by helicopter from Wadowice to the infamous concentration camp of Oswiecim (Auschwitz). He visited cell 18 of block 11 in which Blessed Maximilian Kolbe (N. 16670) died on August 14, 1941. On the bare floor of the narrow cell the Holy Father laid a bouquet of white and red carnations, the colors of Poland, and a paschal candle brought from Rome. He knelt in silent prayer before the wall.

The Holy Father went next by helicopter to the other part of the Oswiecim Camp situated at Brzezinka (Birkenau), a distance of 2 km. Here the prisoners used to arrive by train. At an altar erected in the open space in the middle of the camp, the Pope concelebrated Mass with bishops and priests who had been interned in Nazi concentration camps.

During the Mass, attended by about a million people, John Paul II delivered which he invoked Maximilian Kolbe as a special patron for our times. (For complete text, see Appendix B)

"This is the victory that overcomes the world, our faith" (1 Jn. 5, 4).

These words from the letter of St. John come to my mind and enter my heart as I find myself in this place in which a special victory was won through faith; through the faith that gives rise to love of God and of one's neighbor, the unique love, the supreme love that is ready to "lay down one's life for one's friends" (Jn. 15, 13; cf. 10, 11). . .

On this site of a terrible slaughter that brought death to four million people of different nations, Father Maximilian voluntarily offered himself for death in the starvation bunker for a brother, and so won a spiritual victory like that of Christ himself. This brother still lives today in the land of Poland. . .

I have come then to this special shrine—the birthplace, I can say—of the patron of our difficult century, just as nine centuries ago Skalka was the place of the birth, under the sword, of St. Stanislaus, Patron of the Poles.

I have come and I kneel on this Golgotha of the modern world, on these tombs, largely nameless like the great tomb of the Unknown Soldier. I kneel before all the inscriptions that come one after another bearing the memory of the victims of Oswiecim in Polish, English, Bulgarian, Romany, Czech, Danish, French, Greek, Hebrew, Yiddish, Spanish, Flemish, Serbo, Croat, German, Nowegian, Russian, Romanian, Hungarian and Italian.

In particular I pause with you, dear participants in this encounter, before the inscription in Hebrew. This inscription awakens the memory of the people whose sons and daughters were intended for total extermination. This people draws its origin from Abraham, our father in faith (cf. Rom. 4, 12), as was expressed by Paul of Tarsus. The very people that received from God the commandment "You shall not kill," has itself experienced in a special measure what is meant by killing. It is not permissible for anyone to pass by this inscription with indifference.

Finally, the last inscription in Polish: Six million Poles lost their lives during the Second World War: a fifth of the nation. Yet another stage in the centuries-old fight of this nation, my nation, for its fundamental rights among the peoples of Europe. Yet another loud cry for the right to a place of its own on the map of Europe. Yet another painful reckoning with the conscience of mankind.

Oswiecim is such a reckoning. It is impossible merely to visit it. It is necessary on this occasion to think with fear of how far hatred can go, how far man's destruction of man can go, how far cruelty can go. . . .

Holy is God! Holy and strong! Holy and Immortal One! From plague, from famine, from fire and from war. . .and from war, deliver us, Lord. Amen.

The Minister General of the Order of Friars Minor Conventual, Fr. Vitale Bommarco, on Tuesday, March 2, informed Italian and foreign journalists in a press conference, that Pope John Paul II had fixed the date for the canonization of Bl. Maximilian Kolbe for October 10, of this year.

The following day Father Bommarco issued a letter to all Ministers Provincial, and all the General and Provincial Custodes of the Order. In it he noted that on January 19, 1982, the Holy Father had dispensed from the prescript of Can. 2138, paragraph 1, of the Code of Canon Law, in order to allow the canonization to take place. This prescript requires as a condition for canonization the certification of two miracles that have taken place through the intercession of a Blessed, after his Beatification. Father Bommarco went on to say:

> *We all devoutly believe that this canonization was granted above all as an extraordinary gift to the whole Church through the intercession of Mary, the Immaculate Virgin and Mother of God. . . Moreover, we acknowledge the gift that the Supreme Pontiff John Paul II has offered to the whole Church, since he has decreed that the formal veneration given to the other saints is to be given by her to Maximilian also; from it we hope that all the faithful, by the intercession of Blessed Maximilian, will be able to imitate the examples of his virtues, and especially Charity; and that the entire People of God in the whole world may rejoice in the gifts of justice, charity and peace.*

* * *

AUSCHWITZ, June 5, 1982: At the conclusion or their three-day meeting in Poland, delegates or the German and Polish bishops gathered and prayed in the death cell of Bl. Maximilian Kolbe at Oswiecim (Auschwitz). There they signed a petition requesting Pope John Paul II to canonize Blessed Kolbe as a *Martyr* when he inscribes him in the Register of Saints in Rome the following October 10th.

One year previously, a strong delegation or bishops from West Germany had attended the funeral of Poland's Primate Cardinal Stefan Wyszynski following his death May 28, 1981, while in 1971 the Polish episcopate with Cardinals Wyszynski and Woytila had visited their brother bishops in West Germany.

In the aforementioned June 1982 meeting, Polish Primate Archbishop Joseph Glemp addressed the following words to the West German delegation: "We know that you come to us with words of peace. We know very well the universal good will of the faithful of Germany who have helped and who continue to help the Polish people. All this touches the religious sector first of all, which has its base in our common brotherhood in Christ, and is in the spirit of our responsibilities for the Church in Europe. The Church in fact is the teacher of love for the world...I hope that the visit of the Bishops of the Federal Republic of Germany to Poland may strengthen the Church in Europe, and that the exchange of shared sentiments may encourage a more incisive, strong and faithful witness to Christ."

* * *

VATICAN CITY, October 10, 1982: At 9:30 am his Holiness Pope John Paul II entered St. Peter's Square in procession with twelve concelebrants and numerous other ministers to begin the Canonization Mass for Fr. Maximilian Maria Kolbe. All were wearing red—not white—vestments.

It was a beautiful day. To the north the sky was blue. Above the vast throng filling the square—about 250,000 persons—a soft, white gauze curtain of clouds had veiled the sun, softening its glare and cooling its heat.

Arriving at the altar on the sagrato, or raised open area in front of St. Peter's Basilica, the Pope greeted the applauding multitude from the four sides of the platform successively. He incensed the altar, then proceeded to the papal chair behind the altar atop another many-tiered platform, assisted by two Cardinal Deacons.

When the choir and the huge assembly finished chanting the *Kyrie*, Cardinal Pietro Palazzini, Prefect of the Sacred Congregation for the Canonization of the Saints approached the papal chair and stood before the Pope. In the name of the whole Church he formally petitioned the Holy Father to inscribe Maximilian Maria Kolbe in the Register of Saints, and then read a brief profile of the Blessed's life.

Everyone knelt to chant the Litany of the Saints, which concluded with a prayer by the Pope. Everyone then stood and waited in profound silence for the Holy Father's response to the Cardinal's petition. After a few moments the strong voice of Pope John Paul II rolled out over the vast throng of pilgrims and worshippers, of Roman citizens and tourists.

"For the honor of the Holy and Undivided Trinity,

"For the exaltation of the Catholic faith and growth of Christian life,

"With the authority of our Lord Jesus Christ, of the Holy Apostles Peter and Paul, and our own,

"After careful deliberation and frequent prayer for divine help,

"And on the advice of a great many of our brothers in the episcopate,

"We declare and define Blessed Maximilian Maria Kolbe to be a Saint;

"We inscribe his name in the Register of the Saints, and we establish that in the whole Church he be devoutly honored among the Holy Martyrs.

"In the Name of the Father, and of the Son, and of the Holy Spirit."

A powerful wave of applause greeted the pronouncement. It was what everyone had been waiting for. It was what the throng had assembled in Rome to hear. And yet it went far beyond what most had expected. The

Pope had proclaimed Kolbe to be not only a Saint, but a Martyr as well—and in a manner never before experienced in the history of the Church!

Father Maximilian had been beatified in 1971 by Pope Paul VI as a "Confessor" of the Faith—a man whose stupendous life and miracles prove that he had developed all the Christian virtues to a heroic degree. His beatification and his feast in the Church had been celebrated with white vestments—the liturgical color for Saints and Blesseds who had not shed their blood for Christ.

Now the Pope was telling the whole Church: Not only was Kolbe's whole life an extraordinary witness for Christ and the Gospel, but his death too was a special sign for the whole Church—hence the red vestments for the Canonization Mass.

In his canonization homily, the Pope explained what Kolbe's death—over and above his marvelous life—means for the Church. At Auschwitz, where more than four million persons had been murdered; in our age which continues to be stigmatized by wholesale slaughter of the innocent, Kolbe's voluntary death to save an innocent man condemned to death is a precious witness for every innocent person's right to life. It testifies that God alone has the right over innocent human life.

Moreover, it is in our century a shining sign of the death that Christ underwent on the cross to redeem us, a death having the value of supreme love. "By this we know love, that he laid down his life for us. And we ought to lay down our lives for the brethren" (Jo. 3, 16).

In Kolbe's human death, the Pope said, "there was the clear witness borne in Christ to the dignity of man, to the sanctity of his life, and to the saving power of death in which the power of love is made manifest."

The Pope said that Kolbe seemed to be actually present there in the canonization liturgy. Indeed, the Holy Father's whole demeanor during and after the Canonization Mass—the way in which he seemed to be deeply lost in contemplation—almost in ecstasy, almost unaware of what was going on around him-tended to reflect this.

The inspiration of Kolbe's entire life, the Holy Father said, was Mary the Immaculata. To her he entrusted his love for Christ and desire for martyrdom. In her Immaculate Conception he saw revealed the marvelous supernatural world of grace that God offers to man. Similarly, St. Maximilian saw "his cooperation with divine grace as a warfare under the banner of the Immaculate Conception"—a warfare involving his whole apostolate, the Knights of the Immaculata movement.

Kolbe's agony in the starvation bunker at Auschwitz, the Pope added, was a test that proved him worthy of God, a testing that fulfilled the words of Christ to his apostles that they "should go and bear fruit and that their fruit should abide" (Jn. 15, 16. In other words, it was the final necessary "trimming back" of a fruitful branch on the Vine which is Christ, so that the branch could go on and bear fruit endlessly. Cf. ibid., v. 2). Indeed, the fruit of Maximilian Kolbe's tragic death endures now in the Church and the world, the Holy Father stated.

It was to bring to everyone's attention the full eloquence and definitive meaning of the sign of holiness given us by God in St. Maximilian, the Pope concluded, that he decreed that "Maximilian Maria Kolbe—who after his Beatification was venerated as a Confessor—shall henceforward be venerated also as a Martyr!"

Thus did the apostolic authority of two Popes fulfill in a marvelous, totally unexpected way the promise our Lady had made to young Raymond Kolbe in Poland some 78 years earlier: a white crown for purity, and a red crown for martyrdom. By beatifying Maximilian as a Confessor, the Church certified his white crown of heroic virtue and fruitful apostolate. By canonizing him as a Martyr, she now certifies the red crown given for his singular fulfillment of the words of Christ on laying down one's life for one's friend. And she has declared him to be a special sign in our times proclaiming God's love and the innocent person's right to life.

* * *

In Fr. Maximilian Kolbe and Kommandant Rudolph Hoess at Auschwitz, the clash of two warring worlds at first seemed to bring defeat to the little Catholic priest and the armies of God to which he belonged. In reality it was he and his beloved "Immaculata" who, with Christ, had conquered where it counts most: in the minds and hearts of men, women and youth everywhere. Their victory continues to deepen and spread, as Saint Maximilian Kolbe said it would.

—Editor

Appendix A
Hoess' Farewell Letters

Hoess' Farewell Letter To His Wife

April 11, 1947

My Beloved and good Mutz,

The path of my life is now approaching its end. I am destined to a truly sad fate. How happy are those colleagues of mine who died honorable deaths as soldiers.

I am awaiting my doom peacefully and calmly.

It was quite clear to me from the very outset, that after this world to which I had sold my body and soul had been smashed and destroyed, I would have to perish together with it. Unintentionally I had become one of the large wheels of the gigantic German destructive machines, and I filled one of the most exposed positions. As commandant of the extermination camp in Oswiecim, I was wholly and entirely responsible for everything that took place there, irrespective of whether I knew about it or not. I first found out about the majority of the cruelties and monstrosities that occurred there during the investigation and the hearings.

It is impossible to describe how my subordinates cheated me, how they vitiated my orders, yet everything that happened there was carried into effect supposedly on my command. I certainly hope that the guilty ones will not escape justice.

How tragic it is; I am naturally gentle and mild and always helpful, and yet I became the greatest genocide, who in cold blood and with full knowledge of the consequences, carried out every command of extermination.

The long iron training I had in the SS, which was designed to transform every SS man into a passive instrument for executing all the plans of the Reichsfuehrer, made me an automation that blindly obeyed every order.

My fanatical love for my Fatherland as well as my exaggerated sense of duty, were a good foundation for such training.

It is difficult for a person nearing his end to confess that he has chosen an erroneous path in life and through it brought that end upon himself. But what help will all kinds of reflections be, whether false or reasonable? According to my convictions, all our ways of life are assigned from above through destiny by the Wise Providence, and they are immutable.

This separation from you all is painful, bitter and hard for me; from you, my Beloved and best Mutz and from you, my good and unfortunate loved ones, who are now in want and misery. For you, my poor unfortunate wife, the hardest lot has been destined in our sad fate. Besides the boundless pain of our separation, my deep concern is for your future and the care of our children. Nevertheless, my Beloved, be valiant and do not lose heart.

Time heals the deepest wounds which at first seem unendurable. Millions of families were shattered by this fatal war.

Yet life must go on. The children are growing up. I sincerely hope, my Beloved and best Mutz, that strength and health be granted you so that you will be able to bring up the children until they will be capable of taking care of themselves.

My ineffective life, my Dearest, places upon you the holy duty of bringing up our children in the true spirit of humanity flowing from the depth of your heart. All our darling children are naturally good. Try in all possible ways to develop their good qualities, a compassionate heart and unselfish sensitivity to human misfortunes.

It was here in the Polish prisons that I have learned what humanity is. As a Kommandant of Oswiecim I caused the Polish nation much pain and sorrow and did so much harm, even though it was not done personally, nor from my own initiative; yet they have shown me humane forbearance which deeply abashes me. This has come not only from the higher officers but also from the most common guards. Many of them were prisoners of Oswiecim and other camps. Now, in the last days of my life, I am experiencing humane treatment which I never expected. In spite of everything that happened, yet, they always see a human being in me.

My Darling, good Mutz, please do not become too bitter under the heavy blows of your lot, but keep your good heart always. Do not allow yourself to be led astray by unfavorable circumstances, poverty and misery which you will face in your life, and do not lose faith in people.

Endeavor as much as possible to get away from your present environment. Change your name; adopt your maiden name again. Then, most certainly, you will not have any difficulty. My name is set on a pillory before the entire world and you, my poor loved ones, would continually face new and unnecessary hardships in connection with my name especially the children in their future careers. Klaus most certainly could have had the opportunity of learning his trade if his name was not Hoess. It will be best for my name to disappear with me.

I was permitted to mail my wedding ring in this letter. I recall the springtime of our lives with pain and joy, when we placed the wedding bands on each other's finger. At that time we had no misgivings that our mutual life would end this way. We met eighteen years ago about this time. Although the path before us was difficult, yet we began our life together courageously and joyfully. Not many "sunny days" did we share; on the contrary, there were many difficulties, many, many misfortunes and worries. Nevertheless we tread that path step by step. How happy we were with our children whom you brought into this world so calmly and joyfully! In our children we saw our fulfillment in life. Our constant concern was to bring them up as best we could to be good and useful citizens.

Now, during my arrest, I have reminisced many times about our mutual closeness and the happenings and incidents of our lives. Those fortunate and happy hours we spent together in spite of much misery, sickness, worries and grief!

My Beloved good companion, you have always shared all joys and sorrows with me most heartily and faithfully. I thank you from the bottom of my heart for everything good and beautiful you bestowed upon me and for your incessant love and concern for me. Forgive me, Dearest, if I have ever offended you and caused you grief. How deeply and painfully I now regret every hour which I failed to spend with you, my Beloved and best Mutz, and with the children, for I believed that my service did not permit me to do otherwise, and the other duties I considered more important.

How happy I felt that I could read your loving words during the days of my trial. Your love and concern for me and also the sweet chatter of our darling children afforded me such great pleasure that it renewed my courage and gave me strength to persevere.

To you, my Beloved, I am especially grateful for that last letter which you wrote Sunday morning. It was indeed your intuition, my Poor One, that they would be your last words to reach me. How openly and clearly you expressed yourself about everything. How much bitter sorrow and deep pain were included between the lines! I know well how intimately our lives were bound together. Now, the necessity of parting is very hard!

I have written to you, my Beloved good Mutz, at Christmas, on January 26 and March 3 and 16, and I hope you received my letters. How little one can say in a letter in these circumstances. How much from that which can not be written must remain unsaid! Nevertheless, we must be reconciled with it.

I am very grateful that I heard at least a little about you, and that I had the opportunity, my Dearest, to express to you what was in my heart.

Throughout my whole life I was closed up as in a shell and only with great reluctance did I allow anyone to probe into the depths of my heart, especially if it was something affecting my feelings. I always managed to work out a way within myself to settle my uneasiness. How frequently, my Dearest, you felt sorry for me, and it was painful for you as the closest person to me, that you could do so little for my interior life.

For many years I had been concealing my dejection and low spirits as well as doubt as to the righteousness of my actions and the necessity of performing the severe commands given me. I could not and I was not allowed to mention that to anyone. For the first time now, you will understand, my Beloved and good Mutz, the reason why I was feeling so depressed and more and more unapproachable. You, my best Mutz, and you all, my loved ones, had to suffer on account of that. You could not find any explanation for my dissatisfaction, my distraction and my frequent rough disposition. Nevertheless, that is how it was and I painfully regret it.

During my long isolated sojourn in prison, I have had ample time and peace to reflect thoroughly on my whole life. I have examined thoroughly the whole course of my actions.

In the light of my present convictions, I see today very clearly what for me is very hard and bitter, that the whole ideology and the whole world in which I believed so firmly, were resting upon completely false foundations and certainly had to fall into ruins some day.

My life in the service of this ideology was also absolutely false, although I acted in good faith, believing in the legitimacy of this idea. It is therefore quite logical that it awakened in me many doubts.

Likewise, did not my fall from faith in God depend wholly on my false foundations? This was very difficult to overcome. Nevertheless, I have recovered my faith in God. I cannot write any more about these things, my Beloved, for it would lead me too far. If you, my loved one, my good Mutz, were to find in the Christian faith, strength and consolation in your poverty, follow the dictates of your heart.

Do not allow yourself to be led into any error. In any case, you should not follow my example. In this respect you should make your own decision. After all, the children under the influence of school will follow a different way of life than I did, and which up to this time we both followed. When Klaus becomes mature, he may later on decide for himself in choosing his path. And so from our world only a heap of debris has remained from which the survivors must painstakingly rebuild a new and a better world.

My time is passing. Now, I must bid you my final farewell, my beloved ones, for to me you are something very precious in this world. How hard and painful this parting is for me! Once again, I thank you most heartily, my most loving and best Mutz, for all your love and concern, for everything with which you enriched my life. In our dearest and good children I shall remain forever by you and in this manner I will be by you permanently, my poor unfortunate wife!

I am going away with an unshakable hope that after all your worries and heartaches, just as after a dark and cloudy day a sunshiny tomorrow appears, so too you will be given a place on the bright side of life, and you will find modest possibilities of existence. My Beloved, good Mutz, our loving and good children will create for you a quiet, satisfying and happy life. All my deepest best wishes will accompany you all, my loved ones, in your future way of life.

All the dear, good people who are with you in your need and who are helping you, I thank most sincerely and give them my kindest regards. My last deep respects for Fritz and all my dear old friends.

For the last time, with a deep heartache, I give you my very best heartfelt wishes, my loved ones, to all of you, my dearest good children, my Annemausl, my Burling, my Puppi, my Kindi and my Klaus, and you my dearest and best Mutz, my poor unfortunate wife. Keep me in your memory with love.

To my last breath I am with you, all my loved ones!

Your Daddy

Hoess' Farewell Letter To His Children

April 11, 1947

My Dearest good children!

Your daddy must leave you. Only your dear good Mamma will be left for you. May she be with you for very many, many years. You still do not understand what your good Mamma means to you; what a precious treasure she is for you. A mother's love and concern is most beautiful, most precious of all. At one time I, myself, realized that, when it was too late, and I regretted it through my whole life.

Therefore, to you my dear good children, I am sending my last entreaty, beseeching you never to forget your dearest and good mother! With what great dedication, love and tender care she surrounded you always! Her life was dedicated to you only. How many beautiful moments she gave up deliberately for you. How she feared for your life whenever you were ill; how she suffered and how indefatigably she watched over you! She was never at ease if she did not have you near her. Now, for you only, she must bear the whole bitter sorrow and misery. Never forget that in your life!

Help her all you can to bear this painful lot. Be loving and good to her. Help her as much as I your still weak strength will permit you! In this way you will repay her at least partially for the love she showered upon you day and night.

Klaus, my dear good boy! You are the eldest. You are now going into the world. You must pave the way of life for yourself and therefore endeavor to plan it to the best of your ability. You have a good endowment, take advantage of it.

Always preserve your good heart. Be a man who above all will conduct himself with deep human feeling. Learn to think for yourself and have your own outlook on life. Do not accept everything that you hear without criticism as an irrefutable truth. Learn from life. The greatest mistake in my life was that whatever came from "higher authority" I trusted blindly. I did not dare have the least doubts as to the veracity of the given orders.

Go through life with an open mind. Don't be one-sided; reflect on the pros and cons of all matters. In all that you undertake, direct yourself not only with your understanding, but particularly pay attention to the voice of your heart. Many things for you, my boy, will still not be completely understood. But, remember always my last admonitions. I wish you, my dear

Klaus, much luck in your life. Be a gallant and righteous man who has his heart in the right place.

Kindi and Puppi, my affectionate big girls! You are still too young to understand the whole seriousness of our difficult situation. Just you, my dear girls, have a particular duty in every case to become the most loving and devoted daughters of your poor unfortunate Mamma. Give her your childlike whole-hearted love by which you will show how much you love her and how much you want to help her in her need. I can only beg you fervently, my dear good girls, to obey your dear good mother always. Through her fully dedicated love and concern for you, she will show you the right way and will give you the knowledge you will need in your life to become brave and noble women. In spite of the fact that your characters differ completely, yet both of you, and you my dear little housewife, have soft and sensitive hearts. Keep them so for your later life, for that is most important. You will, however, understand this later, and recall my last words to you.

Burling, my darling little boy! Keep your dear, sweet, happy childlike disposition. Hard life will pluck you from your youthful dream much too soon, my loving boy. I was glad to hear from your dear Mamma that you are making such marvelous progress in your studies. Your dear Daddy cannot tell you anymore now.

Poor boy, you will now have only your dear good Mamma who will care for you. Obey her from your heart; be courteous and continue to remain "your Daddy's dear Burling."

My dear little Annemausl! How little have I experienced your existence. Your loving and good Mamma has you, my little mousey, and let her give you a big hug from me and she will tell you about your dear Daddy, how much he loved you!

Oh, I hope that you will be a little ray of sunshine to your Mamma for a long, long time, and that you continue to give her much joy. Oh, that your loving sunny disposition would help your poor dearest Mamma to endure all her sad hours.

Once again, I beg you from my heart, my dearest good children, take my last words to your hearts. Think of them always!

Keep me in your love,

Your Daddy

Appendix B
The Beatification Of Maximilian Kolbe: Texts Of Some Significant Homilies

Homily of Pope Paul VI at the Beatification of Fr. Maximilian Kolbe October 17, 1971

Maximilian Kolbe—Blessed! What does this mean? It means that the Church recognizes in him an exceptional figure, a man in whom God's grace and the soul have so interacted as to produce a stupendous life. Anyone who observes it closely discovers this symbiosis of a dual operating principle, the divine and the human. One is mysterious, the other can be experienced; one is transcendent but interior, the other natural but complex, and expanded to the point of reaching that extraordinary image of moral and spiritual greatness that we call holiness; that is, perfection reached on the religious parameter, which as we know, soars towards the infinite heights of the Absolute. 'Blessed,' therefore, means worthy of that veneration permitted by the Church in certain places and among certain groups, a veneration that implies admiration of the one who is their object because of some unusual and magnificent reflection of the Sanctifying Spirit in him. It means 'saved and glorious.' It means 'citizen of heaven' with all the peculiar signs of a citizen of earth; it means 'brother and friend' whom we know is still ours, more so than ever, in fact, because he is identified as an active member of the Communion of Saints, which is the Mystical Body of Christ, the Church, living both in time and in eternity. It means, therefore, 'advocate and protector' in the kingdom of love, together with Christ "who is always able to save those who approach God through him, since he forever lives to make intercession for them (Heb. 7, 25; cf. Rom. 8, 34). Finally, it means 'exemplary specimen'—a type of man to whom we can conform our way of life, since he, the Blessed, is recognized as having the apostle Paul's privilege of being able to say to the Christian people: "I beg you the Christian people: "I beg you then, be imitators of me" (I Cor. 4, 16).

This is what we can think of Maximilian Kolbe, the new Blessed, from today onwards. But who is Maximilian Kolbe? We know him well! He is so close to our generation and so imbued with the actual life and experiences of our times that everything is known about him. Rarely does a beatification process deal with such a wealth of documents. Just for the sake of our modern passion for historical truth, we include almost as an epigraph, the biographical sketch of Father Kolbe written by one of the most assiduous of the scholars devoted to him.

Fr. Maximilian Kolbe was born in Zdunska Wola near Lodz on January 8, 1894. In 1907 he entered the Seminary of the Franciscan Conventuals. He was sent to Rome to continue his ecclesiastical studies at the Pontifical Gregorian University and at the Seraphicum of his Order. When still a student, he founded a movement, the *Militia Immaculatae*. Ordained a priest on April 28, 1918, he returned to Poland and began his Marian apostolate, particularly with the monthly publication *Rycerz Niepokalanej* (*The Knight of the Immaculata*), which reached a press run of one million copies in 1938. In 1927 he founded Niepokalanow (City of the Immaculata), a center of religious life and of various forms of apostolate. In 1930 he left for Japan where he founded another similar institution. Returning to Poland permanently, he dedicated himself wholly to his work with various religious publications. The Second World War found him at the head of the most imposing publishing complex in Poland. On September 19, 1939 he was arrested by the Gestapo, who deported him to Lamsdorf, Germany, then temporarily to the concentration camp at Amtitz. Released on December 8, 1939, he returned to Niepokalanow, resuming his interrupted activity. Arrested again in 1941, he was put into Pawiak Prison in Warsaw, and then deported to the concentration camp at Oswiecim (Auschwitz). Having offered his life for an unknown man condemned to death, as a reprisal for the escape of a prisoner from their block, he was sentenced to a starvation bunker. He prepared his co-victims for death, and on August 14, 1941, on the eve of the Feast of the Assumption, he was finished off with an injection of phenol. His body was cremated (Fr. Ernesto Piacentini, OFM Conv.).

But in a ceremony such as this, the biographical data, in a way, dissolve in the dazzling splendor of the principle lines of the many faceted figure of the new Blessed. Let us fix our gaze for a moment on these lines which characterize him and entrust him to our memories.

Maximilian Kolbe was an apostle of the formal religious veneration of the Blessed Virgin, seen in her first, original privileged splendor, as she defined herself at Lourdes: the Immaculate Conception. It is impossible to separate the name, the activity and the mission of Blessed Kolbe from that of Mary Immaculate. It was he who instituted the *Militia Mariae Immaculatae* here in Rome, even before he was ordained a priest, on October 16, 1917. We can commemorate its anniversary today.

It is well known how the humble and meek Franciscan with incredible audacity and extraordinary organizational genius developed the initiative and spread devotion to the Mother of Christ, contemplated as "clothed with the sun" (cf. Rev. 12, 1). This devotion was the focal point of his spirituality, his apostolate and his theology.

Let no hesitation restrain our admiration and commitment to all that our new Blessed has left us as a heritage and an example, as if we too were distrustful of such an exaltation of Mary in view of two other theological movements, the Christological and ecclesiological, which seem to compete today with the Mariological. On the contrary, there is no competition, for in Father Kolbe's Mariology, Christ holds not only the first place but the only necessary and sufficient place in the economy of salvation. His love of the Church and its salvational mission was never forgotten either in his doctrinal outlook or in his apostolic aim. On the contrary, it is precisely from our Lady's complementary, subordinate role in regard to Christ's universal, saving design for man that she derives all of her prerogatives and greatness.

How well we know it! And Kolbe, in accord with the whole of Catholic doctrine, the whole liturgy and the entire theology of the interior life, sees Mary included in God's plan of salvation as the "term fixed by eternal counsel," as the woman filled with grace, as the Seat of Wisdom, as the woman destined from eternity to be the Mother of Christ, as the Queen of the Messianic Kingdom, and at the same time as the Handmaid of the Lord, chosen to participate in the Redemptive Act as Mother of the God-Man, our Savior. "Mary is the one through whose intercession men reach Jesus and the one through whom Jesus reaches men" (L. Bouver: Le trone de la Sagesse; p. 69).

Therefore our Blessed is not to be reproved, nor the Church with him, because of their enthusiasm for the formal religious veneration of the Mother of God. This veneration with its rites and practices will never fully achieve the level it merits, nor the benefits it can bring precisely because of the mystery that unites her to Christ, and which finds fascinating documentation in the New Testament. The result will never be a "Mariolatry," just as the sun will never be darkened by the moon; nor will the mission of salvation specifically entrusted to the ministry of the Church ever be distorted if the latter honors in Mary an exceptional Daughter and a Spiritual Mother. The characteristic aspect, if you like, and the original quality of Blessed Kolbe's devotion, of his "hyperdulia" to Mary, is the importance he attributes to it with regard to the present needs of the Church, the efficacy of her prophecy about the glory of the Lord and the vindication of the humble, the power of her intercession, the splendor of her exemplariness, the presence of her maternal charity. The Council confirmed us in these certainties, and now from heaven Father Kolbe is teaching us and helping us to meditate upon them and live them. This Marian profile of our new Blessed places him among the great saints and seers who have understood, venerated and sung the mystery of Mary.

Next let us consider the tragic and sublime conclusion of Maximilian Kolbe's innocent and apostolic life. It is mainly to this that we owe the glorification of the meek humble, hard-working religious, exemplary follower of St. Francis and Knight in love with Mary Immaculate that the Church celebrates today. The circumstances of his departure from this life are so horrible and harrowing that we would prefer not to speak of them, and never to contemplate them again, in order not to see the depths of inhuman degradation to which the abuse of power can lead, an abuse which seeks to make a pedestal of grandeur and glory from the impassive cruelty it inflicts upon helpless beings that it has degraded to the rank of slaves and doomed to extermination. There were millions of these victims sacrificed to the pride of force and the madness of racism. Nevertheless it is necessary to scan this dark picture again in order to pick out, here and there, the gleams of surviving humanity. Alas, history cannot forget these frightful and tragic pages. And so it cannot but fix its horrified gaze on the luminous points that reveal, but at the same time overcome, their inconceivable darkness.

One of these points, perhaps the one glowing most brightly, is the calm, drained figure of Maximilian Kolbe. A serene hero, always pious and sustained by a paradoxical, yet reasonable confidence. His name will remain among the great; it will reveal what reserves of moral values lay among those unhappy masses, petrified by horror and despair. Over this immense vestibule of death hovers a divine and imperishable word of life, that of Jesus revealing the secret of innocent suffering: to be the expiation, the victim, the burnt sacrifice and, above all, to be love for others. "There is no greater love than this; to lay down one's life for one's friends" (Jn. 15:13). Jesus was speaking of himself in the imminence of his sacrifice for the salvation of men. Men are all friends of Jesus, if they at least listen to his words. Father Kolbe fulfilled his maxim of redeeming love in the fatal concentration camp in Oswiecim. And this by a double title.

Who among us does not recall the incomparable episode? "I am a Catholic priest," he said, offering his own life unto death—and what a death!—To save the life of an unknown companion sentenced to the starvation bunker in blind reprisal. What a magnificent moment! His offer was accepted. It came from a heart trained to give itself. It was as natural and spontaneous as if it were a logical consequence of his priesthood. Is not a priest a "second Christ?" Was not Christ the Priest, the redeeming victim of mankind? What a glory it is for us priests, and what a lesson, to find in Blessed Maximilian such a splendid exemplification of our consecration and of our mission! What a warning he addresses to us in this hour of uncertainty, when at times human nature would like to assert its rights to the detriment of our supernatural vocation to follow Christ through the total gift of ourselves to him! What a consolation it must be for that close-knit, faithful legion, so beloved and noble, of good priests and religious who, filled with the legitimate and praiseworthy desire to transcend personal mediocrity and social frustration, understand their mission just as he did. "I am a Catholic priest, and for this reason I offer my life to save those of others." Such would seem to be the commission which the new Blessed leaves especially to us, ministers of God's Church, and in some way to all in the Church who accept the Spirit.

And to this priestly title we can add another, one which shows that Blessed Maximilian's sacrifice was motivated by a friendship: he was a Pole. As a Pole he was condemned to that unhappy concentration camp, and as a Pole he was willing to give up his life for that of a fellow countryman, Francis Gajowniczeck. How many thoughts come to our minds at the memory of this human, social and ethnical aspect of the voluntary death of Maximilian Kolbe, a son of noble Catholic Poland! This nation's historic destiny of suffering seems to document, in this typical and heroic case, the centuries-old vocation of the Polish people to find in its shared passion a single, united conscience; a Knightly mission for freedom achieved in the pride of the spontaneous sacrifices of its sons and daughters, and their readiness to give themselves for one another and to overcome their vivacity in invincible concord; an indelible Catholic character which makes of it a living and suffering member of the universal Church; a firm conviction that the secret of its renascent prosperity lies in the miraculous but tear-stained protection of the Blessed Virgin. These are the iridescent rays of light issuing from the new Polish martyr: they show us the true visage of his country and lead us to ask Blessed Maximilian, its emblematic hero, for firmness in faith, ardor in charity, prosperity and peace for all his people. The Church and the whole world will rejoice over it together! Amen.

Homily of Pope John Paul II at Auschwitz June 7, 1979

1. "This is the victory that overcomes the world, our faith" (1 Jn 5, 4).

These words from the letter of St. John come to my mind and enter my heart as I find myself in this place in which a special victory was won through faith; through the faith that gives rise to love of God and of one's neighbor, the unique love, the supreme love that is ready to "lay down one's life for one's friends" (Jn 15, 13; cf. 10, 11): A victory therefore, through love enlivened by faith to the extreme point of the final definitive witness.

This victory through faith and love was won in this place by a man whose first name is Maximilian Maria, surname: Kolbe. His profession, as registered in the books of the concentration camp: Catholic priest. Vocation: a son of St. Francis. Birth: a son of simple, hardworking devout parents, who were weavers near Lodz. By God's grace and the Church's judgment: Blessed.

The victory through faith and love was won by him in this place, which was built for the negation of faith-faith in God and faith in man and to trample radically not only on love, but on all signs of human dignity, of humanity. A place built on hatred and on contempt for man in the name of a crazed ideology. A place built on cruelty. On the entrance gate which still exists, is placed the inscription "Arbeit macht frei (Work makes free, etc.)," which has a sardonic sound, since its meaning was radically contradicted by what took place within.

On this site of a terrible slaughter that brought death to four million people of different nations, Father Maximilian voluntarily offered himself for death in the starvation bunker for a brother, and so won a spiritual victory like that of Christ himself. This brother still lives today in the land of Poland.

But was Father Maximilian Kolbe the only one? Certainly he won a victory that was immediately felt by his companions in captivity and is still felt today by the Church and the world. However, there is no doubt that many other similar victories were won. I am thinking, for example, of the death in a gas chamber of the concentration camp of the Carmelite, Sister Teresa Benedicta of the Cross, whose name in the world was Edith Stein. She was an illustrious pupil of Husserl. She became one of the glories of contemporary German philosophy, and was a descendant of a Jewish family living in Wroclaw.

Where the dignity of man was so horribly trampled on, victory was won through faith and love.

Can it still be a surprise to anyone that the Pope born and brought up in this land, the Pope who came to the See of St. Peter from the diocese in whose territory Auschwitz is situated, should have begun his first Encyclical with the words "Redemptor Hominis," and should have dedicated it as a whole to the cause of man, to the threats to him, and finally to his inalienable rights that can so easily be trampled on and annihilated by his fellowmen? Is it enough to put man in a different uniform, and arm him with the apparatus of violence? Is it enough to impose on him an ideology in which human rights are subjected to the demands of the system, completely subjected to them, so as in practice not to exist at all?

2. I am here today as a pilgrim. It is well known that I have been here many times. So many times! And many times I have gone down to Maximilian Kolbe's death cell, stopped in front of the execution wall and passed among the ruins of the cremation furnaces of Brzezinka. It was impossible for me not to come here as Pope.

I have come then to this special shrine, the birthplace, I can say, of the patron of our difficult century, just as nine centuries ago Skalka was the place of the birth under the sword, of St. Stanislaus, Patron of the Poles.

I have come to pray with all of you who have come here today and with the whole of Poland and the whole of Europe. Christ wishes that I who have become the successor of Peter should give witness before the world to what constitutes the greatness and the misery of contemporary man, to what is his defeat and his victory.

I have come and I kneel on this Golgotha of the modern world, on these tombs, largely nameless like the great tomb of the Unknown Soldier. I kneel before all the inscriptions that come one after another bearing the memory of the victims of Auschwitz in Polish, English, Bulgarian, Romany, Czech, Danish, French, Greek, Hebrew, Yiddish, Spanish, Flemish, Serbo, Croat, German, Norwegian, Russian, Romanian, Hungarian and Italian.

In particular I pause with you, dear participants in this encounter, before the inscription in Hebrew. This inscription awakens the memory of the people whose sons and daughters were intended for total extermination. This people draws its origin from Abraham, our father in faith (cf. Rom 4, 12) as was expressed by Paul of Tarsus. The very people that received from God the commandment "You shall not kill," has itself experienced in a special measure what is meant by killing. It is not permissible for anyone to pass by this inscription with indifference.

Finally, the last inscription in Polish: Six million Poles lost their lives during the Second World War; a fifth of the nation. Yet another stage in the centuries-old fight of this nation, my nation, for its fundamental rights among the peoples of Europe. Yet another painful reckoning with the conscience of mankind.

3. Auschwitz is such a reckoning. It is impossible merely to visit it. It is necessary on this occasion to think with fear of how far hatred can go.

Auschwitz is a testimony of war. War brings with it a disproportionate growth of hatred, destruction and cruelty. It cannot be denied that it also manifests new capabilities of human courage, heroism and patriotism, but the fact remains that it is the reckoning of the losses that prevails.

That reckoning prevails more and more, since each day sees an increase in the destructive capacity of the weapons invented by modern technology. Not only those who directly bring about wars are responsible for them, but also those who fail to do all they can to prevent them. Therefore I would like to repeat in this place the words that Paul VI pronounced before the United Nations Organization:

"It is enough to remember that the blood of millions of men, numberless, and the unprecedented sufferings, useless slaughter and frightful ruin, are the sanction of the covenant which unites you in a solemn pledge by which man must change the future history of the world. No more war, war never again. It is peace, peace which must guide the destinies of peoples and of all mankind" (AAS 57, 1965, p. 881).

If however Auschwitz's great call and the cry of man tortured here is to bear fruit for Europe and I for the world also, the Declaration of Human Rights must have all its just consequences drawn from it, as John XXIII urged in the Encyclical "Pacem in Terris."

For the Declaration is a "solemn recognition of the personal dignity of every human being; an assertion of everyone's right to be free to seek out the truth, to follow moral principles, discharge the duties imposed by justice, and lead a fully human life. It also recognized other rights connected with these" (John XXIII, "Pacem in Terris", IV—AAS 55, 1963, pp. 295-296). There must be a return to the wisdom of the old teacher Pawel Wlodkowic, Rector of the Jagellonian University at Krakow, and the rights of nations must be ensured: their right to existence, to freedom, to independence, to their own culture, and to honorable development. Wlodkowic wrote: "Where power is more at work than love, people seek their own interests and not those of Jesus Christ, and accordingly they easily depart from the rule of God's law. . .All kinds of law are against those who threaten people wishing to live in peace; against them is the civil law. . .the canon law. . .the natural law, expressed in the principle 'Do unto others what you would have done to you.' Against them is the divine law, in that. . .the commandment 'You shall not steal' forbids all robbery, and the commandment 'You shall not kill' forbids all violence" (Pawel Wlodkowic, Saevientibus [1415], Tract II, Solutio quaest. 4a; cf. L. Ehrlich, Pisma wybrane Pawla Wlodkowica. Warszawa 1968, t. 1, s. 61; 58-59).

Never one at the other's expense, at the cost of the enslavement of the other, at the cost of conquest, outrage, exploitation and death.

He who is speaking these words is the successor of John XXIII and Paul VI. But he is also the son of a nation that in its history has suffered many afflictions from others. He says this, not to accuse but to remind. He is speaking in the name of all the nations whose rights are being violated and forgotten. He is saying it because he is urged to do so by the truth and by solicitude for man.

4. Holy is God! Holy and strong! Holy and Immortal One! From plague, from famine, from fire and from war. . .and from war, deliver us Lord. Amen.

Appendix C
Pope John Paul II: The Meaning of Maximilian Kolbe's Heroic Death and Canonization

Homily of Pope John Paul II at the Canonization of Fr. Maximilian Kolbe October 10, 1982

"Greater love has no man than this, that a man lay down his life for his friends" (John 15:13).

From today on, the Church desires to address as "Saint" a man who was granted the grace of carrying out these words of the Redeemer in an absolutely literal manner.

For towards the end of July, 1941, when the camp commander ordered the prisoners destined to die of starvation to fall in line, this man—Maximilian Maria Kolbe—spontaneously came forward and declared himself ready to go to death in the place of one of them. This readiness was accepted and, after more than two weeks of torment caused by starvation, Father Maximilian's life was ended with a lethal injection on August 14, 1941.

All this happened in the concentration camp at Auschwitz where during the last war some four million people were put to death, including the Servant of God, Edith Stein (the Carmelite Sister Teresa Benedicta of the Cross), whose cause for beatification is in progress at the competent Congregation. Disobedience to God—the Creator of life who said, "Thou shalt not kill"—caused in that place the immense holocaust of so many innocent persons. And so at the same time, our age has thus been horribly stigmatized by the slaughter of the innocent.

Father Maximilian Kolbe, himself a prisoner of the concentration camp, defended in that place of death an innocent man's right to life. Father Kolbe defended his right to life, declaring that he was ready to go to death in the man's place, because he was the father of a family and his life was necessary for his dear ones. Father Maximilian Maria Kolbe thus reaffirmed the Creator's exclusive right over innocent human life. He bore witness to Christ and to love. For the Apostle John writes: *"By this we know love, that he laid down his life for us. And we ought to lay down our lives for the brethren"* (1 John 3:16).

The Church has venerated Father Maximilian as "Blessed" since 1971. By laying down his life for a brother, he made himself like Christ.

Gathered today before the Basilica of St. Peter in Rome, we wish to express the special value which Father Maximilian Kolbe's death by martyrdom has in the eyes of God.

"Precious in the sight of the Lord is the death of his saints." These are the words we have repeated in today's responsorial psalm. It is truly precious and inestimable! Through the death which Christ underwent on the Cross, the redemption of the world was achieved, for this death has the value of supreme love. Through the death of Father Maximilian Kolbe, a shining sign of this love was renewed in our century which is so seriously and in so many ways threatened by sin and death.

In this canonization liturgy there seems to appear before us that "martyr of love" of Oswiecim (as Paul VI called him), saying: "O Lord, I am thy servant. I am thy servant, the son of thy handmaid. Thou has loosed my bonds" (Psalm 115 (116): 16).

And as though gathering together in one sacrifice the whole of his life, he-a priest and a spiritual son of saint Francis-seems to say: "What shall I render to the Lord for his bounty to me? *I will lift up the cup of salvation and call on the name of the Lord"* (Psalms 115 (116):12).

These are words of gratitude. Death undergone out of love—in the place of one's brother—is an heroic act of man. It is an act through which, together with the one already beatified, we glorify God. For from God comes the grace of such heroism, of this martyrdom.

Therefore let us today glorify God's great work in man. Before all of us gathered here, Father Maximilian Kolbe lifts up his "cup of salvation." In it is contained *the sacrifice* of *his whole life,* sealed with the martyr's death "for a brother."

Maximilian prepared for this definitive sacrifice by following Christ from the first years of his life in Poland. From these years comes the mysterious vision of two crowns—one white and one red. From these our saint does not choose. He accepts them both. From the years of his youth, in fact, Maximilian was filled with the great love of Christ and the desire for martyrdom.

This love and this desire accompanied him along the path of his Franciscan and priestly vocation, for which he prepared himself both in Poland and in Rome. This love and this desire followed him through all the places of his priestly and Franciscan service in Poland and in his missionary service in Japan.

Immaculate Virgin Inspired His Life

The inspiration of his whole life was the *Immaculata*. To her he entrusted his love for Christ and his desire for martyrdom. In the mystery of the Immaculate Conception there revealed itself before the eyes of his soul that marvelous and supernatural world of God's grace offered to man.

The faith and works of the whole life of Father Maximilian show that he thought of his cooperation with divine grace as a warfare under the banner of the Immaculate Conception. This Marian characteristic is particularly expressive in the life and holiness of Father Kolbe. His whole apostolate, both in his homeland and on the missions, was similarly marked with this sign. In Poland and in Japan the centers of this apostolate were the special cities of the Immaculata—Niepokalanow in Poland and Mugenzai no Sono in Japan.

God Found Him Worthy of Himself

What happened in the starvation bunker in the concentration camp at Oswiecim (Auschwitz) on August 14, 1941?

The reply is given in today's liturgy. *"God tested"* Maximilian Maria *"and found him worthy of himself"* (Wisdom 3:5). God tested him "like gold in the furnace and like a sacrificial burnt offering he accepted him" (Wisdom 3:6).

Even if "in the sight of men he was punished," yet "his hope is full of immortality." For "the souls of the righteous are in the hands of God and no torment will ever touch them." And when humanly speaking-torment and death came to them, when "in the eyes of men they seemed to have died...", when "their departure from us was thought to be an affliction...", "they are in peace." They experience life and glory "in the hands of God" (Wisdom 3: 1-4).

This life is the fruit of death like Christ's death. Glory is the sharing of his resurrection.

So what happened in the starvation bunker, on August 14, 1941?

There were fulfilled the words spoken by Christ to the Apostles that they "should go and bear fruit and that their fruit should abide" (John 15:16).

In a marvelous way the fruit of the tragic death of Maximilian Kolbe endures in the Church and the world!

In Their Minds It Was Not "Death"

Men saw what happened in the camp at Auschwitz. And even if to their eyes it must have seemed that a companion of their torment "dies," even if *humanly* speaking they could consider "his departure" as "a disaster," nevertheless in their minds this was not simply "death."

Maximilian did not die but "gave his life...for his brother."

In that death, terrible from the human point of view, there was the whole definitive greatness of *the human act* and of the human choice. He spontaneously offered himself up to death out of love.

And in this human death of his there was the clear *witness* borne to Christ: the witness *borne in Christ* to the dignity of man, to the sanctity of his life, and to the saving power of death in which the power of love is made manifest.

Maximilian's Death a Sign of Victory

Precisely for this reason the death of Maximilian Kolbe became a sign of victory. This was victory won over all systematic contempt and hate for man and for what is divine in man—a victory like that won by our Lord Jesus Christ on Calvary.

"You are my friends if you do what I command you" (John 15:14).

The Church accepts this sign of victory—won through the power of Christ's redemption—with reverence and gratitude. She seeks to discern its eloquence with all humility and love.

As ever *when the Church proclaims the holiness* of her sons and daughters, as also in the present case, she seeks to act with all due exactness and responsibility, searching into all the aspects of the life and death of the Servant of God.

Yet at the same time the Church must be careful, as she reads the sign of holiness given by God in his earthly Servant, *not to allow its full eloquence and definitive meaning to go unnoticed.*

And so, in judging the cause of Blessed Maximilian Kolbe even after his Beatification, it was necessary to take into consideration many voices of the People of God—especially of our Brothers in the episcopate of both Poland and Germany—who asked that Maximilian Kolbe be proclaimed as a *martyr* saint.

Before the eloquence of *the life and death* of blessed Maximilian, it is *impossible not* to *recognize* what seems to constitute the main and essential element of the *sign* given by God to the Church and the world in his death.

Does not this death-faced spontaneously, for love of man-constitute a particular *fulfillment* of *the words* of *Christ?*

Does not this death make Maximilian *particularly like unto Christ-the* Model of all Martyrs –- who gives his own life on the Cross for his brethren?

Does not this death possess a particular and penetrating eloquence for our age?

Does not this death constitute a *particularly authentic witness* of the Church in the modern world?

And so, in virtue of my apostolic authority, I have decreed that Maximilian Maria Kolbe—who after his Beatification was venerated as a Confessor—shall henceforward be venerated *also as* a *Martyr!*

"Precious in the eyes of the Lord is the death of his faithful ones!" Amen.

Address at the Special Audience for Polish Pilgrims
October 11, 1982

The day after Maximilian Kolbe's canonization, Pope John Paul II received in a special audience over 10,000 pilgrims-Poles who came to the canonization from their homeland and from throughout the world. Thousands of Knights of the Immaculata from many countries also attended the audience, overflowing the Paul VI audience hall just inside the Vatican's south wall.

Following is an English translation of the original Polish text of the Holy Father's remarks.

Cordially and with great joy I greet my fellow countrymen gathered here in this hall, corning both from the fatherland and from Polish emigrants abroad. In you, dear brothers and sisters, I greet Poland also—the Poland situated along the Vistula and the Poland scattered throughout the whole world. It is a great event, a solemn circumstance that has brought us together here. Yesterday we participated together with a great multitude of the inhabitants of the Eternal City and of pilgrims from various lands of Europe and of the world in the canonization of Father Maximilian, the martyr of Oswiecim. Today I desire, within this family community to ponder at least briefly the significance which the canonization of our fellow countryman has for us all.

I say "all," having in mind not only those present here but at the same time those millions who are in Poland—who in a special way are living the importance of the event which took place yesterday in the Piazza of St. Peter, and who in a certain sense and special way are identified with it.

The Impact of Polish Saints

The canonizations of Poland's sons and daughters have always had their historic eloquence, not only at Rome but above all in Poland.

We know what an event the canonization of St. Stanislaus was on the background of the Poland of the 13th century Piasts. Certainly there are among you many persons who, like me, recall the last "Polish" canonization, St. Andrew Bobola in 1938. To this succession of centuries there is added today a new and uncommon figure, a figure according to the dimensions of our century and epoch.

I welcome and greet all those who were granted the grace of sharing in the canonization of St. Maximilian Kolbe. In a particular way I greet my brothers in the Episcopate...(The Pope here mentioned various dignitaries from the Church in Poland, from Rome and elsewhere. He also greeted the Government Delegation from the Peoples' Republic of Poland, thanking them for their presence. He then introduced his theme by referring to events taking place in Poland.)

We are all profoundly touched by the eloquence of the fact that Archbishop Josep A. Glemp, Primate of Poland, was not able to come to the celebration of the canonization. Together with him we are living the problem profoundly that forced him to remain at Warsaw, guided by his sense of pastoral obligation and responsibility as Primate. Nor do we hide the fact that the same problem, symptomatic of the actual situation in the homeland, profoundly touches and affects all of us. It is a question (and here once again I use the words of the Metropolitan of Cracow) of "not losing anything of what is grand and just of that which has taken place in the course of the last two years and thanks to which today we feel more than ever masters of this land."

"A Son of that Polish Earth"

St. Maximilian Maria Kolbe is a son of that land, of that Polish earth. In a particular manner we can think of him as "our" saint. He was born into the great society of Polish labor. He entered into the Order of Franciscans on Polish soil. From that land he departed for the missions in Japan and to that land, to its Niepokalanow, he returned at the approach of the Second World War. On that earth he shared the lot of so many fellow countrymen in the course of the horrible years 1939-1945.

When as Metropolitan of Cracow I wanted to offer to the Bishops participating in the Synod of 1971 (during which Paul VI included Father Maximilian among the Blessed) some relic of his, I was not able to give anything but a bit of soil taken from Oswiecim, a bit of the land of martyrs. All the rest had been devoured by the flames of the crematory's furnace.

Written into History of Nation, Church

Father Maximilian, while growing up from the Polish earth, was at the same time putting roots down into it, into its society, into the nation, whose spiritual patrimony he lived, whose language he spoke, whose historical experience he considered with all his person. The new Saint is profoundly written into the Polish history on the 20th century, into the history of the nation and of the Church.

His holiness grows together with this history. From it in a certain sense he draws his particular "raw material." It developed in various stages, but particularly in that decisive stage which unfolded in the months of the occupation of 1941, in the concentration camp of Oswiecim, and above all in the days between the end of July and August 14th of that year. It is there that we find the definitive "raw material" for the holiness of this martyr who is tied to that period of history forever, and to that terrible test of men. Some of those men still live and are among us. To them I give particular greeting. I give it to the prisoners of the concentration camp of Auschwitz and of the other camps. Among them I salute Francis Gajowniczek, a person bound most closely to Father Maximilian.

Kolbe Opens Up the Future

Can one therefore say that the holiness of Father Maximilian was constructed from specifically "Polish" material? I think that one can and one must say so. The Polish earth should harvest this fruit which, once matured, it has restored to heaven. This is the particular fruit of "its time," which the past ages now behold. At the same time it opens up the future. In this fruit we recall the history of generations, the testimony that the nation has left to its children and grandchildren. If the contribution that the Saints have made figures in the history of a nation, then the story of Poland in the 20th century cannot be understood without the figure of Father Maximilian, the martyr of Oswiecim.

Nevertheless, there are opening before us through this figure horizons that are universal. This is not only because the Church, who proclaims Maximilian a Saint, is "Catholic"—that is to say "universal"—but also by reason of that which constitutes the "raw material" of his holiness. I said earlier that this "material" is Polish. Now I have to note that it is at the same time profoundly "human." It is taken from the history of man and of the humanity of our century. It is tied to the experiences of various nations, first of all those of the European Continent.

This, one can easily verify by stepping into the camp of Oswiecim at the great monument to the victims. How many are the languages used for the inscriptions that speak of those who suffered terrible torments there and finally underwent death! In fact the holiness of Maximilian Kolbe was built in the final analysis from the same "material." So therefore, one finds at the foundations of this holiness the great, profoundly sorrowful human cause. One can say that from the very heart of this cause the immortal God and the Lord on human history draws forth inexhaustible testimonies, in order that they too may remain in the history of humanity as "signs of the times."

Kolbe: Sign of Love Stronger than Death

In like manner the figure of Maximilian remains as a testimony of the age and belongs to the "signs of the times." This difficult and tragic epoch, stigmatized by horrible debasement of human dignity, has brought about at Oswiecim the birth of its salvific sign. Love has shown itself more powerful than death, more powerful than anti-human systems. Love for man has achieved its victory there where hatred and scorn for man seemed to triumph. In this victory of love at Oswiecim the victory of Golgotha presented itself in a particular way. Men saw the death of their prison companion not as still another defeat for man, but a saving sign-the sign of our time, of our age.

The Church is rereading the meaning of such signs. It is in this that its link with the history of humanity, of men and of nations, consists. Yesterday she reread to the very end the meaning of the sign of Oswiecim that Maximilian Kolbe established by his martyr's death. The Church has reread this sign with profound veneration and emotion in proclaiming the holiness of the Martyr of Oswiecim. The Saints are in history in order to establish permanent points of reference as a background for the future of man and the world. That which shows through in them is lasting and unfailing. It bears witness to eternity. From this testimony man always draws a renewed awareness of his vocation and renewed assurance of all that awaits him. This is the direction in which the Saints guide the Church and humanity. Among these spiritual guides we include today St. Maximilian, our fellow countryman. In him the man of our times discovers a wonderful "synthesis" of the sufferings and the hopes of our age.

The Power of Self-Consecration

There is in this synthesis-molded by the life and death of this Martyr-an evangelical appeal of great clarity and power. Look at what the man who entrusts himself absolutely to Christ through the Immaculata is capable on But in this synthesis there is also a prophetic warning. It is a cry addressed to man, to society, to humanity, to the systems responsible for the life of man and of his societies. This modern day Saint has come forth from the very center of man's humiliation by man, of the humiliation of his dignity, of cruelty and of slaughter. This Saint cries out therefore with all the syntheses of his martyrdom for a consistent respect for the rights of man and also of nations since in fact he is the son of a nation whose rights have been terribly violated.

There are many facets to the eloquence of yesterday's canonization. I wish, venerable and dear brothers and sisters, that as you return to the homeland or to the other countries in which you live, that you take this eloquence with you, that you enter into it deeply with your thoughts and heart. This is what I wish for you.

I wish also for my homeland and the Church in Poland that St. Maximilian Kolbe—the Knight of the Immaculata, the Martyr of Oswiecim—may become for us all a mediator before him who is the Lord of the future age; that he may become also the daily witness for that which is great and just, and thanks to which human life on earth is worthy of man and becomes, by means of saving grace, worthy of God himself.

Excuse me if I add still another thing or two. They are reflections that have occurred in this hall. They do not enter into the context of this discourse but even so they have to be said. First of all, as I was passing through the midst of this hall which bears the name of Paul VI, there came to mind another occasion when I passed through I here in the midst of Polish pilgrims who had come I from the homeland and from the other lands in which they live. We were gathered here in this' very place in 1971. Then it was Pope Paul VI who I was passing through, accompanied by the Polish Cardinals of that period: Cardinal Stefan I Wyszynski, Primate of Poland; Cardinal John Krol, and, like today, the one who is speaking these I words. I have the custom that while passing through the midst of this hall during the general audiences I try to make contact with the persons that stand along the passageway and greet personally at least them. While I was passing through this hall today I heard many words. Above all assurances that people would pray for me. For this prayer I want to thank you all, and each of you individually. I have also heard many requests to give blessings to families, to individual persons, to parishes. I acknowledge that I have been able to respond personally only to a small part of these requests since there are hundreds and hundreds of persons more or less distant from the security barrier.

"That There Be No More of These Tears"

I want to respond, dear brothers and sisters, to all your requests, and to the intentions with which everyone of you have arrived here. I want to tell you that I take them to heart and I make them the object of my prayer before God.

Finally, passing through the midst of this hall, I noted many tears. It is not good when fellow countrymen come to a canonization of one of their compatriots with tears in their eyes. They are not tears of joy. To these tears there were at times joined words and appeals—appeals not only from this hall, appeals from far away. And so I desire to respond to these appeals by means of you who are present. I want to respond to those who are not here, and above all to those who find themselves in internment camps, in prisons.

I want to respond to those who are in some manner suffering in the land of Poland and I address myself from this place to the authorities of the Peoples' Republic of Poland, asking them that there be no more of these tears. Polish society, my people, do not deserve having tears of desperation and despondency wrung from them, but that there be built for them a better future.

Appendix D
A Man Who Knew Maximilian Kolbe

A Man Who Knew Maximilian Kolbe
By Richard Cowden

(Editor's Note: Sigmund Gorson is a Polish Jew now working as a radio and TV producer in the United States. A keynote speaker at the recent National Right-to-Life Committee Convention in New Jersey, Gorson spent his adolescence in Nazi prison camps in Poland, where he was befriended by the recently canonized St. Maximilian Kolbe.)

There's a pin that many Jews and others wear, with the Hebrew letters that mean, "Never forget!" Are you inclined to describe or talk about what you have remembered?

Gorson: To describe it to you fully, to portray it in detail and with justice, would require the pen of a Dante or the brush of a Rembrandt. . .but, the German and Austrian Nazis, they rounded us up, Polish Jews and Christians, marched us to the railway station with beatings and shooting above our heads, they stuffed us like sardines into the cattle cars, with no room to sit down or lie down or even stand up. We had no air, no food nor water, and for some four or five days as we headed toward Auschwitz, no facilities to urinate or defecate, and of course, many died. The stench of death and decay was horrible, and when the wailing of the women and children became too much for the Nazi barbarians, they began to shoot at random into the sealed cars, through the wooden walls. How to say, we envied those who died. Some prayed, many screamed and wailed, some literally went mad, some laughed, wildly, with madness.

I do not know how to describe this, in English. For many tried to kiss, and embrace, and say goodbye. It was heartbreaking.

At Auschwitz itself, kickings, beatings, attack dogs were constant. Children or husbands or fathers who tried to stop beatings of their mothers or daughters or wives were killed immediately, shot, or torn apart by dogs. Human flesh, you smelled it, the burnings and gassing were constant, but these savages murdered by every method imaginable.

Every day and every night trains kept arriving from all over occupied Europe. Everyone was stripped. Auschwitz prison camp director Joseph Mengele himself chose who would die immediately, in the chambers, and who would work for the German war effort. The Nazis photographed everyone, to humiliate them, to destroy their identity, and then they gassed them, hundreds at a time, babies and mothers, people with their hands clasped, frozen stiff, covered in slime.

Do I remember? Yes, yes, I will never forget, though I still cannot believe.

How long were you in Auschwitz, and the other camps?

Gorson: A total of six years. I was liberated by the British in 1945.

Did you meet Blessed Maximilian Kolbe?

Gorson: I held him in my arms. He was. . . everything to me. He was a humble Polish village priest, a refuge to me, he was an escape from madness.

He took it upon himself to take special care of me because my parents were not alive. He stroked my head many times, because we were completely shaved. He was a refuge from insanity. I remember I risked my life once. I stole some potato peelings from a kitchen cart. And though Fr. Kolbe was very, very hungry, he didn't ask for any food. He gave his food away, the little food we received, twice a day. The average American doesn't realize, even the Catholics don't realize, of his existence, his greatness. He gave away his food. He taught me so many things. His lips were swollen from hunger, but he was always smiling, always cheerful, the only one. God spoke through him. It was always raining at Auschwitz and Fr. Kolbe said it was God crying with us.

Do you think he had the same effect on the other inmates of Auschwitz, as he did on you?

Gorson: Well, lots of people had links with relatives, that the Nazis weren't aware of. I had no one, and it was people like me that Fr. Kolbe took a special interest in.

You have said that you attribute your survival of the Nazi camps to Fr. Kolbe's intercession. Do you mean while he was still alive, or did you pray to him after he died?

Gorson: Both. There must be something stronger than I in the world, or why would I survive? I believe that Fr. Kolbe's prayers saved me, absolutely. I still pray to him today. I believe with all my heart in his powers, his closeness to God.

You've also been quoted as saying that Fr. Kolbe was your confessor? Do you mean as a friend, or formally, as a priest?

Gorson: No, we suffered the same thing, so there was no need to confess. We all knew what the others were suffering.

Have you converted to Roman Catholicism?

Gorson: I don't like to talk about religion. Humility is my religion, and mankind. I believe in God with all my heart, but religion is a private affair with me. I was born of a lovely, highly educated Jewish-Polish mother, who studied at Sorbonne. So I am a Jew. But I believe in Fr. Kolbe, too, that he was very close to God. Incidentally, I see Sergeant Gajowniczek from time to time, the man Fr. Kolbe died for..

Did you give testimony at the Vatican hearings on Fr. Kolbe's beatification?

Gorson: No, I never wanted publicity. . . .John Paul II happens to be a personal friend. I knew him after the war. He was a humble village priest in Cracow. And we have talked of Fr. Kolbe.

Why are you accepting publicity now?

Gorson: Because of abortion, because I saw the Nazis dragging babies from their mother's bellies to experiment on them, and. . . well, it is happening again, in my beloved America. Legalized abortion is legalized murder, just like the vicious Nazis, nothing less. If we condone these things it won't stop, it is just a continuation of what the Nazis did. These 17,000 fetuses they found in plastic jars, and some judge won't even let them be buried, it's a continuation. Just like the Nazis. You begin with the very young, and then its a straight line to the feeble-minded, the sick, the old, the gypsies, Jews, Poles, Christians, rabbis, priests. There was no stopping then, and it won't be stopped here unless we stop it at the beginning, at abortion. And so I cannot be silent, I will fight and sacrifice all the time I can to this noble cause, this basic cause. To a Jew, to save one life is to preserve all mankind, and so I must, so I cannot be silent.

When did you come to the United States, and are I you a citizen?

Gorson: We came, my wife and I, on Dec. 2nd, 1949, my birthday. I became a citizen in 1955, and I live in Delaware.

When you knew the Pope, back when he was a Cracow priest, did you have any idea he would become the Successor to St. Peter?

Gorson: No, but he was a great human being, and so I knew he would help the Catholic Church in Poland, that he would get promotions. But I didn't know he would become Pope.

There was a recent German magazine that accused Blessed Kolbe of being anti-Semitic on the grounds that one of his publications seemed to have some anti-Semitic inferences. Is there any substance to this?

Gorson: Oh, I wouldn't be alive today if it weren't for Fr. Kolbe. That is a heinous accusation. I don't even want to dignify it with an answer, but let me tell you something. They came up with the most heinous attacks on the Catholic Church. An infamous play was on Broadway recently, called "The Deputy" accusing the Catholic Church of aiding and abetting in the killing of Jews. It is not true, and I went to New York to tell that to the author of this ugly play. People in America can't understand. I escaped twice from the concentration camps when we were being transferred, and I hid out with other Jewish kids in convents and seminaries. And the nuns who helped us, they were brutally raped and killed. How can anybody say these things? The Catholic Church in Poland helped us, constantly, and Fr. Kolbe saved me personally. I don't understand how people can say such things.

Gorson, you were prisoner no. 52821 at Auschwitz, your parents and three sisters were murdered there, and you lost 58 members of your family to the Nazis. So when you call abortion America's silent holocaust, you speak with painful authority. Do you think the roots of the Nazi culture and the abortion culture are the same, and, it so, what can be done to uproot it?

Gorson: The direction is the same. The solution is to realize that, and just stop it, legally, actually, in every way.

Do you think President Reagan is doing enough to aid that cause?

Gorson: I'm against any politician who speaks with a forked tongue. God forbid that this should be true of President Reagan. But any candidate who is not embracing this noble philosophy to save lives does not deserve to serve the public.

Do you think the right-to-life movement in the United States, as far as you have seen, is headed in the right direction?

Gorson: I'm an optimist. If I weren't, I wouldn't be alive today. I feel this noble cause will eventually win. Laws will be passed which will express that this united nation cannot continue to allow for this heinous situation.

Given the ferocity of the pro-abortionists, do you think there will be violence when abortion does become illegal again?

Gorson: No, I don't think Americans are a violent people. Really, you are a very nice people, the nicest in the world. I think and I hope soon, Americans will come to realize they cannot destroy what God has given us. Abortion is murder, legalized murder, nothing less, and Americans will reject it.

Do you know much about the history of Planned Parenthood?

Gorson: I have read quite a bit, unfortunately.

Do you know that eugenicists who worked for the Hitler government used to write for Planned Parenthood's official publication, the **Birth Control Review,** *and that Planned Parenthood sent a number of delegates to Nazi eugenical conferences in the 1930's? Or that Planned Parenthood's found-er, Margaret Sanger, openly called for the elimination of the Negro race?*

Gorson: I pity these people, I don't hate them, I pity them. If they had gone through the experience I had gone through, they would not feel as they do, they would not do the things they do.

So you think they are more ignorant than malicious, or racists?

Gorson: Yes I think so, I think they are ignorant.

A lot of pro-abortionists maintain that really only Catholics are against abortion, and that most people think one should have the right to abort one's child. Is that just propaganda or do you think there is some truth in it?

Gorson: I'm a Jew. Most religious Jews, rabbis, Orthodox, Hasidim, most people who think about this question, agree with the Catholics. The only conspiracy is to stop Americans from becoming what Germany became.

Photo Section

The church of the Immaculata at Niepokalanow. It was planned by Saint Maximilian but not built until after World War II. Consecrated in 1954, it is dedicated to Mary the Immaculata, Mediatrix of All Graces. Kolbe saw the Immaculata as a mediatrix in the sense that through her perfect union with God through Christ she obtains all she asks for, and always asks for all that perfectly glorifies God.

Interior of the church of the Immaculata at Niepokalanow. About half of the work of construction and interior decoration was done by the friars themselves.

Auschwitz survivors Sigmund Gorson (l.) and Francis Gajowniczek (r.) participate in the Conventual Franciscans' national Mass of thanksgiving at St. Patrick's cathedral in New York City two months after Saint Kolbe's canonization in Rome. Between them is Bro. John Baptist Zint, O.F.M. Conv. of Marytown, the U.S. National Center of the Knights of the Immaculata movement. Gajowniczek is the man whose life Saint Maximilian saved by his heroic self-sacrifice. Gorson, now a television producer in Wilmington, Del., was a 13-year-old boy who lost 58 family members and relatives including his parents, grandparents and three sisters in the Holocaust. He credits his friendship with Saint Maximilian at Auschwitz for the preservation of his sanity.

"He was like an angel to me," Gorson told Patricia Treece, author of A Man for Others. "Like a mother hen, he took me in his arms, he used to wipe away my tears. I believe in God more since that time. Because of the deaths of my parents I had been asking, 'Where is God?' and had lost faith. Kolbe gave me back that faith.

"He knew I was a Jewish boy. That made no difference. His heart was bigger that persons - that is, whether they were Jewish, Catholic, or whatever. He loved every-one. He dispensed love and nothing but love. For one thing, he gave away so much of his meager rations, that to me it was a miracle he could live. Now it is easy to be nice, to be charitable, to be humble, when times are good and peace prevails. For someone to be as Father Kolbe was in that time and place—I can only say the way he was is beyond words.

"I am a Jew by my heritage as the son of a Jewish mother, and I am of the Jewish faith and very proud of it. And not only did I love Maximilian Kolbe very, very much in Auschwitz, where he befriended me, but I will love him until the last moments of my life." (From A Man for Others. Harper and Row: San Francisco, 1982, p. 153. Copy-right 1982 by Patricia Treece. Used with permission.)

Sunday, October 17, 1976, outdoor Mass commemorating fifth anniversary of Maximilian Kolbe's beatification. Far left, Ted Wojtkowski carrying ashes of victims killed in Auschwitz. He was in the same lineup with Francis Gajowniczek (to his left), and Kolbe the day Kolbe offered to take Gajowniczek's place in the starvation bunker. On the right side of Kolbe's picture is John Dagis, one of the original group of friars who went to Japan with Father Maximilian.

Pope John Paul II pauses in prayer before a new bronze statue of St. Maximilian Maria Kolbe after the Canonization Mass October 10th. The statue, blessed by the Pope, was sent as a gift to Niepokalanow, the huge center of the Knights of the Immaculata for prayer and evangelism established by Saint Maximilian in Poland.

Panoramic view of the out-of-doors canonization of St. Maximilian Maria Kolbe in St. Peter's Square in Rome on Sunday, October 10, 1982. Scene includes papal altar set up on the "sagrato" or raised open area in front of the Basilica, Pope John Paul II on the papal throne behind the altar, and part of the 250,000 pilgrims, Roman worshippers and tourists who participated. (L'Osservatore Romano Photographic Service photo)

Pope John Paul II greets some of Saint Maximilian's Conventual Franciscan confreres after the canonization. L. to r.: Most Rev. Vitale Bommarco, Minister General; the Pope; Fr. Gaetano Stano, Consultor to the Holy See; Fr. Cornelian Dende, Dir. of Fr. Justin's Rosary Hour Radio Apostolate, U.S.A.; Fr. Bernard M. Geiger, U.S. National Director of the M.I., holding a specially boxed proof copy of *Kolbe and the Kommandant* which is surrounded by a hand-made onyx rosary featuring the first center of St. Kolbe and the Blessed Mother struck in silver, also a product of the publishers of this book on St. Kolbe. The cased book and rosary was presented as one of the many gifts received by Pope John Paul II on October 10, 1982.

SECRETARIAT OF STATE

FROM THE VATICAN, December 28, 1982

Dear Father Geiger,

    I am writing at the direction of the Holy Father to express his thanks for the rosary and volume which you offered for his acceptance on behalf of the Knights of the Immaculata in the United States. His Holiness wishes you to know how appreciative he is of your thoughtfulness and devoted sentiments.

    The Holy Father willingly assures you of his prayers and cordially imparts his Apostolic Blessing to you and all associated in this kind gesture, invoking upon you the grace and peace of Christ.

                     Sincerely yours in Christ,

                     Msgr. G.B. Re
                     Assessor

The Reverend Bernard M. Geiger, O.F.M. Conv.
National Director
Knights of the Immaculata
1600 West Part Ave.
Libertyville, IL   60048